BITTERSWEET
ENCOUNTER

Contributions in Afro-American and African Studies

Contributions in
Afro-American and African Studies, No. 5

BITTERSWEET ENCOUNTER

The Afro-American and the American Jew

ROBERT G. WEISBORD
and ARTHUR STEIN

Foreword by C. Eric Lincoln

Negro Universities Press
Westport, Connecticut

For our children
Lisa Natanya, Jody Arielle,
Steven Darrow, Aaron King,
and Joanna Sanger

Library of Congress Catalog Card Number: 72–127828

SBN: 8371–5093–0

Negro Universities Press
51 Riverside Avenue, Westport, Connecticut 06880

Printed in the United States of America

CONTENTS

FOREWORD

AMERICA IS PERHAPS THE FIRST MODERN NATION IN THE WORLD whose establishment was consciously and confidently rested on a foundation of religious assurance and political idealism. It proclaimed its intentions of political sovereignty as an indivisible nation under God, where liberty, justice and the pursuit of happiness would be guaranteed to every citizen. The political intentions of nations, like the private intentions of individuals do not always find their maturation in fact. Between the intention and the act, often there falls the shadow. So with American democracy. The ambitious intention to weld an indivisible cultural and political entity from a multiplicity of national, racial and ethnic subentities has enjoyed some success; but its failures are increasingly apparent, and relationships considered settled, or at least viable a hundred years ago, a generation ago, or even a decade ago, are threatening to come unglued. Relationships that were never really settled want restructuring. The whole society is in for a shakedown which has been unnaturally delayed for more than a hundred years. Wars abroad and clever (often crude) political and economic maneuvering at home, ad hoc responses to continuing crises, paper rapprochement, luck, and the emotional attractiveness of the American dream for the millions who could not possibly experience it, all helped to delay the day when Americans would look at themselves with critical appraisal and ask "why?" We are in a situation of crisis today because the people to whom we have always looked for answers—the politicians, the educators, the clergymen, the businessmen—have

vii

but one set of rhetoric, and it has proved itself an irrelevant and ineffectual response to the new questions and the new issues being raised by a generation demanding new solutions to old problems. The "bittersweet encounter," the way in which Jews and Blacks have experienced each other in their common pilgrimage from exclusion toward increased participation in the full range of options available to the "assimilated" society, is the history of cooperation and conflict between two cultural subentities with superficially similar, but fundamentally disparate experiences, historically, and in America as well. Historically, they (or their ancestors) have met before under circumstances not precisely replicated in their American experience. Jews and Blacks are not strangers to each other. Their western experience is in some sense but a resumption of a relationship that is rooted in antiquity, but well documented in the peculiar nuances of their common and separate histories.

This generation of Jews and Blacks may well see themselves in isolation as they confront each other in personal and local situations. They are in fact a part of a larger context in which they, and others, are involved in the reconstruction of American history, or at least the modification of a society which has grown stagnant on its own excesses. Included in those excesses has been the deliberate and systematic alienation of Jews and Blacks from the American mainstream and whatever values mainstream America may represent for the assimilated.

The bittersweet encounter is a play within a play, backdropped by the peculiar American racial canvas which predetermines who cannot be the protagonist, and sets the conditions for the way the play will end. No matter how long the list or how broad the spectrum of the dramatis personae, within the context of American racial ideology, to this date, it has not been possible for the Blackamerican to leave the stage a *living* hero. This could come as no news to the Jews, who for so many generations found themselves cast in roles no less susceptible to denigration, saved only by the color of their skins.

At a time before American idealism learned to discipline itself with observation, the expectation was that this new outpost of western development was destined to become a supercivilization of European cultural eclecticism under the controlling preemptions of the Anglo-Saxon experience. The rhetoric of politics and the premature conclusions of untested social theory proclaimed America to be a vast melting pot from which countless millions of immigrant Poles, Czechs, Hungarians, Irish, Italians, Jews, and the like would emerge after proper annealing as a new entity: *American*. Was it not Emma Lazarus, a Spanish Jew, who wrote the official welcome a confident America caused to be inscribed on the Statue of Liberty, the national symbol of its belief in its destiny to mold and give to the world a new people?

> give me your tired your poor
> your huddled masses
> yearning to breathe free

And so they came by the millions—among them the Jews—in search of the promise of being American in America. All that was required was the urge to merge—to "melt," as it were, and to be one with the prevailing developing American archetype.

It is evident by hindsight, of course, that there were some for whom the urge to merge held no attraction. They left the Old Country less with the intent of being molded into the New American than with the hope of having increased opportunities for remaining what they were. The notion of being shorn of their treasured cultural or ethnic identity and being melted into an anonymous general population was abhorrent to some of the immigrant groups. To be sure, they paid the price for their recalcitrance, and indeed, some have continued to pay to this day.

Others found the melting process to exist mainly in the imaginations of its true believers. There were barriers to assimilation, and some of them were formidable. Perhaps it could be for their children, or for their children's children. But not for themselves. For them, maybe it would be better to give priority to immediate, visceral needs—keeping to their own communities, looking after their own. These, too, paid a price—for their defeatism.

For the true believers, assimilation was the narrow gate to the real America and to being real Americans. It was the access-way to the American dream. If the annealing process was slow and uncertain, it could be catalyzed by certain strategies guaranteed to close the gap between the dream and reality. For example, if one were both enterprising and committed, he could swallow his accent, find himself a new religion, and learn to get along without the last syllable of his name. If the dream was worth more than identity, he could adopt a new name altogether. And to make his conversion complete, he could foreswear the comforts of endogamy and take a wife from the reference group of which he intended to be a part.

The point is that one (or more accurately, *certain* ones) could be melted and assimilated, but like so many other theories of human behavior, the melting pot theory of American assimilation was notable for its exceptions. It was not an adequate projection of what could (and did) happen to millions of European immigrants, and it did not address itself in any serious way to the Black experience in America. It was politically and intellectually misleading, and it provided the grounds for a jumble of false assumptions which still condition our thinking about why some have made it in America, and some have not.

At the height of the European exodus to America in the late nineteenth century, Blacks already constituted a sizeable population. But they were not by reason of certain continuing disabilities assimilated into the general population. To call them "American" was to observe a political courtesy scarcely grounded in fact. It did not seem to matter that they already spoke the language, having learned it over three centuries or so of intimate proximity and experience. The Blacks had no unpleasant accents, only the approved regional inflections of indigenous old stock. Since they were already Methodists and Baptists by faith, there seemed little need to apostatize; (although legend has it that Episcopalianism was, in the case of the more assiduous immigrants, a more attractive religious catalyst for people being melted at the bottom with hopes of being assimilated at the top).

Again, Black people interested in this melting process shouldn't have had to worry about changing their names. They had good euphonious "American" names already, without any troublesome suffixes like "witz" or "berg" or "stein" or "ski" or "sky." And as for exogamy as a strategy of assimilation, in most states Blacks were prevented by law (and everywhere discouraged by custom) from exercising any marriage options *except* endogamy.

In spite of all this, it was inevitable that some Blacks would want to do what everybody else was doing, social theory, law, and convention notwithstanding. While others changed their names and their religion, assimilation-minded Blacks simply changed their race. After all, unlike national or ethnic identity, *race* (in America) is a matter of complexion. So, never mind the genes: if you're light enough, and changing from the identity of the oppressed to the identity of the oppressor holds no trauma for you, then why not? If assimilation is the prerequisite for the meaningful pursuit of the American dream, and if you are non-assimilable by reason of race, then why not indeed?

Some did. Over the generations of our experience together in America, enough Black people have become white people to seriously qualify the meaning of being white. If, (as the laws and conventions dealing with the matter have declared it to be), "a person having any Negro blood whatever is, with all his descendants, forever and eternally of the Negro race," then race in America is not a state of being, but a matter of who knows about it. If by some divine benevolence every white American with Black ancestry or Black kinfolks developed black splotches on his cheeks whenever he contemplated an act of bigotry, the race problem would be over.

The Blackamericans who opted for assimilation by passing, however, are not the subjects of this work. Nor are the Jews who compromised their identity and forfeited their history by changing their names and becoming Episcopalians. The Blacks and the Jews who have, for whatever reasons, remained Blacks and Jews are the principals who are now, and who have been for most of their experience in America, involved in the bittersweet encounter. They are both in some sense in pursuit of the American dream, insofar as that dream means a reasonable participation in the privileges and the responsibilities of citizenship. But the pursuit has been on different terms and under disparate circumstances, and they have arrived at their present state of relationships via different routes and through vastly different circumstances. Historically, the Blackamerican has wanted to be *American*. American racism has always precluded that possibility; and now the Blacks are rethinking the whole question of Black identity and its meaning in America. Historically, the Jew too has wanted to be American, but he has insisted on retaining his Jewishness. From the point of view of most Jews, the options for entering the American mainstream at the sacrifice of religious and cultural identity were scarcely viable, although there is evidence that Jewishness is not a high priority for some contemporary youth from Jewish families. But to Black people it has often seemed that the Jew has had it both ways. He could be "white" when it was convenient, and he could be "Jewish" when he pleased. But he was *never* Black, so whatever disabilities he suffered were in a sense (1) voluntary, and (2) relative.

While such a view is undoubtedly simplistic, it is true that anti-Semitism in America has always been comparatively mild in comparison to the hatred for Blacks for a number of reasons which can be documented. In the first place, the American dislike for the Jew was a secondary, or even tertiary experience. Jewish oppression was something that occurred elsewhere—in the ghettoes of Europe. It was something Americans read about, or learned about from non-Jewish immigrants, or from the Jews themselves. There was no direct cause-and-effect relationship between American anti-Semitism and its objects. On the other hand, white racism, for all practical purposes, *originated* in America. It grew out of a direct experience in which white men enslaved Black men and have sought continuously since to justify that behavior. As a consequence of this primary, personal experience, guilt, fear, and the need for vindication all contributed to the severity of the oppression directed toward Blackamericans. To the degree that the Jew has identified with other whites in abusing Black people, he may well share their guilt and fear. To the degree that he has remembered his own bondage and oppression and has refused to participate in the racism that has sought to dehumanize Blacks, he has reason to expect that his own identity distinction will be recognized and respected by Blacks.

The Black man's visibility made him a readily recognizable target, and if the uncritical opinion held by some Blacks that the Jew could change identities like a chameleon is somewhat overdrawn, it at least has a basis in fact. White is the color of privilege in America. *Anybody* who is white is automatically *presumed* to warrant certain prerogatives, privileges and protection. Anyone who is Black is not. The Jew does not have to take advantage of his color. It is an advantage thrust upon him. But being white must never be an excuse for oppressing people who are not.

The authors of this book go to some pains to make it clear that Jews are white, and that being white they have, as individuals, behaved more or less like other whites among whom they have elected to live. It is interesting, though perhaps not generally known outside the Black community, that traditionally, Blacks have made a sharp distinction between "Jews" and "white" men. For better or for worse, most Blacks seldom think of a Jew in terms other than what they perceive as his Jewishness, and in Black conversation, Jews are almost never lumped with Caucasians. It is usually "the white man *and* the Jew"; or idiomatically, it is "Charlie *and* Goldberg." In most instances this has permitted an interpretation of racial attitudes and behavior (toward Blacks) in which the Jew consistently appears less vicious and less bloodthirsty if more cunning and deceitful. In recent times three new factors have emerged which tend to modify the Black "folk" concept of Jews: the Jews themselves increasingly stress their "white" identity; Jews have become increasingly visible in the white power structure; and many Jews have identified with the war in the Middle East.

The first is probably a manifestation of increased self-confidence Jews have come to know as more barriers continue to fall between them and their rightful participation in American life. But the barriers have not fallen because mainstream America suddenly recognized Jews as white. That was never the question at issue in their case. It was their religion and their culture which placed them beyond the pale, but America never pursued these objections more than half-heartedly. The objection to Roman Catholics, though usually more subtle, was probably more intense for most of our history than our religious antipathy for Jews. But it was hard to tell who was a Catholic six days a week, while the Jew maintained a persistent cultural visibility which made him hardly less targetable than the Blackamerican—which brings us to the point to be made here: the new levels of acceptability enjoyed by contemporary Jews derive to a significant degree from the determined *Black* push from beneath. Jewish philanthropy and Jewish participation in the civil rights movement were important factors contributing to what developed into the Black Revolution, but if the Jews had done nothing at all, they still would have reaped some major benefits of the Black Revolution before Blacks themselves. In short, American acceptability presupposes an order of priority. In order for the Blacks to move up, some other group has to be moved out of the way.

So goes the rule. The problem now is that Blacks don't want to play by the rules because all the rules seem contrived to make them "it" whatever the name of the game. The increased abrasiveness characterizing contemporary Black-Jewish relations reflects the Jew's apparent willingness to go along with the system, and the Blackamerican's repudiation of an arrangement that gives him the scrapings *every time*. For the Jew, the American dream has taken on substantial form and substance. Overt acts of bigotry toward Jews are greatly diminished, or have been directed toward new targets. There are fewer bars across the doors to Jewish success. For the Jew, life is sweeter in America than anywhere else in the world. The American dream is beginning to look like the stuff of reality. For the Blackamerican, the dream is still a will-o-the-wisp, and for longer than he intends to continue, he has been chasing it over an impossible terrain, where the natural quagmires and quicksands have been mined with every conceivable booby trap known to human invention. From the Black man's point of view, he is always chasing what other Americans—who came later and have given less—always seem to have, or always get before he does. Every time he lays his hand on a piece of the so-called American dream, before he can grab hold he finds somebody else's hand under his. So he is about ready to damn the dream and whomever he feels has taken his share.

The Jew qua Jew is not the adversary. The adversary is whosoever subscribes to the cold, calculated racist ideology which, having identified selected Americans as "Negroes," then moves to deprive them of their fair share of privilege and responsibility; whosoever takes advantage of their disability; and whosoever stands in the way of their recovery. That is the enemy, whatever his race, color, or religion.

The bittersweet encounter is the record of two minorities trying to gain parity in a society which is intolerant of racial and cultural differences. Blacks and Jews are not the only groups involved in the struggle, although they are, for the moment the most prominent, and possibly the most competitive. They have pursued this goal with differing degrees of success, a matter largely determined by factors not within the control of either of them. Their separate struggles have been conditioned by their separate histories, and rewarded or negated by the attitudes and intentions of the larger society from which they have both been excluded. Had their travail been a common struggle rather than an encounter, the history of America might have been written differently.

As Jews qua Jews have never represented a focus of anti-Black feeling, it is also true that classical anti-Semitism has never curdled the emotions nor perverted the behavior of Black people. As a matter of fact, the Blackamerican has, for most of his history, been so desperate in his efforts to establish his humanity and his right to belong, that there has been little energy left for finding a scapegoat, or for hating anybody—except himself. The concerted weight of white American opinion that Black people were different and should be treated differently from anybody else took an inevitable toll of self-appreciation and perceptivity. The American discrimination against Blacks has been so common, so harsh, and so unremitting that much of the time ordinary Black people did not know they were being discriminated against and could not identify the discriminator if they did. A woman who had lived all her life in Selma, Alabama, admitted that she had no sense of discrimination or oppression until Martin Luther King, Jr., went there. Differential treatment was so "normal" as to be unrecognized. Who then could single out the Jew as a special target for "anti-Semitism" if he was behaving the way "white" people normally behave?

The truth is that the Black man's animus was for the most part vague and unfocused. He was vaguely aware that "Polacks" and "Jews" and "Italians" and "Irishmen" and "poor whites" were against him. But then, weren't *all* whites? And if the "Hunky" or the "Polack" took his job, or the Irish cop busted his skull, or the "poor whites" lynched him while the "good whites" took his land, if the Jew merchant cheated him out of his money and the "Dago" sold him bad meat, who was he going to single out to hate? He hated *himself,* for being the object of so much hatred. And so long as he hated himself he lacked the self-confidence necessary to say to any particular group, *"you are oppressing me and I intend to fight you."*

Undoubtedly, Black concern about "the Jewish position" has taken on more serious dimensions as the new struggle for Black liberation has gradually affected the Blackamericans' total spectrum of relationships. This new concern is in part a fallout of the growing Black interest in international politics, and an increasing willingness on the part of an increasing number of Blacks to see themselves and all Black people in the context of world affairs. As political reactions to the Arab-Israeli conflict, or to our possible involvement in another foreign war, Black "anti-Semitism" may be no more than a response to perceived self-interest. It may, or may not be translated into anti-Jewishness at home. On the other hand, Jewish visibility in the larger cities where Black anti-Semitism is more likely to exist is increasingly pronounced—physically, economically, culturally, and politically, and at a time when Black determination to break all the bonds and symbols of oppression has taken on an evangelistic zeal. It is inevitable that abrasions between Blacks and Jews (and Blacks and others) will occur, and those Jews who are caught up in the pattern of conventional attitudes towards Blacks will find the new Black resistance to convention especially hard to interpret rationally and to find acceptable. To such Jews, some Black antiniggerism may look like Black anti-Semitism. But the Black man's unwillingness to be America's nigger any longer is assuredly not the same as adopting a blanket hostility toward Jews, their culture, or their aspirations.

So far as the Arab-Israeli fight is concerned, and the Jewish fretfulness that Blackamericans are pro-Arab, or are becoming pro-Arab, it ought to be understood that while Blacks have a right to their opinions and sentiments as do other Americans, the suspicions of Arab support and Jewish hostility are very grossly overdrawn, if not altogether figments of fantasy. There are small Muslim groups in the United States who understandably feel an affinity for other Muslims as Christians (and Jews) do for their coreligionists in other parts of the world. And there are "Third World" revolutionaries (including some American Jews) who have romantic notions about Jews and the western military-economic establishment, and about "the underdogs of the Middle East" who were dispossessed of their ancient homeland in Palestine to make way for the modern state of Israel. But in America, the Arab presence and Black support of the Arab cause, where it exists at all, is low profile. Few Blackamericans would even know where to look for a real live Arab, while everyone knows a Jew, what he's like, and where to find one. As a result, the "common" Jew may well suffer in comparison to the "exotic" Arab at a low level of uncritical response. But this is hardly hardcore anti-Semitism. It is more like American students who wear Viet Cong flags and cheer for Ho Chi Minh because they are disenchanted by the common Americans they know so well, but willing to be charmed by the exoticism and the romanticism of people they know little about and whose own failings are blotted out by a self-induced, selective myopia.

When the pot boils, the first action is at the top. The Jews stand to benefit substantially from the Black Revolution, no matter how abrasive the Black-Jewish encounter may become. But it is also true that a hard boil stirs up the sediment at the bottom, and all elements are set in motion. It is reasonable to predict that as the Black struggle for parity intensifies, the normal order of priority will be upset and some groups now ahead of Blacks in the order of social progression will be outdistanced by them. The Jews are safe from this possibility, and the bittersweet encounter should logically be less bitter and more functional for both groups.

C. ERIC LINCOLN
Accra, Ghana

July 11, 1970

ACKNOWLEDGMENTS

WE WISH TO EXPRESS OUR GRATITUDE TO THOSE WHO WERE most helpful in the preparation of this book. We are indebted to Mrs. Jean Blackwell Hutson and Ernest Kaiser of the Schomburg Library in Harlem who made available to us the excellent collection of materials on Negro history and literature and to the staff of the New York Public Library, especially the Jewish division. Harry Fleischman, Haskell Lazere, and Edward Moldover of the American Jewish Committee; Kenyon Burke, Ben Epstein, and Nat Belth of the Anti-Defamation League; and the various officials of the American Jewish Congress who kindly provided materials written for or compiled by their respective organizations.

Thanks are also due Herbert Aptheker, for sharing with us his recollections of W. E. B. DuBois; Floyd McKissick, for making available to us reprints of his articles in the *Amsterdam News* on Negro-Jewish relations; Toby Kurzband for telling of his experiences as an administrator in the New York school system, and Ira Glasser of the New York Civil Liberties Union for his help in our research on the New York school strike and its effect on race relations.

Mr. Stein wishes to thank a number of teachers and administrators of Public School 271 in Ocean Hill-Brownsville who were receptive and helpful during his visit to that school.

We also greatly appreciate the interest in our project of Abner Gaines, associate librarian at the University of Rhode Island. Mrs. Julia Hoxsie did a yeoman's job, with occasional assistance by

Mrs. Gail Rabasca and Mrs. Donna Fisher in rendering our hand-written manuscript scrawl into typescript. Zechariah Gaiya, a graduate student at the University of Rhode Island, helped with the bibliography. Mr. Weisbord would also like to thank the National Endowment of the Humanities and Mr. Stein, the University of Rhode Island, for summer fellowships in 1969 which helped support their work. In addition, Mr. Weisbord would like to thank the University of Rhode Island for a grant-in-aid.

Parts of chapters 4 and 6, "Negro Perceptions of Jews Between the World Wars" and "Black Nationalism and the Arab-Israeli Conflict," have appeared, respectively, in somewhat different form in *Judaism* (Fall 1969) and *Patterns of Prejudice* (November–December 1969); we thank the editors of those journals for permission to include those portions in this book.

Words cannot adequately express our gratitude to Cynthia Weisbord and Karen Stein who made valuable suggestions, proofread the manuscript, and minimized our share of the household chores while we were researching and writing this book.

INTRODUCTION

IN THE FALL OF 1966 A JEWISH WRITER TOOK A "HARD LOOK" AT Negro-Jewish relations and concluded "we are faced with the most fateful domestic issue since the 1930s, and perhaps in all American Jewish history."[1] Few Jews would have agreed at that time. More recently, the 1968 New York City school dispute brought to the public's attention a growing confrontation between blacks and Jews. Fairly typical of Jewish opinion in the fall of 1968 was the statement of the president of the Zionist Organization of America, Jacques Torczyner: "We have a *new* brand of anti-Semitism—black anti-Semitism" (italics added).[2] Tension gripped much of the New York Jewish community.

For those Jews accustomed to thinking that Negroes and Jews were natural allies, that Jewish liberals were the black man's most loyal friends and his most dedicated defenders, the rift that was occurring between two of America's ethnic minorities was astonishing and frightening. Partly responsible for the surprise and fear were a relatively small number of widely publicized anti-Jewish slurs. These incidents occurred at a time when the tensions between blacks and whites were rapidly mounting. The events of the last several years have thus necessitated a rethinking of the relationship between Jews and blacks in America.

Academics, no less than other mortals, are of necessity influ-

[1] Judd L. Teller, "Negroes and Jews: A Hard Look," *Conservative Judaism* 21, no. 1 (Fall 1966): 13.
[2] *New York Times,* 13 September 1968.

xxi

enced by their societal heritage and upbringing. Inevitably they are affected by their family backgrounds, their circle of friends and colleagues, and their own personal experiences. The authors of this book are both Jews. We have striven to be impartial and objective, but as Jews, and as Americans concerned with righting the injustices perpetrated on black people for three hundred and fifty years, we have not sought to be clinically detached. With what success, the reader must judge.

All Jews, of course, do not view the problems we discuss in the same way. We certainly do not claim to speak for the American-Jewish community or even for a majority of it. It seems reasonable, however, to assume that two black Americans, or other white scholars for that matter, would have an angle of vision different from ours. It is therefore desirable that this book be followed by other studies on the same general subject.

Most of the writing on relations between Negroes and Jews in the past has been done by Jews and their principal concern has been black anti-Semitism, its causes and its cures. In point of fact this volume also deals more with the black reactions, favorable and unfavorable to Jews, than it does with the range of Jewish attitudes toward Negroes. This is the case not because Jewish attitudes toward blacks are friendlier and more sympathetic than the blacks' toward Jews. There is no evidence to support this notion. We believe that Dick Gregory, the black social critic and humorist, was essentially correct when he said: "Every Jew in America over 15 years old knows another Jew that don't like niggers."[3]

While it is true that among white Americans, Jews, individually and organizationally, have been represented out of all proportion to their population in the battle for racial justice, we believe it is equally true that, in general, the racism of many Jews is inseparable from—and indistinguishable from—white American racism. Of course, Jewish anti-Negro sentiment is seldom expressed in such a way as to justify newspaper headlines. Typically, direct individual Jewish-Negro encounters have been unequal-status encounters—between landlords and tenants, between merchants and consumers,

[3] *New York Times*, Entertainment Section, 7 September 1969. The remark was quoted from a Gregory recording entitled "The Light Side: The Dark Side."

between housewives and domestics. Ordinarily, Negroes have been at a distinct disadvantage in the relationship. Where the relationship has been a frustrating one, it has usually been the black man who has felt put upon. The Jew's feelings about the Negro in those situations may be no more wholesome, but obviously he does not feel the need to cry out, to castigate, or to hurl an epithet. We do not mean to suggest that all contacts between Jews and blacks have been abrasive. They have not. Hopefully, we will not neglect the areas of accord and harmony between Jewish-Americans and Afro-Americans, or advance an unduly pessimistic analysis.

Our purpose is twofold: to provide a study which places contemporary Jewish-Negro relations in historic perspective; and hopefully to shed some light on an area of interracial relations that has already generated much heat and misunderstanding in recent years.

We have not sought to provide an exhaustive treatment of all manifestations of the historic and contemporary relationship between Negroes and Jews. Admittedly, our somewhat eclectic approach leaves gaps. Fascinating but somewhat tangential subjects such as the black Jewish cults which have been located in several American cities since World War I have been given little attention. Their origin or origins have long been a matter of dispute. Rabbi Wentworth A. Matthew, spiritual leader of Harlem's largest black congregation, in an interview published several years ago by a Negro newspaper, maintained: "The black man is a Jew because he is a direct lineal descendant of Abraham."[4] Moreover, he said flatly that "all genuine Jews are black men." According to the author of a book on the black Jews of Harlem, the members are convinced that they, indeed all Negroes, are descended from the tribes of Israel. Some aver that Afro-Americans are, in reality, Falashas or Ethiopian Jews, who were deprived of their heritage and religion in the slave era.[5] Because of their small numbers and their very limited contact with white Jews, black Jews in the United States have not been able to act as a buffer or a liaison between their

[4] Roi Ottley, *New World A-Coming: Inside Black America* (Boston: Houghton Mifflin Co., 1943), p. 144.
[5] Howard Brotz, *The Black Jews of Harlem: Negro Nationalism and the Dilemmas of Negro Leadership* (New York: Free Press, 1964), pp. 15, 46.

black non-Jewish brethren and their white coreligionists in times of strife. Most white Jews know next to nothing about the life and religious practices of black Jews, and it would be very valuable if more were written by black Jews themselves of their own experience.

Although we have discussed Negro-Jewish relations in a number of localities, New York City has received the greatest amount of attention for two simple reasons. One has to do with the fact that Gotham had the unhappy distinction of serving as the cockpit for the battle over community control of education. The second is bound up with the fact that nowhere else in the country are both Jews and Afro-Americans found in such large numbers in such close proximity. New York City has the largest Jewish community in the world. Jews comprise 28 percent of the city's total population. Negroes are only 14 percent of the population, but Harlem is the symbolic capital of Negro America and Brooklyn remains the center of the storm over community control.

We have devoted relatively little space to the period before the 1920s because contacts between the two ethnic groups were sporadic until then. Close, sustained contacts resulted from the mass migration of southern blacks to the North which reached its zenith during World War I. After that, Jews and blacks became infinitely more aware of one another. Jews, often one generation removed from the old country, moved up the economic ladder rapidly. Negroes remained an underclass, scorned by the same white society which oppressed them. Jewish-Negro relations, in large measure, reflect this basic difference.

There has been much tragedy in the histories of both the Jews and of the ancestors of the American Negroes. Jews in Europe over the past six centuries have suffered medieval inquisitions, have been repeatedly exiled en masse, and have been subjected to countless pogroms. The nadir of their misfortunes, of course, was the Nazi holocaust. Equally horrendous for centuries was the lot of the East and West Africans at the hands of the slaver. Less well known is the story of the Congolese who for more than a quarter of a century beginning around 1885 were at the mercy of Belgium's King Leopold. Barbaric mutilation and outright murder were committed in the name of economic progress and western civilization. Famine, forced labor, epidemics, and massacres decimated the black population.

In America the fortunes of Jews and blacks have been markedly dissimilar. But despite the enormous differences between their histories in the United States, differences which are discussed at some length in Chapter 1, Jews and Negroes have been linked or compared with one another. The comparisons have sometimes been made by Jews, sometimes by black Americans, sometimes by anti-Semites.[6]

In the latter half of the twentieth century, blacks have been acutely aware of and vocal about the profound differences between their own position in America and that of the white American of the Jewish faith. Still, there are parallels between the Jewish experiences of facing systematic persecution in Europe and the Negro experience in America. In assessing the black man's predicament the Hitlerian tragedy of the Jews is often referred to by young blacks who have taken militant stances in the struggle for black liberation. For example, in 1966 Stokely Carmichael commented wryly: "To ask Negroes to get in the Democratic party is like ask-

---

[6] At the beginning of this century, for example, a white man, one Arthur T. Abernathy, actually claimed that Jews were the descendants and kinsmen of the African "holding the Negro's features and characteristics through the long years of racial transmutations." The Jews, whom the author viewed as exploiters and exacters of the pound of flesh, are alleged like Negroes to be "pathetically devoid of regard for the truth." He characterized both minorities as cunning and susceptible to bribery. Even the Ku Klux Klan to whom Jews and Negroes are anathema, has not suggested such a coincidence of traits, much less an identity of racial descent. See Arthur T. Abernathy, *The Jew a Negro* (Moravian Falls, N.C.: Dixie Publishing Co., 1910). Interestingly, almost sixty years later a black nationalist claimed that Americans of African descent were actually God's chosen people in the Old Testament sense of that term. The Reverend Albert B. Cleage, Jr., has denied that the Nation Israel whose history is chronicled in the Bible was ever a white nation. American Jews are really converts to Judaism. Middle Eastern Jews, on the other hand, are "black" as were their forebears. In enunciating his theology of black power Cleage has described Jesus as "a revolutionary black leader . . . seeking to lead a black nation to freedom." Mary was a black woman, he contends, and Moses was nonwhite. See Albert B. Cleage, Jr., *The Black Messiah* (New York: Sheed & Ward, 1968), pp. 4, 40–41.

ing Jews to join the Nazi party."[7] Others, including H. Rap Brown have promised that in the event of a racial showdown black people would not play Jew to the white man's Nazi.

Harry Edwards, a prime mover in the black athletes' revolt against racism in organized sports, has drawn upon Jewish tradition in recommending punishment for black "traitors." "If a Jew turns against his religion, the Jewish people mourn for him, as if he were dead. They write him off, as dead. He is dead spiritually. The black man who cooperates with . . . pigs will be written off, ignored."[8]

Eldridge Cleaver, the exiled Black Panther leader, has seen a fascinating parallel between the present dilemma of the Afro-American and the plight of European Jews at the end of the nineteenth century when Theodor Herzl, the founder of modern political Zionism, appeared on the stage of history.

The Jews had no homeland and were dispersed around the world, cooped up in the ghettos of Europe. Functionally, a return to Israel seemed as impractical as obtaining a homeland for Afro-Americans now seems. Renowned Jewish leaders were seriously considering transporting the Jews to Argentina, en masse, and developing a homeland there. Others seriously considered obtaining from England the territory of Uganda in East Africa for the same purpose. . . .[9] The Jewish people were prepared psychologically to take desperate and unprecedented action. They saw themselves faced with an immediate disastrous situation. Genocide was staring them in the face and this common threat galvanized them into common action. Psychologically, black people in America have precisely the same outlook as the Jews had then, and they are therefore prepared to take common action for the solution to a common problem.[10]

Coming from a strong critic of present day Zionism, the preceding is particularly interesting. Cleaver was by no means the first to see an analogy between Zionism and certain forms of black nation-

---

[7] *New York Times,* 22 May 1966.

[8] *New York Times Magazine,* 12 May 1968.

[9] In point of fact the territory considered by the Zionist Organization from 1903–1905 was the East Africa Protectorate, now Kenya. See Robert G. Weisbord, *African Zion* (Philadelphia: Jewish Publication Society, 1968).

[10] Robert Scheer, ed., *Eldridge Cleaver: Post-Prison Writings and Speeches* (New York: Random House, 1969), pp. 67–68.

alism. "A certain similarity" between Herzl and the man whom many remember as the progenitor of black power, the flamboyant Marcus Mosiah Garvey, was noted by sociologist Arnold Rose. From the time of his arrival in America in 1916 this charismatic Black Moses exalted everything black. He disparaged the history of the white man and glorified the history of the African. He taught that black was not inferior; on the contrary, it represented beauty and power. Race purity was praised by Garvey, and the amalgamation of the races derogated.

This remarkable West Indian founded the Universal Negro Improvement Association (UNIA) to accomplish his full-blown black nationalist program. Its motto was "One God! One Aim, One Destiny" and its anthem "Ethiopia: Thou Land of Our Fathers." In his journal, *The Negro World,* Garvey repeatedly asserted that the only hope for the black man was flight from the white man's oppression and return to African soil.

Arnold Rose observed that both Herzl and Garvey responded to prejudice by favoring escape to another land rather than trying to overcome it at home. As leaders they both shunned assimilation and embraced nationalism.[11]

It should be added that just as Jewish nationalists included territorialists—those who sought a homeland for Jews but not necessarily in Palestine—there have been separatist-minded black nationalists who have not set their sights on Africa. Counted among these would be the Black Muslims and the New Republic of Africa, who favor the creation of an independent black nation within what are now our national boundaries. However interesting and valid the Zionism-black nationalism analogy may be, it has had little relevance to the encounters between Afro-Americans and Jewish-Americans. So striking have been the disparities in their experiences in this country that they have overshadowed the common factors in their respective histories.

[11] Arnold Rose, *The Negro's Morale: Group Identification and Protest* (Minneapolis: University of Minnesota Press, 1949), p. 43.

BITTERSWEET
ENCOUNTER

} 1 {

THE JEW AND THE
NEGRO IN AMERICAN
HISTORY: A COMPARISON
AND A CONTRAST

AMERICA'S FIRST BLACKS ARRIVED IN VIRGINIA IN 1619, ONE YEAR
before the *Mayflower* dropped anchor in Plymouth Bay. The first
Jewish community in America was founded in 1654 in New York,
then New Amsterdam, by Sephardic Jews who had fled persecution
by the Portuguese in Brazil.

Historically, Jews victimized by a nominally Christian world and
blacks by a white world are in a sense brothers in adversity. But
since the seventeenth century the historical experiences of the two
groups in the United States have been significantly divergent.

One noteworthy difference can readily be discerned in the circumstances of the transatlantic journey. Woebegone Africans en
route to enslavement in the New World endured the infamous and
inhuman Middle Passage. Chained like animals, the Africans on the
slave vessels were fed a monotonous, unbalanced diet which ren-
dered them vulnerable to a variety of diseases. Smallpox and flux
were commonplace. Overcrowding afforded the slave little room to
move about. The area provided for a male slave was probably
about seventy-two inches long, sixteen inches wide, and thirty-one
inches high.[1] Sanitary facilities were, when they existed, wholly inadequate. Female slaves were fair game for the crew, particularly

[1] Daniel P. Mannix and Malcolm Cowley, *Black Cargoes: A History of the
Atlantic Slave Trade* (New York: Viking Press, 1962), p. 107.

1

the ships' officers. Incredible brutality was exhibited toward the black cargo. Insubordinate captives were dealt with unmercifully. In short, the slaves were regarded as subhuman creatures and treated accordingly.

To appreciate how ruthless the slave trade was, one has only to look at a case such as that involving the Liverpool slave ship, *Zong*. In September 1781 the *Zong* sailed from the Guinea coast of Africa bound for Jamaica. Seventeen whites and approximately 440 Negro slaves were on board. In late November as the vessel was approaching her destination, she suddenly veered off course. Seven whites and over sixty Africans had already perished. Many more of the latter were gravely ill. They would certainly be of no market value in the West Indies. Chances were they would not even survive the journey. The dead and dying slaves represented a significant loss to the owners of the *Zong*. Apparently, it occurred to the ship's captain that the potential loss could be transferred to the underwriters. If part of a cargo were jettisoned to save the rest, a claim for damages could be filed. The captain made a fateful decision to throw 133 of those sickly slaves least likely to recover into the sea. A trial followed, made inevitable by the adamant refusal of the insurers to honor the claim of the *Zong*'s owners. However, the claim was upheld and the Chief Justice, Lord Mansfield, opined that "though it shocks me very much, the case of slaves was the same as if horses had been thrown overboard."[2]

There are no reliable statistics regarding the number of Africans involuntarily transported to the Western Hemisphere. Estimates vary from less than fifteen million to more than fifty million. Africans who survived the Atlantic crossing and the heavy toll taken by the seasoning period in the New World faced a bleak future. Those who were not marketable might be left on the wharves to starve to death. For the remainder, life probably meant perpetual servitude. Moreover, their children and grandchildren would inherit the same lowly status.

Historians may question the assertion that slavery in America

2 *Gregson* v. *Gilbert* Henry Roscoe, *Reports of Cases Argued and Determined in the Court of King's Bench (1782–1785)* (London: S. Sweet and Stevens & Sons, 1831) 3: 233–234. For the complete story see Robert G. Weisbord, "The Case of the Slave Ship *Zong*," *History Today*, August 1969, pp. 561–567.

was "the most awful the world has ever known."[3] They may differ about the relative harshness of slavery in the United States, Latin America, and the West Indies. But clearly the "magnolia and mint-julep" version of antebellum bondage is a distortion. Transplanted Africans were not the primitive, banjo-strumming, single-dimension figures textbooks have made them out to be. They were not contented to toil from dawn to dusk under the overseer's lash. Almost certainly they were not the docile, infantile beings which Ulrich B. Phillips and Stanley Elkins have etched in their respective writings. Black resistance took many forms: running away, malingering, self-induced injury, slave strikes, and insurrections.[4]

There is no reason to believe that masters were, for the most part, benign and paternalistic. Especially in the colonial period, slave codes allowed hideously cruel punishment to be meted out to Negroes who misbehaved. Castration, a penalty unknown to English law, was used exclusively for Negroes and Indians.[5] Where the law expressly forbade gross maltreatment of slaves, it could be easily circumvented. Slaves could not testify against whites in court, and racial solidarity prevented other whites from doing so. White juries, as one might expect, were extremely loath to convict a fellow Caucasian of committing a crime against chattel in human form.

The "peculiar institution," to use John C. Calhoun's euphemism for slavery, also did violence to the Negro family. Slave marriages were not recognized in law because bondsmen could not make contracts. Adultery and fornication had no legal significance where unfree blacks were concerned.[6] Human rights could not be permitted to interfere with property rights, and blacks, it must be emphasized, were mere property. After all, the venerable Constitution had declared that the Negro, for purposes of taxation and representation, was to be counted as three-fifths of a man.

[3] See Nathan Glazer's introduction to Stanley Elkins, *Slavery: A Problem in American Institutional and Intellectual Life* (New York: Grosset & Dunlap, 1963), p. ix.

[4] Kenneth Stampp, *Peculiar Institution* (New York: Vintage Books, 1956), pp. 128–132.

[5] Winthrop Jordan, *White Over Black: American Attitudes Towards the Negro 1550–1812* (Chapel Hill: University of North Carolina Press, 1968), p. 155.

[6] Stampp, *Peculiar Institution*, p. 198.

No legal obstacle prevented the separation of slave "husbands" and "wives" or parents and children. The master's conscience was the only barrier to the dissolution of families. All too often, judging by contemporary accounts, his conscience served a purely decorative purpose. Black couples were joined in "wedlock" by one Negro preacher in Kentucky "until death or distance do you part." An advertisement in the *New Orleans Bee* described slaves for sale under these flexible conditions: "A negro [sic] woman, 24 years of age, and her two children, one eight and the other three years old. Said negroes [sic] will be sold separately or together, as desired."[7] Kenneth Stampp has cited the case of a slave owner in Virginia who offered to sell a female slave "with one or more Children, to suit the purchaser." A slaveholder in Kentucky indicated his willingness to dispose of a mother and her four offspring "together or separately."[8]

Contrary to popular thinking in the twentieth century, repression of blacks before the Civil War was not a phenomenon peculiar to the South. Above the Mason-Dixon line, the Negro was quasi-free at best. As Leon F. Litwack has documented in his incisive *North of Slavery,* persons of African extraction were limited legally and extra-legally in almost every facet of their daily lives.[9] Determined and often successful attempts were made by states to bar additional immigration of Negroes. Jacksonian democracy, specifically the extension of the franchise, bypassed the hapless "free" Negro. Twenty years before the Civil War, only 7 percent of the Africans in the North lived in states that allowed them to vote.[10] Not a single state admitted to the Union from the Missouri Compromise to 1865 gave Negroes the ballot.[11]

Equal justice did not exist in the antebellum North. In five states Negroes were legally prevented from testifying in a court of law in those instances where a white man was a party.[12] Only in one state,

---

[7] Frank Tannenbaum, *Slave and Citizen: The Negro in the Americas* (New York: Vintage Books, 1946), p. 77.

[8] Stampp, *Peculiar Institution,* p. 267.

[9] Leon F. Litwack, *North of Slavery: The Negro in the Free States 1790–1860* (Chicago: University of Chicago Press, 1965), p. 64.

[10] Ibid., p. 75.

[11] Ibid., p. 79.

[12] Ibid., p. 93.

Massachusetts, were Negroes eligible for jury service. Where Negroes were not completely excluded from places of public accommodation, they were Jim Crowed. That was the lamentable situation in land and river transportation, in entertainment and recreation facilities, in most restaurants, hotels, and churches. Furthermore, according to Litwack, Negroes "were often educated in segregated schools, punished in segregated prisons, nursed in segregated hospitals and buried in segregated cemeteries."[13]

And, as if such degradation were not enough, they were the targets of sporadic individual and mob violence. Periodic anti-Negro eruptions occurred in Philadelphia in the 1830s and 1840s wreaking death and destruction.[14] Cincinnati's black enclave was put to the torch in 1862 as the result of Negroes' being employed as longshoremen on the Ohio River docks. Perhaps the most serious manifestation of anti-Negroism in the North took place the following year in New York City during the draft riots in which Negroes were indiscriminately beaten and lynched. Homes and businesses owned by Negroes were burned to the ground. Even the Colored Orphan Asylum was not spared.[15]

Negro hopes for freedom and equality which had been raised by the Emancipation Proclamation, the Union victory, and the adoption of the Thirteenth, Fourteenth, and Fifteenth Amendments to the Constitution were quickly dashed after Reconstruction. What followed were four decades of betrayal. Various devices were used to disfranchise the freedmen in the South. Worse still, their very lives were jeopardized by a society determined to consolidate white supremacy. From 1889 to 1918 more than 3,200 persons were lynched in the United States. Of those 2,522 were black.[16] No fewer than seventy Americans of African descent were lynched in 1919. Some were returning servicemen, still in uniform. They had fought for their country ostensibly to make the world safe for democracy.

---

[13] Ibid., p. 97.
[14] Ibid., p. 100.
[15] August Meier and Elliot Rudwick, *From Plantation to Ghetto: An Interpretive History of American Negroes* (New York: Hill & Wang, 1966), pp. 129–130.
[16] *Thirty Years of Lynching In The United States 1889–1918* (New York: NAACP, 1919), p. 7.

The summer of 1919 in John Hope Franklin's estimation "ushered in the greatest period of interracial strife the nation had ever witnessed."[17] Race riots comparable to those which had virtually devastated Atlanta, Georgia, Brownsville, Texas, and Springfield, Illinois earlier in the century, took place in the nation's capital, in Chicago, and in more than twenty other cities in the last seven months of 1919. Twenty-three Negroes were killed in the Chicago upheaval alone.[18] Unlike the urban convulsions of the 1960s, riots in the early part of the twentieth century were little better than antiblack massacres. With considerable justification an east St. Louis race riot in 1917 has been likened to a Russian pogrom.[19]

By the beginning of World War I the rigid separation of white and black Americans permeated southern society. Schools, hotels, restaurants, theaters, buses, trolleys, trains, drinking fountains, toilets, even courtroom bibles, were segregated.[20] Both the executive and legislative branches of the federal government were totally unresponsive to the infringement of Negro rights. As for the federal judiciary, the Supreme Court in *Plessy* v. *Ferguson* (1896) put its stamp of approval on Jim Crowism by setting forth the "separate but equal" doctrine which was not overturned until 1954. Needless to say, during the almost six decades that the doctrine was the law of the land, in practice the emphasis was on separation with lip service paid to equality.

White illusions about ghetto conditions in the 1960s have been shattered by the Kerner Commission report. That study disclosed inter alia that in 1966 median black family income was 58 percent of median white family income.[21] Small wonder. By and large, Negroes continue to hold low-status, low-paying jobs. Rates of unemployment, according to the report, were twice as high for blacks

17 John Hope Franklin, *From Slavery To Freedom: A History of Negro Americans* (New York: Alfred A. Knopf, 1967), p. 480.
18 *Ibid.*, p. 482.
19 Arna Bontemps and Jack Conroy, *Anyplace But Here* (New York: Hill & Wang, 1966), p. 153.
20 The standard work on "Jim Crowism," its etiology and significance is C. Vann Woodward, *The Strange Career of Jim Crow* (New York: Oxford University Press, 1966).
21 *Report of the National Advisory Commission On Civil Disorders* (New York: Bantam Books, 1968), p. 251.

as for whites.[22] Health statistics are even more shocking. Nonwhite mothers have a maternal mortality rate four times higher than their white counterparts. Under the age of one month the white infant mortality rate is 58 percent lower than it is for nonwhite babies. From one month to a year the nonwhite death rate is almost three times as high. On the average, as of 1965, whites could expect to live 6.9 years longer than nonwhites.[23] From these data one is forced to conclude that America's promise to her black citizens is still far from fulfillment.

American-Jewish history has followed a different pattern. During the colonial era Jews suffered amazingly few disabilities. There were recorded anti-Jewish incidents and there were occasional anti-Jewish utterances frequently predicated on the Shylock canards. Isolated statutes adversely affecting Jews can also be cited. But Jacob Rader Marcus, a leading authority on American-Jewish history, has concluded: "there was probably not a single law in the land, in the eighteenth century, that had been enacted for the purpose of imposing a disability on Jews alone."[24]

Jews as such, Marcus has written, were not assaulted. Socially they were often more acceptable than Roman Catholics. They enjoyed civil liberties, economic privileges, and sometimes political rights as well. Neither a ghetto nor a ghetto spirit existed. "If the times are taken into consideration," Marcus concludes, "their [the Jews] economic, social, religious, civil and political status was good, excelled by no conditions in no land of Europe."[25] Of course, the Jewish population was very small. As late as 1850 there were only fifty thousand American Jews. The influx would not occur for three more decades when East European ghetto Jewry found itself in desperate straits. Once again the wandering Jew departed for a new land.

Crossing the Atlantic at the end of the last century was a memorable experience for the Jewish immigrant. For one thing, he was heading for a great unknown. For another, the trip was ordinarily made under circumstances that were far from comfortable.

[22] Ibid., p. 253.
[23] Ibid., p. 270.
[24] Jacob Rader Marcus, *Early American Jewry* (Philadelphia: Jewish Publication Society, 1961), II, 526.
[25] Ibid.

Immigrants' quarters were congested and privacy almost impossible. Their food was of poor quality and many suffered seasickness.[26] Many of the uprooted, having been fleeced by unscrupulous steamship agents, arrived in the United States penniless. Bearing a few bundles containing personal possessions, the immigrant had to run the gauntlet of immigration officials at Ellis Island and other ports of entry. For the great majority, those physically and mentally healthy, those not likely to become public charges, the journey was over. Those with obvious deformities, e.g., the feeble-minded and those patently not employable, might have to repeat the Atlantic ordeal on a ship bound for Europe. As Oscar Handlin, an authority on the history of immigration, has written: "The crossing in all its phases was a harsh and brutal filter."[27] But however trying, however inhuman the transatlantic journey was for multitudes of East European Jews, it was a veritable luxury line cruise compared with the nightmare of the slave ship's Middle Passage.

Adjustment would be difficult for the Jewish immigrants. But they had not come in chains; they had come as free men. In addition, needy newcomers were given a helping hand by Jewish charitable agencies. Outstanding was the Hebrew Sheltering and Immigrant Aid Society or HIAS as it was popularly called. Temporary shelter was found for the homeless. Food and clothing were provided as was information useful to the greenhorn. Some of the lucky new arrivals were taken under the protective wing of their relatives or *landsmen*. None were left to starve on the docks.

Most of the hundreds of thousands of Jews who were part of the immigration that reached tidal-wave proportions after 1882 settled in a few urban areas of the Northeast. Unable to speak, read or write English, they relied upon their coreligionists for jobs and sustenance. Their adjustment to strange surroundings was also facilitated by a host of associations: mutual aid societies, burial societies, social clubs, settlement houses, etc.

To the already established and assimilated immigrants in America, Jews, Negroes from the rural South, and other new-

---

26 Oscar Handlin, *The Uprooted: The Epic Story Of The Great Migration That Made The American People* (New York: Grosset & Dunlap, 1951), pp. 53–54.
27 Ibid., p. 61.

comers were an offensive breed, unassimilable and a danger to America's social fabric and moral fiber. Talking of the Jewish denizens of New York's Lower East Side in the not-so-gay nineties an unidentified contributor to *The New York Times* offered his opinions of the newest Americans. Those opinions have a distinctly déja vu quality.

A writer might go on for a week reciting the abominations of these people and still have much to tell. One of their greatest faults is that they have an utter disregard for law. There is a certain hour when they are required to set out their garbage and ash cans, but they pay no attention to that. . . . Filthy persons and clothing reeking with vermin are seen on every side. . . . Cleanliness is an unknown quantity to these people. They cannot be lifted to a higher plane because they do not want to be.[28]

Ironically, some of the children and grandchildren of immigrants so maligned—Jews, Italians, Poles, Hungarians, and the Irish, now uncritically repeat such characterizations regarding Negroes and Puerto Ricans almost verbatim.

The impoverished Jew in America was viewed as the perennial Shylock stereotype described by Jacob Riis in his *How the Other Half Lives*. "Thrift is the watchword of Jewtown . . . Money is their God. Life itself is of little value compared with even the leanest bank account."[29]

Many Jewish immigrants did in fact live in poverty in New York's East side. In his classic *Jews Without Money,* Michael Gold reminisces of his childhood:

Pimps, gamblers and red-nosed bums, peanut politicians, pugilists in sweaters; tinhorn sports and tall longshoremen in overalls. An endless pageant of East Side life passed through the wicker doors of Jake Wolf's saloon. . . . East Side mothers with heroic bosoms pushed their baby carriages, gossiping. Horse cars jingled by. A tinker hammered at brass. Junkbells clanged. Whirlwinds of dust and newspaper. The prostitutes laughed shrilly. A prophet passed, an old-clothes Jew with a white beard. Kids were dancing around the hurdy-gurdy. Two bums

---

[28] Originally published in 1895, the letter was republished in *The New York Times,* 28 January 1969.

[29] Jacob A. Riis, *How the Other Half Lives: Studies Among the Tenements of New York* (New York: Charles Scribner's Sons, 1902), p. 106.

slugged each other. Excitement, dirt, fighting, chaos! The sound of my street lifted like the blast of a great carnival or catastrophe. . . .

The East Side of New York was then the city's red light district, a vast 606 playground under the business management of Tammany Hall.

The Jews had fled from the European pogroms; with prayer, thanksgiving and solemn faith from a new Egypt into a New Promised Land.

They found awaiting them the sweatshops, the bawdy houses and Tammany Hall. There were hundreds of [Jewish] prostitutes on my street. . . . The pious Jews hated the traffic. But they were pauper strangers here; they could do nothing. They shrugged their shoulders and murmured: "This is America." They tried to live.[30]

In fact sweatshop life was harsh. It meant extremely long hours of arduous labor under hazardous conditions for criminally low pay. After work the Jewish immigrant returned home. For almost all, home was a grimy, cold-water flat in an overpopulated tenement. In 1902 Jacob Riis, writing of the Jewish district in New York City, observed that, "nowhere in the world are so many people crowded together on a square mile as here."[31]

Ghetto-living does not seem to have changed much. Just a decade ago the United States Civil Rights Commission advanced a thought-provoking hypothesis: "If the population density in some of Harlem's worst blocks obtained in the rest of New York City, the entire population of the United States could fit into three of New York's boroughs." Juxtaposition of the plight of the Jew and the predicament of the Negro, however poignant, can be misleading. The Jews assumed, and rightly so, that by diligence and industry they could hurdle the barriers of the ghetto. They could see the light at the end of the proverbial tunnel. Jews in America have worked hard, very hard. That fact cannot be gainsaid. But so has the black American. In his case, Horatio Alger has been as relevant as Mother Goose.

Social discrimination against Jews became noticeable in the last quarter of the nineteenth century. It emerged simultaneously with the escalation of Jewish immigration. However, the social exclusion of Jews was not confined to flotsam and jetsam from Eastern Europe. Well-to-do, highly assimilated German Jews were also ex-

[30] Michael Gold, *Jews Without Money* (New York: Avon, 1965), pp. 5–6.
[31] Riis, *How The Other Half Lives,* p. 105.

cluded. In 1877 a scandal arose over the denial of admittance of a distinguished Jewish banker, Joseph Seligman, to a hotel in Saratoga Springs, New York. Indignant newspaper editorials were sharply critical of the hotel. During the next few years summer resorts and clubs such as the Union League Club of New York were known to restrict their clientele to Christians.[32] The Jew was also persona non grata in many private schools. Clearly though, the pattern of social discrimination was never as extensive as that which affected the Negro. Jews have not been forced to walk across southern towns to get a drink of water. There were signs reading "No Jews Wanted" or the euphemistic "Churches Close By" which plainly indicated distaste for Jewish patronage. But these were comparatively rare and were not legally sanctioned. Until virtually yesterday apartheid was mandated by the law in many regions of America. Even if white Gentile America had desired to set the Jew completely apart, enforcement would have been difficult for an obvious reason—the Jew is white.

Urban Jews in the 1880s were sometimes annoyed, insulted, and abused in the streets. Some were even stoned or had their beards seized by street toughs.[33] Hatred against foreigners was especially marked in the eighties and nineties. It was a time of class cleavage, an era of heightened nativism. The so-called gilded age was also bloody.

Hysterical chauvinism led to the lynching of eleven Italians in New Orleans in 1891. Although violence directed against Jews was rare, there were a few such incidents in the lower South where Jewish merchants were conspicuous. On one occasion farmers, burdened with debt, ran amuck in Delhi, Louisiana, and demolished the stores of four Jewish entrepreneurs. Their objective appears to have been to cancel their indebtedness.[34]

As far as the Jews were concerned, the year 1893 was the nadir.

---

[32] Nathan Glazer, *American Judaism* (Chicago: University of Chicago Press, 1957), p. 45.

[33] Louis Wirth, *The Ghetto* (Chicago: University of Chicago Press, 1928), pp. 180–181.

[34] C. Vann Woodward, *Origins Of The New South 1877–1913,* Vol. IX of *A History of the South,* ed. by Wendell Holmes Stevenson and E. Merton Coulter (10 vols.; Baton Rouge: Louisiana State University Press, 1951), p. 188.

Farmhouses owned by Jewish landlords were reduced to rubble in Mississippi and terrorized Jewish storekeepers were driven out of Louisiana. Sporadic incidents were reported in the North as well. In 1891 five hundred youngsters who worked in a New Jersey glass factory went berserk when fourteen Russian Jews were employed. Jews living in the area found it necessary to move.[35] Religious billingsgate was frequently directed at Jews in various sections of the country.

No loss of life resulted from these nativistic outbursts which bore little resemblance to the anti-Negro mob violence. In fact, there are only two cases on record in the United States of a Jew being lynched.[36] Near Marietta, Georgia, in August 1915, Leo Frank, a New Yorker who had married into an Atlanta Jewish family, was hanged and horribly mutilated. Two years earlier when he was superintendent of a pencil company in Atlanta he was convicted under highly suspicious circumstances of the rape-murder of "little Mary Phagan," a fourteen-year-old employee at the pencil factory. Never before had a white man been found guilty of a capital crime by a white southern jury on the testimony of a black man. For Tom Watson, the malevolent Georgia Populist, Frank's violent death—he refrained from using the word "lynching"—put "Jew Libertines on notice."[37] Ironically, at an earlier stage of his career Watson had professed his intention to "make lynch law odious to the people." By 1915 he defended lynch law and warned: "The Next Jew Who Does What Frank Did Is Going to Get Exactly The Same Thing We Give Negro Rapists."[38]

There is no doubt that the Frank case was a disgrace—the conviction as well as the hanging by a frenzied mob. It became a cause célèbre at the time, and at least two full-length books have since been written about the case.[39] Contrast this with the more than

[35] John Higham, *Strangers in the Land: Patterns of American Nativism 1860–1925* (New York: Atheneum, 1963), pp. 92–93.

[36] There was a case of a double lynching of a Negro and a Jew in Tennessee in 1868. See Morris N. Schappes, ed., *Documentary History of the Jews in the United States* (New York: Citadel Press, 1952), p. 515.

[37] Harry Golden, *A Little Girl Is Dead* (New York: Avon, 1965), p. 291.

[38] Ibid., p. 281.

[39] In addition to the popular treatment of the case by Harry Golden, there is Leonard Dinnerstein, *The Leo Frank Case* (New York: Columbia University Press, 1968).

twenty-five hundred recorded Negro victims of lynchings previously mentioned who remain, almost without exception, nameless and faceless.[40] Their comparative obscurity attests to the fact that for most of American history the basic humanity of blacks has been rejected, explicitly or implicitly, by American society at large.

The disillusionment which set in following World War I was accompanied by an upsurge in xenophobia. One historian has written aptly of "The Tribal Twenties." Of all the foreigners who had inundated America's shores for more than four decades, the Jews were singled out for sustained nativist mistreatment. Job discrimination was rife, as was prejudice in higher education. New York University and a number of Ivy League colleges instituted quotas governing the maximum percentage of Jews to be admitted.[41] Medical schools were notorious for their discrimination. To fully comprehend the significance of such anti-Semitism the reader must be familiar with the Czarist numerus clausus which imposed a 10 percent quota on the number of Jewish admissions to high schools and universities located in the pale of Jewish settlement. For education-minded Jews the numerus clausus, Russian or American style, was among the vilest of disabilities.

Anti-Semitism was also generated in the twenties by the dissemination of the fraudulent Protocols of the Elders of Zion purported to be proof of a worldwide Jewish conspiracy. A gullible Henry Ford lent his support to the anti-Jewish crusade in the columns of his weekly, the *Dearborn Independent*. The weekly slanders against the Jewish people were collected and distributed under the provocative title, *The International Jew*. During the depression-ridden thirties there was no shortage of Jew-baiters. This is not surprising. Bigotry thrives on despair. Preëminent among the bigots was Father Coughlin whose tirades skillfully blended the blessings of isolationism and the dangers of international Jewish capitalism. Despite the professional Jew-baiter, and despite the widely publicized incidents of black anti-Semitism in recent years, the preponderance of evidence suggests that overt anti-Semitism has now reached its lowest ebb.

[40] The names are actually recorded in *Thirty Years of Lynching In The United States.*
[41] Higham, *Strangers in the Land,* p. 278.

An examination of the respective histories of the African American and the Jewish American leads to an inescapable conclusion: the contrast is vivid. Given the conventional measure of success in America, the Jew has succeeded. He sought religious freedom and economic opportunity. Essentially, he found both. Hated and persecuted for centuries he has "made it" in America. This is not to say that millions of Americans do not harbor hostility toward Jews. They do. This is not to say that unfortunate stereotypes of Jews do not persist. Most assuredly, they do. This does not mean that one does not occasionally hear a blatantly anti-Semitic jibe. "Jew bastard" is a single word in the vocabulary of some Gentiles. Jewish executives in banking and insurance are few and far between, the myth of Jewish financial dominance to the contrary, notwithstanding.[42] In more than a handful of social circles snobbery toward Jews continues.[43] Jews, regardless of ability to pay, are still unwelcome in certain neighborhoods.

But who can deny that Jews are privileged, not deprived? In the main, they are comfortably ensconced as members of America's bourgeoisie. When they are barred from country clubs, Jews build their own, just as big and just as gaudy as those that exclude them. If Jews live in ghettos today they are golden ghettos for the most part, and Jews are there by choice. Fully 70 percent of Jewish high school graduates go on to college, an incredibly high figure unmatched by any other ethnic minority. Therefore, a Jew who tells a Negro that he, too, understands bigotry and brutality may actually enrage the latter. James Baldwin states: "For it is not here, and not now, that the Jew is being slaughtered, and he is never despised, here, as the Negro is, *because* he is an American. The Jewish travail occurred across the sea and America rescued

---

[42] A corollary of the exclusion of Jews from managerial roles in large corporations is the preponderance of Jewish small businessmen in positions of great visibility in ghettos. This lack of ethnic anonymity perpetuates the Shylock stereotype and keeps some Jews in a social position similar to that which they occupied in medieval society.

[43] According to a seven-year study made public in May 1969, "the Jewish religion stands alone as a major negative factor in the lives of American business executives." The inability of Jews to obtain membership in athletic, country, and golf clubs hindered "their climb up the executive ladder in the world of big business." *New York Times,* 16 May 1969.

him from the house of bondage. But America is the house of bondage for the Negro, and no country can rescue him."[44]

Eric Hoffer, the colorful San Francisco longshoreman-writer, has a different outlook. Hoffer, never reticent about expressing his views, has written that the city is simultaneously "the greatest opportunity and the worst influence."[45] He contends that to the Jew it has been the former and to the Negro it has been the latter. Why? Simply because to "thrive in the city one must have ambition and persistence to make the most of its opportunities and discipline to resist temptation. Most Negroes have neither." But the Jews, he maintains, are altogether different. Their example "shows what persistent, patient striving and a passion for education can do for man in this country even in the teeth of discrimination. This is a fact which the Negro vehemently rejects. It sticks in his gullet." Hoffer goes on to explain that, "The Jew impairs the authenticity of the Negro's grievances and alibis. He threatens the Negro's most precious possession: The freedom to fail."[46]

Foes of Negro-Jewish amity doubtlessly relish the foregoing. For those having even a nodding acquaintance with American history it is unadulterated nonsense. Hoffer is really making the fallacious argument that the Jewish and the black experiences were fundamentally the same. Jews have been achievers and Negroes have not, only because the former have the character traits required for success. Coming from a man of Hoffer's stature this explanation is irresponsible. He completely overlooks the major stumbling blocks confronting the Negro in his quest for social, political, and economic equality.

Some of these impediments to the Negro should be mentioned here. For instance, Jews and other white immigrants were never stigmatized by their color. They lacked, fortunately for them, what the sociologists call "high visibility." English-speaking, second-generation Jews who were not averse to changing their foreign-sounding names could cloak their past identities. Despite hair-

[44] James Baldwin, "Negroes Are Anti-Semitic Because They're Anti-White," *New York Times Magazine*, 9 April 1967.

[45] Eric Hoffer, "The Reason for Negro Hostility Towards Jews," *San Francisco Examiner*, 18 November 1968.

[46] Ibid.

straightening and skin-lightening, Negroes were left with what the dominant white society chose to see as a badge of inferiority, namely their blackness.

Chronology is another factor ignored by the Hoffer school of thought in asking the loaded question: "Why can't Negroes climb the ladder of success as other immigrants have done?" Ethnic minorities which came to the United States at the end of the nineteenth century encountered an expanding economy, one which cried out for unskilled labor. A strong back was the only qualification necessary for gainful employment. Figuratively speaking, the Afro-American in the sixties has just reached Ellis Island. His timing could not have been worse. A technological revolution has reduced to a minimum the industrial demand for unskilled labor. For example, elevators which required human operation a few decades ago are now increasingly being run automatically. Today there are still many thousands of elevator operatives, mainly black, mostly middle-aged and older, usually unskilled, faced with displacement. In the South crops which were picked by Negro hands for generations are machine-harvested. Tractors and electric milking machines are part of the same mechanization trend. Consequently, jobs for the uneducated and unskilled are hard to come by.

Unions, too, have made a crucial difference in the collective ethnic histories of Jews and Negroes. Who can adequately measure the contribution of the trade unions, the International Ladies Garment Workers Union (ILGWU), for instance, to Jewish economic progress?[47] Compare this with the traditional exclusion of Americans of African descent from the building trades unions.

The Kerner Commission has also taken cognizance of the political opportunities that facilitated the escape from ghetto poverty by strangers in our land. Urban political machines which have lately been at least partially eclipsed by reform clubs, were in the ascendance earlier in the century. Tammany Hall and its nefarious counterparts in a score of metropolises, struck a bargain of sorts with the immigrants. Votes on election day were exchanged for patronage. Work on the construction of public projects fell into

[47] The racial practices of the ILGWU, one of the more progressive unions, have been criticized by Herbert Hill, the NAACP's expert on labor relations, and by Kenneth Clark. See Kenneth B. Clark, *Dark Ghetto: Dilemmas of Social Power* (New York: Harper & Row, 1967), pp. 43–45.

this category. And it was no coincidence that certain municipal departments, e.g., fire, police, and sanitation, were practically monopolized by particular ethnic groups.[48]

Jews, it should also be recalled, came to this country without any experience as chattel slaves in the modern era. Jewish ghetto dwellers who came to America may have come without worldly goods, but they carried with them something more valuable—a highly developed culture. They hungered for education, and they were, by and large, literate although rarely in English. Without a long heritage of literacy, rapid advancement in the academic, legal, and scientific worlds would have been well-nigh impossible for the Jews.[49] Slaves, on the other hand, were kept unskilled. Teaching bondsmen to read and write was actually prohibited by law in many southern states.

Brief reference has already been made to the corrosive effect of the plantation system on the Negro family. Jews, to the contrary, found their close-knit families a vital source of strength in their trying years of adjustment to the American way of life. Jews brought with them a tradition of mercantile entrepreneurship. If initially they lacked the capital to enter business, they didn't lack the self-confidence or the expertise. In this respect, as in so many others, the plantation in Dixie was a poorer preparatory school for life in a highly competitive American milieu than the *shtetl,* the Jewish ghetto in the Russian pale of settlement.

The plantation system greatly affected the psychology of the Negro by fostering the passive traits of obedience and submission rather than the more self-assertive traits which helped the white immigrant worker to "make it" in America. To survive within the system the Negro turned to flattery, hypochondria, and self-abnegation, thus fulfilling the master's stereotyped notions about the slave mentality. Nor did the characteristics implanted in the black man during several centuries of slavery immediately disappear as the result of his "emancipation." In 1903 W. E. B. Du Bois analyzed this problem in his *The Souls of Black Folk:* "These workingmen have been trained for centuries as slaves. They exhibit,

[48] *Report of the National Advisory Commission on Civil Disorders,* p. 279.
[49] Bayard Rustin, "From Protest To Politics," in *Negro Protest Thought in the Twentieth Century,* ed. by Francis L. Broderick and August Meier (Indianapolis: Bobbs-Merrill Co., 1965), pp. 408–409.

therefore, all the advantages and defects of such training, they are willing and good natured, but not self-reliant, provident or careful. . . . [They are] handicapped by a training the very opposite to that of the modern self-reliant democratic laborer."

Though persecuted for centuries, Jewish refugees who set foot in America in the pre-World War I era had a psychological advantage. They harbored positive self-images. They took pride in their centuries-old culture. Black Americans were stripped of their African heritage. They were brainwashed into believing that they were descended from naked, cannibalistic savages. Without European intervention Africa and Africans would have remained benighted and barbaric, according to this distorted version of the black man's past. The considerable cultural achievements of medieval Sudanic kingdoms such as Ghana, Mali, and Songhay along with Axum, Kush, Benin, and Zimbabwe—if known at all by American historians—were conveniently ignored. For the most part, until the black revolution of the sixties, Afro-Americans have been embarrassed by their color and ashamed of their African roots. Happily, this state of affairs is rapidly changing.

Familiarity with social studies curricula and textbooks provide an explanation for the widespread ignorance of the true history of the black man. Until quite recently the Negro in almost all American history books used on the primary and secondary school levels was the "invisible man," to use author Ralph Ellison's apt phrase. In other words, black history more often than not has been bypassed or ignored. If white Americans had been exposed to the whole melancholy truth, chances are they would understand what the late Malcolm X meant when he commented bitterly: "We didn't land on Plymouth Rock, it landed on us."

Willingness to remedy social evils is contingent upon the realization that those evils exist and, in the case of the black man, have existed for nearly three and a half centuries. So long as white America is allowed to delude itself into believing that the black man's problems are of his own making, are ascribable to laziness and innate incapacity rather than to enslavement and oppression, remedies will be slow in coming. And so long will dialogue between and about Afro-Americans and other hyphenated Americans be conducted against a background of misunderstanding and myth.

}2{

EARLY SPORADIC ENCOUNTERS

INTERACTION BETWEEN NEGROES AND JEWS IN THE UNITED STATES can be traced as far back as the colonial period. There was, however, no contact then on the scale that has occurred in twentieth-century urban America. Blacks were principally unfree agrarian workers. In 1790 the first decennial census revealed that all but 59,000 of the nearly 760,000 Negroes were chattel slaves, mostly field hands. By 1860 there were approximately 488,000 "free" Negroes and almost 4,000,000 black bondsmen.[1] The overwhelming majority of the latter were engaged in raising cotton, rice, sugar, tobacco, and hemp on southern plantations.

Jews who numbered about 150,000 in 1860—three times as many as there had been a decade earlier—found the urban environment more congenial. On the eve of the Civil War Jewish communities existed in New York, Chicago, Pittsburgh, Philadelphia, Cincinnati, Baltimore, St. Louis, Newark, and a host of other metropolitan manufacturing and commercial centers.[2] Hence, by dint of geography and sheer numbers, encounters between Jews and African-derived peoples were limited.

Insofar as Jews did relate to Negroes, in general they related as did other white Americans. Jews were both proslavery and anti-

---

[1] John Hope Franklin, *From Slavery to Freedom: A History of Negro Americans* (New York: Alfred A. Knopf, 1967), p. 217.
[2] Bertram Wallace Korn, *American Jewry and the Civil War* (Cleveland and New York: World Publishing Co., 1961), p. 1.

slavery. There were Jewish slaveholders and Jewish abolitionists. There were Negrophobes and Negrophiles.

Of the colonial period Jacob Rader Marcus has observed that, "As far as can be determined . . . Jews were no different from non-Jews in their treatment of Negroes."[3] And Bertram W. Korn, a scholar specializing in American-Jewish history, has written that although Jews in the Old South were not among the major slave-dealers, "they participated in every aspect and process of the exploitation of defenseless blacks."[4] This included purchasing, owning, and selling slaves. It included apprehending runaways and meting out punishment. Both in their thinking about and behavior toward slaves, Jews were indistinguishable from their southern Gentile neighbors.

In the early federal era, Abraham M. Seixas, a Jewish businessman whose merchandise included slaves, was living in Charleston. Apparently he had a penchant for inserting poetic advertisements in newspapers such as the one which was published by the *South Carolina State Gazette* in 1794.

Abraham Seixas	He has for sale
All so gracious	Some negroes, male,
Once again does offer	Will suit full well grooms
His services pure	He has likewise
For to secure	Some of their wives
Money in the coffer	Can man clean dirty rooms.[5]

From the available evidence it seems that Jews were neither more likely nor less likely than other southerners to question the morality of commerce in black flesh. There were Jewish civic leaders, businessmen, and politicians ready, even eager, to justify the twin evils of slavery and the slave trade. The year after Appomattox one Solomon Cohen in Savannah wrote that slavery was "refining and civilizing to the whites—giving them an elevation of sentiment and ease and dignity of manners only attainable in societies under the restraining influence of a privileged class—and at

[3] Jacob Rader Marcus, *Early American Jewry* (Philadelphia: Jewish Publication Society, 1961), I, 419.

[4] Bertram Wallace Korn, *Jews and Negro Slavery in the Old South 1789–1865* (Elkins Park, Pa.: Reform Congregation Keneseth Israel, 1961), pp. 34, 45.

[5] Marcus, *Early American Jewry*, II, 255–256.

the same time the only human institution that could elevate the Negro from barbarism and develop the small amount of intellect with which he is endowed."[6]

Cohen's defense of slavery is similar to that offered on occasion by John C. Calhoun and James Henry Hammond, two United States senators from South Carolina. Sometimes called the mudsill theory, their argument usually ran as follows. Down through history in all advanced societies a civilized leisure class lived off the sweat and toil of a menial class. In the South the infantile, docile African, inferior in intellectual capacity, constituted that menial class.

Another champion of the slave system was Judah P. Benjamin. Of Spanish-Jewish ancestry, he was born in the Virgin Islands. Benjamin became a successful sugar grower and business promoter, an outstanding orator and debater, and is best remembered as a senator from Louisiana and secretary of war under the Confederacy. Not surprisingly, Benjamin shared the common notion of that day that the Negro's intellect was not as acute as the white man's. Yet one of Benjamin's statements raises interesting questions about his racial ideology. "What is a slave? He is a human being. He has feelings and passion and intellect. His heart like the white man's swells with love, burns with jealousy, aches with sorrow, pines under restraint and discomfort, boils with revenge and ever cherishes the desire for liberty."

The foregoing observation, unusual for the antebellum South in its recognition of the basic humanity of the black man, prompted Benjamin's biographer to speculate: "could Benjamin, a member of a race that had known its share of oppression have had, therefore, a greater sympathy for the Negro?"[7]

A few southern Jews did object to the slave system. Isaiah Isaacs, for example, advocated manumission of the unfree. Perhaps the first Jewish resident of Virginia, and a partner in a prosperous Richmond firm, he freed his own slaves in his will because "all men are by nature equally free."[8]

The efforts of other rare souls on behalf of individual Negroes

---

[6] Korn, *Jews and Negro Slavery in the Old South,* p. 61.
[7] Robert Douthat Meade, *Judah P. Benjamin and the American Civil War* (Chicago: University of Chicago Press, 1944), p. 9.
[8] Marcus, *Early American Jewry,* II, 183.

have also been recorded. Peter Still, forty years a slave in Kentucky and Alabama, attributed his liberation to the generosity of two German Jews. Joseph Friedman and his younger brother, Isaac, were the first Jews to settle in the Tuscumbia region of Alabama. Their Christian neighbors doubted that "mercenary" Jews could harbor the tender feelings which they, the true southerners, allegedly felt for their slaves. Yet Peter believed that only to Joseph Friedman could he confide his longing for personal freedom. Under an arrangement whereby the Jew purchased Peter, the latter was allowed to sell his labor to others. He could keep his earnings to buy his freedom which he did in 1850.[9]

Why weren't there many more Joseph Friedmans and Isaiah Isaacs? Why did southern Jews, in the main, acquiesce in the status quo antebellum? How can one explain Jewish compliance with and involvement in the slave system?

Bertram Korn has contended that although Jews were few in number and vulnerable to the wrath of the larger community, it was not the spectre of anti-Semitism that militated against a distinctively antislavery position. Instead, Korn has pointed to the need of Jewish Americans to be accepted as equals by their neighbors. By copying the example set by Gentile slave masters they would achieve a psychological and social parity. Thus their accommodation to a new and potentially uncomfortable milieu was accomplished at the expense of the black man.[10]

Race consciousness in Dixie resulted in benefit to the Jew as a white man. Differences between whites were submerged in a society that was preoccupied with maintaining the subordinate status of blacks. In this vein Korn has analyzed the loftier political and social status enjoyed by southern Jews than by their northern co-religionists: "The Negroes acted as an escape valve in Southern society. The Jews gained in status and security from the very presence of this large mass of defenceless victims who were compelled to absorb all of the prejudices which might otherwise have been expressed more frequently in anti-Jewish sentiment."[11]

---

9 Kate E. R. Pickard, *The Kidnapped and the Ransomed* (Syracuse: William T. Hamilton, 1856), pp. 212–213, 228–229.

10 Korn, *Jews and Negro Slavery in the Old South,* p. 26.

11 Korn, *American Jewry and the Civil War,* p. 67.

North as well as south Jewish racial views were not appreciably different from those of Christians. Before the American Revolution which gave considerable impetus to the antislavery crusade above the Mason-Dixon line, some Jews were identified with the institution of slavery. Examples can easily be cited in Newport, Rhode Island, which figured prominently in the traffic in black cargo throughout the eighteenth century. Newport's early Jewish settlement was built in part by refugees from the Portuguese Inquisition. A particularly enterprising mercantile partnership in the community was that of Rivera and Lopez. Among their broad business interests was traffic in slaves. Beginning in the 1760s the company sent vessels to the West African coast on a regular basis.

Isaac Eliezer and Samuel Moses, business associates in Newport, also participated in the lucrative commerce in slaves. In a 1762 letter addressed to one of the captains in their employ, Eliezer and Moses' instructions were to: "make the best of your way to the windward part of the coast of Affrica [sic], and at your arrival there dispose of your cargo for the most possible can be gotten and invest the neat [sic] proceeds into as many good merchantable slaves as you can, and make all the despatch you possible can."[12]

Writing of Elmina, the old slave fortress on the Gold Coast which he visited, Harold Isaacs "had the small but consoling thought that my ancestors, whatever other sins they might have been committing at the time, were sequestered in some Eastern European ghetto and could not have been among the slavers who waited out there on those ships."[13] If Isaacs was thinking specifically of his own forbears he may well have been justified in making this statement. If, however, he was thinking in broader terms of Jews, especially those involved in transatlantic commerce, he was mistaken.

Slaves were hired to build the famous eighteenth-century Touro synagogue in Newport, the oldest Jewish house of worship in the

---

[12] Marcus, *Early American Jewry*, I, 127–128.

[13] Criticizing Isaacs' article that was published in the 13 May 1961 issue of *The New Yorker*, Horace Mann Bond pointed to Jewish slave importers in New Orleans, Mobile, Charleston, and to those in the Hanse and Dutch cities. See Horace Mann Bond, "Howe and Isaacs in the Bush: The Ram in the Thicket," *Apropos of Africa*, ed. by Adelaide Cromwell Hill and Martin Kilson (London: Frank Cass & Co., 1969), pp. 278–279.

United States and today a national historic site.[14] The eminent philanthropist, Judah Touro, was born in Newport and raised in Boston, but lived most of his life in New Orleans. His aversion to the institution of slavery was so strong that he often bought slaves just for the purpose of manumitting them. In several instances, his biographer has disclosed, he established the former bondsmen in businesses of their own.[15] Touro's abhorrence of slavery was by no means unique. But precisely how many Jews acted as did Touro or Haym M. Solomon, who in 1812 freed his ten-year-old female slave, Anna, will never be known.[16]

While it did not permeate the Jewish community, antislavery feeling did exist. Illustrative are the activities of a New York merchant, Moses Judah. For many years Judah was affiliated with the New York Manumission Society which worked not only for the liberation of blacks still in bondage, but also tried to prevent re-enslavement of freed Negroes. Judah's name appears very frequently in the minutes of the Society.[17] Several Philadelphia Jews played notable roles in the Quaker-inspired work of the Pennsylvania Society for Promoting the Abolition of Slavery.[18]

An interesting individual example of Jewish opposition to slavery is the case of the Bavarian-born Louis Stix who arrived in Cincinnati in the 1830s. He began his career as a pack peddler and when he died in New York in 1902 he was an extremely wealthy man. His reflections on "the peculiar institution" are worth quoting. "From the day I first landed in this most glorious country, until the present time, my principles have not undergone any radical change. I was then, as I am now, an outspoken opponent of all involuntary serfdom, and against the acquisition of any new territory to perpetuate this unfortunate evil. . . . My open opposition

14 C. M. Andrews, *Colonial Folkways: A Chronicle of American Life in the Reign of the Georges* (New Haven: Yale University Press, 1919), p. 199.
15 Leon Hühner, *The Life of Judah Touro (1775–1854)* (Philadelphia: Jewish Publication Society, 1946), p. 69.
16 M. Vaxer, *Haym M. Solomon Frees His Slave.* Publication of the American Jewish Historical Society, no. 37 (1947), 447–448.
17 Morris V. Schappes, ed., *Documentary History of the Jews in the United States* (New York: The Citadel Press, 1952), p. 118.
18 Edwin Wolf II and Maxwell Whiteman, *The History of the Jews of Philadelphia from Colonial Times to the Age of Jackson* (Philadelphia: Jewish Publication Society, 1957), pp. 190–191.

to slavery had cost me the goodwill of many Southern customers, and at no time before the war was it considered safe for me to venture south of Mason and Dixon's line."[19]

When John Brown confronted the slave power in "bloody Kansas" in the 1850s, three young Jewish pioneers were at his side. They were, respectively, a Pole, a Bohemian, and a Viennese. The Viennese, August Bondi, although purportedly more moderate in his views than Brown, observed that the small team of free-state men were united by brotherly love for the great abolitionist. Bondi credited Brown's "tender words and wise counsel" with preparing them "for the work of laying the foundation of a free Commonwealth."[20] As Bondi explained in his autobiography, his revulsion toward slavery was partly the product of his own observations of the plantation system. En route to New Orleans soon after his arrival in America he saw Negroes for the first time. A few years later he viewed the callous and inhuman treatment of Negroes in Texas. "When in Galveston the howling of the slaves receiving their morning ration of cowhiding woke me at 1 A.M." As a young man Bondi refrained from marrying any slaveowner's daughter because "my father's son was not to be a slavedriver."[21]

Another opponent of slavery was Moritz Pinner who worked in Missouri in the 1850s. In 1859 he edited an avowedly abolitionist newspaper in Kansas City.[22]

Stix and Bondi and Pinner were extraordinary. Most Jews did not take a stand against slavery. In this respect Jews were not dif-

---

[19] Jacob Rader Marcus, *Memoirs of American Jews 1775–1865* (Philadelphia: Jewish Publication Society, 1955), I, 338.

[20] Leon Hühner, *Some Associates of John Brown,* reprinted from *The Magazine of History,* 1908, p. 18.

[21] August Bondi, *Autobiography of August Bondi 1833–1907* (Galesburg, Ill.: Wagoner Printing Co., 1910), p. 30; Schappes, *Documentary History of the Jews,* p. 352.

[22] Max J. Kohler, *The Jews and the Anti-Slavery Movement,* Publication of the American Jewish Historical Society, no. 5 (New York, 1896): 152. It has been suggested that one reason why Jews were not attracted to the abolitionist banner was that the abolitionists themselves were not concerned with the rights of Jews. Korn says that some had "anti-Jewish leanings." A contrary view advanced by Louis Ruchames is that the abolitionists hated "oppression and discrimination of every kind" and "their devotion to equal rights extended to the Jew." Louis Ruchames, *The Abolitionists and The Jews,* Publication of the American Jewish Historical Society, 42, no. 2 (December 1952):132.

ferent from most other ethnic groups. On the whole their record was superior to some immigrant communities. Oscar Handlin, in his celebrated *Boston's Immigrants,* has explained that the Irish were virtually united in their opposition to the abolitionist movement, to the enfranchisement of blacks, to what was generally termed "niggerology." Unskilled Irishmen felt threatened. Freedmen who might flock to Boston would compete for available jobs.[23] In addition, for the Irish as well as for the Jews and other white minority groups, the knowledge that the Negroes were "permanently" relegated to a lower rung on the social ladder must have been psychologically satisfying.

While Jews as individuals often expressed themselves unequivocally on the moral, economic, and political implications of slavery, organizationally, for all practical purposes, American Jewry was mute. This fact has not gone unnoticed. In its thirteenth annual report presented in New York in 1853 the American and Foreign Anti-Slavery Society stated: "The Jews of the United States have never taken any steps whatever with regard to the slavery question. As citizens they deem it their policy to have every one choose which ever side he may deem best to promote his own interests and the welfare of his country. . . . It cannot be said that the Jews have formed any denominational opinion on the subject of American slavery."[24]

More than four decades later in an essay entitled "The Jews and the Anti-Slavery Movement," Max J. Kohler commented, "it may well be doubted if a single church other than the Jewish neglected to expound its attitude in the pamphlet and tract literature of the day."[25] Most recently, black author Harold Cruse in *The Crisis of the Negro Intellectual,* wrote: "As a body, American Jewry took no action, either pro or con, on the slavery issue, even while the Christian churches were rent by warring factions over the issue."[26]

Slavery had in fact split *some* of the major Protestant sects.

[23] Oscar Handlin, *Boston's Immigrants: A Study in Acculturation* (Cambridge: Harvard University Press, 1959), pp. 132–133.

[24] Schappes, *Documentary History of the Jews,* pp. 332–333.

[25] Kohler, *The Jews and the Anti-Slavery Movement,* p. 138.

[26] Harold Cruse, *The Crisis of the Negro Intellectual* (New York: William Morrow & Co., 1967), p. 478.

The Presbyterian schism occurred in 1838; the Methodist rift took place in 1844 and the Baptists became, to all intents and purposes, Northerners and Southerners in 1845. However, it was different with the Episcopalians and the Roman Catholics who stubbornly refused to be divided by the slavery issue.

Catholic attitudes in particular deserve a closer look. The entire range of opinion on Negro slavery was to be found among America's Roman Catholics. But by 1860, Madeleine Rice had written, the majority strongly condemned abolitionism.[27] Moreover, the leaders of the Church, determined not to be drawn into bitter public controversy, maintained a policy of official silence. Reflective of a significant segment of Catholic thinking were the ideas expounded in a Boston weekly, the *Pilot,* founded in 1829 by Bishop Benedict Joseph Fenwick. A *Pilot* editorial published in 1831, the year William Lloyd Garrison launched his *Liberator* in Boston, pointed out that "Slavery . . . has existed in the world ever since the fall of Adam, and what is still more, will continue till the end of time." The editorial went on to invoke the wage-slave argument ordinarily associated with the name of George Fitzhugh: "the slave of the South enjoys more comfort, is often more moral, and certainly more exempt from care, and the temptations to vice, than the free black or indigent white man of the North." Abolitionists were "fanatical and evil minded preachers."[28] With the same perspective, in 1856 the *Pilot* accused the free-soilers or "Black Republicans" of undermining the Constitution.[29]

As far as the Church was concerned there was theological prohibition against slaveholding. Slavery per se was not evil. Therefore, the preservation of harmony and unity within the Catholic edifice became the overriding consideration, the more so in the 1850s when nativism was widespread and Catholics were suspect by a segment of Protestant America. In some situations Know-Nothings reviled Catholics for being proslavery. In other situations Catholics were abused for their antislavery stance. To blunt such

---

[27] Madeleine Hooke Rice, *American Catholic Opinion in the Slavery Controversy* (New York: Columbia University Press, 1944), p. 155. Also see John Tracy Ellis, *American Catholicism* (Chicago: University of Chicago Press, 1956), pp. 87–89.

[28] Rice, *American Catholic Opinion,* pp. 77–78.

[29] Ibid., p. 95.

contradictory criticism the Catholic Church adhered to a legalistic and constitutional approach to the critical ethical question of human bondage. Anything less, it was believed, could tragically sever the bonds between Catholics in Maryland and Louisiana and those in Boston, thus irreparably damaging the Church.

There were other factors. The Roman Church in Europe was frightened by radicals and in the United States abolitionism appeared to be the quintessence of radicalism. Beyond that, because of their close affiliation with the Democratic party, Catholics were still more likely to look askance at abolitionists.[30]

It has been suggested that the absence of a national Jewish organization, at least in the formal sense, was partially rooted in the fear that an identifiable Jewish structure would be as vulnerable to Know-Nothingism as the Catholic hierarchy.[31] Centuries-old insecurity was an integral part of the heritage which Jews had carried to these shores. Why draw attention to themselves by collectively challenging the status quo? The ethnic and linguistic diversity of American Jews, plus the irreconcilable differences between reform and traditional Judaism, also militated against a nationwide body. There were, of course, some Jewish fraternal orders in the antebellum period. In 1843 German Jews had established the Independent Order of B'nai B'rith (Sons of the Covenant). But mutual aid, charity, and cultural activities were its foci, not social action. Organizationally it stood aloof from the slavery dilemma.

In the pre-Civil War era there was no recognized spokesman, lay or spiritual, for American Jewry. Such leadership as there was came from rabbinical quarters. But in their pronouncements on the great questions of the day, rabbis spoke for themselves and not always for their congregations. Predictably, with reference to slavery, they were in disagreement with one another.

This can be seen in the bitter controversy that was touched off by Rabbi Morris Jacob Raphall in his sermon to Congregation B'nai Jeshurun in New York. Scriptural justifications for slavery were nothing new when Raphall delivered his discourse, "Bible View of Slavery," on 4 January 1861, a national fast day. The

30 Ibid., pp. 92–94.
31 Korn, *American Jewry and the Civil War*, p. 13.

previous year Raphall had become the first rabbi to offer an opening prayer at a session of the United States Congress. As a rabbi
of some repute, his interpretation of the scriptual basis of bondage
carried considerable weight. Raphall, who was later to support the
Union cause, pointed out that although there were Negro slaves
whose general circumstances paralleled those of ancient Hebrew
bondsmen, the two slave systems were significantly different. He
argued that under Biblical slavery "The slave is a person in whom
the dignity of human nature is to be respected."[32] The South, alas,
had adopted the system of heathen Rome which reduced the slave
to a thing devoid of rights. Slaveholding itself, Rabbi Raphall
preached, was not sinful and he admonished Northerners not to
be self-righteous. He urged the Southerners to discard Roman
slavery and replace it with the Old Testament brand.

This advice was totally ignored by those advocates of chattel
bondage who loudly praised Rabbi Raphall's sermon. What they
chose to hear was his assertion that involuntary servitude in some
form was divinely approved. They had also heard a respected man
of God declare that next to family relationships, those between
master and slave were the oldest, even preceding the Great Flood.
Noah had cursed the descendants of his son Ham, saying that
they should be the "meanest of slaves." More than four millennia
before, the doom of Ham's descendants, i.e., the African people,
had been prophesied, according to Raphall. The Rabbi went
further, stating categorically that the Biblical injunction, "Thou
shalt not surrender unto his master the slave who escaped from
his master unto thee" (Deuteronomy 23:16), did not warrant cir-
cumvention of the Fugitive Slave Law.[33]

Among those who took Raphall to task for his sermon was
Michael Heilprin, an erudite Polish Jew and a rabid opponent of
slavery. His impassioned response to the national fast day homily
appeared in the pages of the *New York Tribune*. Heilprin was
outraged by Raphall's "sacrilegious words." He rejected out of
hand the notion that slavery was not sinful in the eyes of the God
of Israel. He painstakingly refuted the Noah and Ham arguments.
More important, he contended that Talmudists had repudiated

[32] Schappes, *Documentary History of the Jews,* p. 417.
[33] Ibid., p. 416.

much in Scripture which they found "contradictory, unjust and even barbarous." Slavery was not sanctioned by divine law any more than were bigamy, polygamy, and concubinage.[34]

Best known of the rabbis who had espoused the abolitionist cause and who assailed the Raphall sermon was Reverend Dr. David Einhorn. Born in Bavaria, Einhorn was a leader of the Reform movement in Judaism in central Europe. In 1855 he accepted a pulpit in Baltimore, a slave city in a slave state. Both in his sermons and his German language "black republican" journal, *Sinai,* he took every opportunity to attack the institution of chattel slavery which he called "the cancer of the union." So explosive was the situation in Baltimore in April 1861 that Einhorn, the abolitionist, had to flee.

Einhorn ridiculed the idea that the God of Israel was a God who condoned slavery.[35] To him the Raphall thesis was "a defamation of Judaism." Slavery, he reminded his Philadelphia congregation in 1864, had reduced defenseless black human beings to a condition of merchandise. Through violence husbands and wives and parents and children had been criminally separated. History provided no justification whatsoever. Customs could not change an atrocious wrong into right any more than a disease of long duration ceased to be an evil.[36] "Was not the enslavement of Israel in Egypt equally a historic right for Pharaoh and his mercenaries?" he asked pointedly.

The Biblical justification was equally unconvincing. Advocates of bad causes had long sought support in a literal interpretation of Holy Writ. Einhorn, concerned with the spirit rather than the letter, could not bring himself to believe that the book which proclaims "break the bonds of oppression, let the oppressed go free, and tear every yoke," was meant to "raise the whip and forge chains."[37]

It was Einhorn's conviction that the fortunes of Negroes and

[34] Ibid., pp. 418–428.
[35] Ibid., p. 446.
[36] David Einhorn, *War With Amalek: A Sermon Delivered on March 19, 1864* (Philadelphia: Stein & Jones, 1864), p. 4.
[37] Ibid., p. 5.

Jews were inextricably interwoven. At that juncture, given America's racial dichotomy, few Jews would have agreed and even fewer were as outspoken in championing Negro rights as Rabbi Einhorn. In retrospect this is not surprising although it is to be regretted for, as an antislavery society report lamented, "The objects of so much mean prejudice and unrighteous oppression as the Jews have been for ages, surely they, it would seem, more than any other denomination, ought to be the enemies of Caste, and the friends of Universal Freedom."[38]

The same sectional and intrasectional divergence of Jewish attitudes toward Negroes which existed before 1865 are easily discernible in the decades after Appomattox. There were still a dedicated few who vigorously advocated the cause of justice and racial equality. The majority accommodated themselves to a system which continued to dehumanize and emasculate the black man. Their attitudes mirrored those of the Gentile Americans in whose midst they dwelt and worked and upon whom their livelihood might depend. In the main they bore out Otto von Bismarck's pithy observation: "As the Christian, so goes the Jew."

In the South Jewish merchants established themselves with little difficulty, the Ku Klux Klan notwithstanding. One historian has even asserted that, "Probably in no other region of the United States have they been so integrated with the general population or subjected to less discrimination."[39] Even where Jews did not actually subscribe to southern white prejudices toward the Negro, as businessmen they were peculiarly open to the wrath or merely the displeasure of their customers. Such was the conclusion reached by a David Pierce, "a young American of Jewish descent who has suffered both for his religion and for his friendship to the Negro race." His 1925 article entitled "Is the Jew a Friend of the Negro" was published in the *Crisis,* the journal of the NAACP. Inter alia, Pierce addressed himself to the "enforced silence of the Jewish entrepreneur. "With economic security as an impetus and with complete acceptance as a social equal of the Gentile as a goal,

---

[38] Schappes, *Documentary History of the Jews,* p. 333.
[39] John Samuel Ezell, *The South Since 1865* (New York: Macmillan Co., 1963), p. 227.

the Jew must shun the black man. And if he lives in the South, the Jew must acquiesce completely in the assumption that the Negro must confine himself to the hewing of wood and the drawing of water."[40]

Jews were certainly not in the front ranks of the oppressors of the Negro. Neither were they in the vanguard of his defenders— a miniscule group to begin with. Finding themselves in a precarious situation, southern Jews for the most part tried to be as inconspicuous and as inoffensive as possible. Despite the tragic European past of their own people, they must have found it extremely difficult to identify with their degraded, darkskinned neighbors. If they were able to empathize at all, practical considerations prevented southern Jews from demonstrating their concern.

In July 1910, Baruch Vladeck, a visiting Jewish socialist, witnessed an anti-Negro riot in Virginia, which he likened to a Russian pogrom. Racial strife in Norfolk and a number of other cities throughout the nation was precipitated by the boxing ring victory of Jack Johnson over Jim Jeffries, "the great white hope." Johnson, to the considerable annoyance of white America, had become the first black world heavyweight champion. When a shocked Vladeck urged the Jews of Norfolk to intervene on behalf of the hapless blacks, he was told that he did not comprehend the situation. Blacks were "nothing but animals."[41] How many Jews in Norfolk actually believed that Negroes were subhuman is a matter of conjecture. What is certain is that the small Jewish community was helpless to stop the butchery even if disposed to do so.

In the course of his southern travels Vladeck was profoundly moved by the brutal treatment of Negroes. Slavery had not been succeeded by true freedom. Instead it had been replaced by peonage, a form of disguised bondage. In his autobiography, Vladeck recalled an occasion on which he had witnessed the Savannah police acting as labor agents. Young Negroes whose only crime was being black were arrested and put to work on the chain

---

[40] David Pierce, "Is The Jew a Friend of the Negro," *Crisis* 30, no. 4 (August 1925): 184–185.

[41] Franklin Jonas, "The Early Life and Career of B. Charney Vladeck: A Study in Political Acculturation" (Ph.D. diss., New York University, 1970), chap. 2.

gangs. Vladeck's protest was laughable to the police chief of Savannah who informed him: "My boy, you don't belong here—go back to your goddam New York."[42]

Few rabbis with southern congregations were courageous enough to make the proverbial waves in what whites thought of as tranquil racial seas. One who did have ample courage was Benjamin Goldstein, spiritual leader of Temple Beth Or in Montgomery, Alabama. In the early 1930s the spotlight of public attention was focused on the previously obscure town of Scottsboro, where a racial tragedy was being played out. Nine Negro youths, the internationally known "Scottsboro boys," had been convicted and sentenced to death for allegedly having raped two white girls on a freight train.

Rabbi Goldstein believed them to be the innocent victims of bigotry and became active on their behalf. He spoke out publicly and raised money for their defense. As the drama unfolded, hate and hysteria became rampant. The Jewish community in Alabama was fearful of being labeled "red" because of Communist involvement in the cause célèbre. In 1933, alarmed by anti-Semitic utterances, Rabbi Goldstein's congregation told him to dissociate himself from the Scottsboro case or resign. He resigned and within a few months he was intimidated into leaving Alabama for the more hospitable environment of New York.[43]

Hostility to Jews had been engendered in some degree by the legal activities of Samuel S. Leibowitz in the Scottsboro case. Unmistakable displeasure with Leibowitz came through in the comment of the Athens, Alabama, *Courier* that, "The New York Jew says there is no such thing as a fair trial in Alabama."[44] During the 1933 trial of Haywood Patterson, a nineteen-year-old Scottsboro defendant for whom Leibowitz was chief defense attorney, Wade Wright arguing the state's case, implored the jury to demonstrate by their verdict that "Jew money from New York can't buy and sell Alabama justice."[45] The jury complied willingly.

While some of the members of Temple Beth Or privately shared

[42] Ibid.
[43] Dan T. Carter, *Scottsboro: A Tragedy of the American South* (Baton Rouge: Louisiana State University Press, 1969), pp. 258–259.
[44] Ibid., p. 245.
[45] *New York Times,* 10 April 1933.

the convictions of Rabbi Goldstein and Samuel Leibowitz that Scottsboro was a mockery of justice, they thought it prudent to keep their own counsel. In so doing they conformed to the southern Jewish pattern which, by and large, persists to this day.

In the post-Reconstruction period, contact between Negroes and a variety of European immigrants occurred with increasing frequency in the North. The contacts took place in circumstances which were not at all conducive to the creation and maintenance of harmonious relations. Job competition between groups of have-nots usually produces bitterness if not strife. Negro-Irish tensions that led to the draft riots in New York City in 1863 lingered. With the accelerated pace of immigration in the waning years of the century, Negro–foreigner conflicts multiplied.

From the vantage point of the Negroes unrestricted immigration constituted a distinct threat to their already fragile economic position. It was widely understood by the Negro population that the moment the European newcomer stepped off the boat he enjoyed fundamental rights which were unattainable for the nonwhite. It was generally and correctly assumed that the new arrivals at the end of the century would be given preference in housing and employment. Consequently, James Weldon Johnson and Booker T. Washington, to cite just two distinguished Negroes, and such newspapers as the *New York Age* took a rather dim view of uncontrolled immigration.[46]

Nevertheless, antiforeign sentiment, whether it emanated from Negro or nativist quarters, was futile in terms of curtailing the influx of aliens, at least until the time of World War I. Long before then Negroes and white "strangers in the land" found themselves living cheek by jowl in some of our burgeoning urban centers.

In 1897 *Harper's Weekly* carried a piece entitled "The New Ghetto" in which the author detailed the encounter between Negroes and Polish Jews in midtown west side Manhattan.[47] To be

[46] Seth Scheiner, *Negro Mecca: A History of the Negro in New York City 1865–1920* (New York: New York University Press, 1965), p. 130; John Higham, *Strangers In The Land: Patterns of American Nativism 1860–1925* (New York: Atheneum, 1963), p. 169.

[47] Edwin Emerson, Jr., "The New Ghetto," *Harper's Weekly*, 9 January 1897, p. 44.

found in that section were rows of Jewish shops bearing signs in a variety of languages. The Jews lived in their stores or in dark, dank basements for which they paid exorbitant rents. Many of the merchants dealt in cast-off clothing, much of it ostentatious, which they sold to unemployed Negroes most of whom occupied squalid apartments above the shops. Although the Negro residents had deeper roots in the area, by custom and practice, they were confined to dilapidated dwellings.

According to the author, Edwin Emerson, Jr., whose proclivity to generalize about group traits is apparent to his readers, the Jewish businessmen had no objection to selling to a Negro clientele because "pizzness is pizzness," but they disapproved of their own children playing with Negro children. They themselves did not ordinarily socialize with Negroes whom they regarded as an unclean people. If this portrayal of Jewish racial attitudes was accurate, it reveals that little time was needed to absorb the white supremacist mythology which prevailed in America. It is not improbable that Negrophobia, albeit latent, existed in Europe and was transported to the United States where it germinated under propitious social conditions.

Be that as it may, historian Seth Scheiner, in his fine study of the Negro in New York City during this period, has written of a 1905 incident which involved a band of young Jews who harassed an elderly Negro woman with cries of "Nigger" and "Schwartze." A few years later Jewish property owners—and they were so identified by the Negro press—acted collectively to keep Negroes out of an area in lower Harlem.[48]

There were, of course, other Jews with markedly different racial outlooks. There were the Jewish philanthropists, most notably Julius Rosenwald. There were the Jews who helped to found the NAACP in 1910 and who served on its executive board at a time when the NAACP was suspect as a radical force in race relations. Dr. Henry Moskowitz, a Jewish social worker in New York, was one of three persons—the other two were Mary White Ovington and William English Walling—who met in 1909 and decided to ask Oswald Garrison Villard to issue "the call" for a biracial or-

[48] Scheiner, *Negro Mecca*, p. 133.

ganization to fight for full racial equality.[49] Dr. Joel E. Spingarn, a professor of English at Columbia University, was elected chairman of the Board of Directors of the NAACP in January, 1914. His passion for racial justice won him the praise of Langston Hughes and W. E. B. Du Bois. The latter eulogized Joel Spingarn as "one of those vivid, enthusiastic but clear-thinking idealists which from age to age the Jewish race has given the world."[50] Du Bois also stated in his *Dusk of Dawn* that had it not been for Joel Spingarn, no black army officers would have been appointed and trained in World War I.[51] Arthur Spingarn, Joel's brother, was for more than a quarter of a century the unpaid chairman of legal defense of the NAACP.[52]

There were those who in 1919, working through the Jewish Welfare Board, enabled Negro soldiers awaiting demobilization to acquire a precious knowledge of correct English usage and vocational subjects.[53] Those Jews were in a manner of speaking the spiritual godfathers of Andrew Goodman and Mickey Schwerner. In other words, Jewish bigots and Jewish humanitarians, although nominally adherents of the same faith, were as dissimilar as night and day.

Apparently, Negroes have held a comparable diversity of opinion about Jews in America and in Europe. Jews were frequently seen as brothers in affliction who could provide a model for black men to follow. Through their unity and industriousness Jews could point the way to equality. Frederick Douglass, the ex-slave who utilized his extraordinary talents as an active opponent of slavery, an adviser to Lincoln, and as American minister to Haiti, belonged to that school of thought. "The Jew was once despised and hated in Europe, and is still so in some parts of that continent," he said in 1884, "but he has risen and is rising to higher consideration,

[49] Charles Flint Kellogg, *NAACP: A History of the National Association for the Advancement of Colored People* (Baltimore: Johns Hopkins Press, 1967), I, 12; Langston Hughes, *Fight for Freedom: The Story of the N.A.A.C.P.* (New York: Berkley Publishing Corp., 1962), p. 21.

[50] W. E. B. Du Bois, *Dusk of Dawn: An Essay Toward An Autobiography of a Race Concept* (New York: Schocken Books, 1968), p. 255. *Dusk of Dawn* was dedicated to "Joel Spingarn, Scholar and Knight."

[51] Ibid., p. 249.

[52] Langston Hughes, *Fight For Freedom*, p. 27.

[53] *New York Age*, 18 February 1919.

and no man is now degraded by association with him anywhere."
In the same manner, he predicted black people would climb the
social ladder.[54]

A college administrator and ex-Congressman, Thomas E. Miller,
in 1902 stated that by dint of cooperative effort and economic
power Jews virtually ruled Europe. Similar success was not beyond
the grasp of the colored man.[55]

Douglass was unduly sanguine about the prospects of European
Jewry then faced by a recrudescence of virulent anti-Semitism,
often with racial as well as religious overtones. And Miller surely
exaggerated Jewish control over European destinies, but both men
were using Jewish history as they understood it to chart a course
for the American Negro. Booker T. Washington also found "a
very bright and striking example" in the much-vaunted Jewish
sense of ethnic brotherhood. Critics of the Jews disdainfully called
it "clannishness." Because of his accommodationist philosophy of
race relations which was embodied in his Atlantic Exposition address in 1895, Washington is today out of favor with many blacks.
But at the turn of the century he was by far the most influential
Negro in America. In 1900 in his book, *The Future of the American Negro,* Washington spoke of the Jews who had suffered so
long in Europe, but who had clung together. "They have had a
certain amount of unity, pride, and love of race; and, as the years
go on, they will be more and more influential in this country,—
a country where they were once despised, and looked upon with
scorn and derision. It is largely because the Jewish race has had
faith in itself. Unless the Negro learns more and more to imitate
the Jew in these matters, to have faith in himself, he cannot expect to have any high degree of success."[56]

Negro perceptions, including those of Washington, were often
ambivalent. Anti-Semitism, especially Czarist anti-Semitism, was
denounced without reservation. But such denunciation did not pre-

---

[54] Quoted in Richard C. Wade, ed., *The Negro in American Life: Selected
Readings* (Boston: Houghton Mifflin Company, 1965), p. 83.

[55] August Meier, *Negro Thought in America, 1880–1915: Racial Ideologies
in the Age of Booker T. Washington* (Ann Arbor: University of Michigan
Press, 1966), pp. 248–249.

[56] Booker T. Washington, *The Future of the American Negro* (Boston:
Small, Maynard & Co., 1900), pp. 182–183.

clude enmity toward Jews any more than the Negro press' condemnation of British colonialism in Ireland guaranteed Irish-Negro amity in the United States. While the Jews were held up as exemplary because of their respect for the law, the chastity of their women, and above all, their group solidarity and business acumen, they were simultaneously criticized for their parasitism, avarice, trickery, and their supposed obsession with moneymaking. Isolated incidents of exploitation by Jewish merchants were related by some Negroes. Others were deeply impressed by Jewish resourcefulness and the support given by Jews to their own commercial enterprises.[57]

In 1915 the short-lived *Colored American Review* indicted northern Negroes for their myopia in patronizing white industries and stores rather than colored businesses. Negro spending habits were all the more asinine because white firms refused to employ Negroes. Colored merchants were not completely blameless: their business methods required improvement. But the most guilty were the foolish Negroes who regularly "fill the coffers of the Jew and the Italian, without complaint at the filthy conditions of many of the stores." Those merchants, it was charged, practiced robbery. Summing up the case for race patronage, the editor, Cyril V. Briggs, wrote that there were a thousand positions in Harlem alone that should be open to Negroes and would be "could we but play the Jew for only a few weeks, insisting within that period and after on spending our money with our own enterprises and only those white stores that give the race something in return."[58] Jobs-for-Negroes campaigns with almost identical themes became common phenomena in Harlem in the thirties.

While the Jews were mentioned more than any other ethnic minority, they were at times coupled with the Italians or even the Chinese. Though not white, of course, the latter in common with other immigrant groups, owned their communities—the shops, the restaurants, the homes. Only the black man was an exploited alien in his own neighborhood.

[57] *The New York Age,* 14 June 1917 is illustrative. It stated editorially, "the solidarity of the Jews causes them to deal exclusively among their own people in the matter of trade and patronage of professional men, except when greater profit is to be made by dealing with outsiders."
[58] *The Colored American Review,* 1 October 1915.

As has previously been indicated, the period from the end of Reconstruction to Versailles was a nightmare for Afro-Americans. They had been disfranchised, Jim-Crowed, and lynched on an incredible scale. They continued to be dehumanized or "thingified." Quite understandably, the North was seen as the promised land by southern Negroes who hungered for justice and thirsted for economic opportunity. "To die from the bite of frost is far more glorious than at the hands of a mob," the *Chicago Defender* asserted during World War I when wholesale migration to the urban North reached its pinnacle.[59] This demographic shift was a watershed in black history. Conflagrations in our cities have recently demonstrated that it was nothing less in the domestic history of the nation as a whole.

The forty years before Versailles had also been tragic for East European Jews. After the assassination of the Czar in 1881, pogroms occurred with unprecedented fury and frequency. As a result, swarms of Jewish immigrants sought and found asylum in many of the same cities that served as havens for the southern Negro. Historic destiny had set the stage for more sustained and extensive contact between the two peoples.

[59] John Hope Franklin, *From Slavery to Freedom: A History of Negro Americans* (New York: Alfred A. Knopf, 1967), p. 472.

} 3 {

NEGRO PERCEPTIONS OF JEWS BETWEEN THE WORLD WARS

MANY OF THE ENCOUNTERS BETWEEN AFRO-AMERICANS AND American Jews in northern urban centers were scarcely the kind that promoted goodwill and intergroup understanding. Instead, they were unequal-status, friction-generating contacts, between merchants and consumers, between landlords and tenants, between housewives and domestics. In almost every instance, the black was in a subordinate position, essentially the position he had hoped to finally escape from in his flight to the North.

Underhanded business practices by white entrepreneurs in the black enclaves have long been a source of racial friction. There was often ample justification for allegations of overcharging and shortweighting, and these were but two of the malpractices which frequently occurred between the two world wars. Of course, for the poor eking out a marginal living, even fair prices have always seemed outrageously high. Installment buying also caused irritation. Penurious Negroes in the Depression economy became embittered when pressed to make regular payments which they could ill-afford.

That retailers of many faiths and national backgrounds were guilty of unethical business habits is incontrovertible. Jews as a group were probably no more or less culpable than Gentiles. However, significantly, they were identified more easily, either by name

40

or manner of dress. A popular misconception in some urban ghettos where rent gouging was a constant irritant was that *all* white landlords and shopkeepers were Jews. In certain cities, Jews constituted a majority in those categories and were present out of proportion to their numbers in the overall population. This was particularly the case in cities where the black ghettos were previously Jewish neighborhoods. Boston's Roxbury, sections of Philadelphia, South Providence, and Harlem, among others, fit this description.

Just before the turn of the century the face of Harlem was drastically altered by a boom in real estate. Almost overnight houses were erected. Many of these were occupied by East European Jews, shortly before denizens of the lower east side. Moving uptown earned them considerable prestige in the eyes of their coreligionists and bespoke their growing affluence. So dense was the Jewish population of lower Harlem that the district was dubbed "Little Russia" by the press. Synagogues, Hebrew schools, and a host of social and fraternal institutions were founded or transplanted. Harlem's newest residents were not universally welcome. Gilbert Osofsky in his fascinating *Harlem: The Making of a Ghetto* cites a to-let sign which read in German, "No Jews, No Dogs."[1]

Afro-Americans, at first those with some resources, began to filter into the area after the real estate bubble burst in 1904–1905. Many segments of Harlem's white population tried to stem the tide of nonwhite southern migrants. Their efforts were doomed to fail. By the time of the Great Depression the metamorphosis of Harlem from an elegant, expensive section to a segregated Negro slum was complete. Virtually en masse its Italian inhabitants moved elsewhere. Jews did likewise. Many relocated further north in the Washington Heights area or in the Bronx. Shopkeepers and landlords did not necessarily dispose of their property. But regardless of the actual proportion of Jewish landlords in Harlem, their number was often exaggerated. Abetting this process of selective perception was the fact that not infrequently in the 1920s, 1930s, and 1940s, Christian firms used Jews to manage apartment houses

[1] Gilbert Osofsky, *Harlem: The Making of a Ghetto* (New York: Harper & Row, 1968), p. 89.

and to collect rents. The percentage of Jewish-owned shops in that era is not known, but a few of the very large department stores on 125th Street symbolized Jewish commercial domination of Harlem. Also, pawnbrokers, who customarily deal with people in dire straits, were predominantly Jewish.

A comparable situation existed in Philadelphia. On specific streets in the Negro districts of north and south Philadelphia, Jewish ownership was conspicuous. When black Americans and Jews met in the City of Brotherly Love the encounters were not likely to result in feelings of brotherly affection. Typically, they involved Jewish retailers and landlords on one hand and Negro consumers and tenants on the other. Stereotypes, more likely than not disparaging ones, emerged and were disseminated by word of mouth and by the printed word. A writer in the *Philadelphia Tribune* in 1934 painted the Jews as "dollar crazy" people who were always prepared to invade black communities.[2] In 1942 Philadelphia was bluntly described by a Negro as a "hotbed of Negro anti-Semitism."[3]

Competition between nascent colored entrepreneurs and established Jewish businessmen also bred ill will in the inner cities during the interwar years. On the basis of their research in Chicago, St. Clair Drake and Horace R. Cayton concluded that most black storekeepers sincerely believed that there was a functioning Jewish conspiracy designed to victimize them.[4] A not uncommon complaint with a great deal of validity was that Jews, having gotten in on the ground floor, so to speak, had a distinct advantage over black competitors. The Jews enjoyed the best locations. In addition, because they had capital, they could cut prices and extend credit. An editorial in a weekly magazine charged that, "an organization of Jewish businessmen arbitrarily holds down competition. No colored merchant is permitted to operate a competing estab-

[2] Lunabelle Wedlock, *The Reaction of Negro Publications and Organizations to German Anti-Semitism* (Washington, D.C.: Howard University Press, 1942), p. 126, quoting from the *Philadelphia Tribune*, 26 July 1934.

[3] Wedlock, *The Reaction of Negro Publications and Organizations*, pp. 136–137.

[4] St. Clair Drake and Horace R. Cayton, *Black Metropolis: A Study of Negro Life in a Northern City* (New York and Evanston: Harper & Row, 1962), II; 448.

lishment in a good location except under conditions which make bankruptcy inevitable."[5] Following the formation of a Biracial Business Association with a membership 80 percent Caucasian, the same editor was quoted as saying that a goodly number of the members lived in "Master Race" communities and were signers of restrictive covenants.[6]

There was also a feeling among black Chicagoans that people of African descent had more confidence in Jewish storekeepers than in their black counterparts. Drake and Cayton quoted a shoemaker to the effect that, "the Negro has no faith in colored business. He thinks I can't fix his good pair of shoes. He don't know that the Jew down the street brings his work for me to do."[7]

Jews, who were once held up as examples for Negro entrepreneurs, increasingly became the target of their rancor. Jews who had "milked" the ghettos of millions of dollars did not deserve Negro patronage. To offset the advantages of their more experienced Jewish rivals, black businessmen appealed for racial solidarity.

Black chauvinism in the dog-eat-dog business world can only be appreciated if it is recognized that the expanding commercial initiative among Negroes was a tremendous development. After all, the bulk of them were only a few generations removed from slavery. Black enterprises in predominantly black areas were a vehicle by which black Americans could advance in material terms without relying on "whitey." One could say that it was an embryonic form of black power.[8]

Outside the ghettos, department stores in some cities refused to serve Negro customers. That was the state of affairs in Baltimore, for example, in the late 1930s. It was not just a question of ice-cream sodas and other refreshments. Wearing apparel, furniture, and a myriad of other basic items could not be purchased by

[5] Harold L. Sheppard, "The Negro Merchant: A Study of Negro Anti-Semitism," *American Journal of Sociology* 53, no. 2 (September 1947): 98.

[6] Ibid., p. 99.

[7] Drake and Cayton, *Black Metropolis*, II, 441.

[8] Sheppard, "The Negro Merchant," pp. 96–97; although Roi Ottley credited Jewish doctors with making it possible for black doctors to associate themselves with some of the nation's largest hospitals, there was competition among Jewish and Negro physicians. Jewish-Negro relations suffered as a consequence.

Americans of African descent. According to a *Crisis* editorial in 1938 the majority of the stores which so humiliated the black population were Jewish-owned or managed by Jews.[9] Rabbi Edward L. Israel had previously written in *Crisis* that only a few Jewish department storeowners refused to sell to black people. Several had a completely different customer policy. Moreover, Rabbi Israel commented, Negroes were universally barred from Gentile department stores in Baltimore.[10] Negroes were infuriated and quite properly so. Such a situation was almost certain to adversely affect Negro views of Jews if they were associated with that exclusion, rightly or wrongly.

Discriminatory hiring practices were another sore point exacerbating Jewish-Negro relations. E. Franklin Frazier, the noted Negro sociologist, observed that New York employers in the 1920s were of two kinds, those who adamantly refused to employ black people at all and those who hired them only in low-paying, menial capacities.[11] Gimbels belonged in the first category and Macy's in the second. Companies owned by Christians pursued essentially the same personnel policies as did these large Jewish-owned department stores. In 1930 the Metropolitan Life Insurance Company rationalized its total exclusion of Negroes by predicting strong objections on the part of white employees to a nondiscriminatory policy.[12]

On the eve of the Great Depression, Negro workers in the urban North were already severely depressed. The "promised land" envisioned by migrants from the South had failed to materialize. If Pullman porters, janitors, elevator operators or waiters were needed, black men could apply. If servants, charwomen or waitresses were required, black women would be taken on. Unskilled manual labor was one thing, but higher paying "clean work" was another. Attempts by skilled or semiskilled Negroes to obtain clerical, managerial, or professional jobs were ordinarily futile. As Drake and Cayton indicated in their classic *Black Metropolis,* just prior to the onset of the Depression 56 percent of all black females employed

[9] *Crisis* 45, no. 4 (April 1938): 177.
[10] Edward L. Israel, "Jew Hatred Among Negroes," *Crisis* 43, no. 2 (February 1936):39, 50.
[11] Osofsky, *Harlem: The Making of a Ghetto,* p. 136.
[12] Ibid., pp. 136–137.

and more than 25 percent of all black males who held jobs were servants of one type or another. Taking into consideration their percentage of the total population, this was more than four times the Negro's proportionate share of such work.[13] They were also grossly overrepresented in the ranks of the unemployed. In short, they were the last to be added to the work force and almost invariably for "Negro jobs." Needless to say, they were the first to be fired.

If prejudice in employment degraded and belittled the Negro in downtown shopping areas, then the discrimination in recruitment and promotion which was rife in the ghetto itself, was unbearably galling. Some of the same merchants who earned their livings in the black neighborhoods refused to employ Negroes except in lowly positions. Roi Ottley writing in 1943 offered as a prime exhibit, Blumstein's, a sizeable department store which is still doing business today on 125th Street in Harlem. Although willing to retain black people to run his elevators and to do cleaning work, the owner, William Blumstein, refused to hire Negroes to sell or to perform clerical work.[14]

Claude McKay, the distinguished Jamaican novelist and poet, told of a white southerner who managed a large five-and-dime store in Harlem. When asked to hire a fixed quota of black clerks he retorted that where he had been born in the South, Negroes could not be customers in the better stores, much less employees. As long as he was in charge "not a damned 'nigger' would work behind his counters" even if his customers were "niggers."[15]

So deplorable was this state of affairs that jobs-for-Negroes direct action campaigns were launched in a number of cities—Saint Louis, Baltimore, Chicago, and, of course, New York. Indignant blacks brought considerable economic pressure to bear by picketing and boycotting the guilty storekeepers. On the whole, the campaigns in the 1930s met with only moderate success. They did bring to the fore a covey of flamboyant nationalists whose rhetoric was rabidly anti-Semitic.

[13] Drake and Cayton, *Black Metropolis,* I, 220.
[14] Roi Ottley, *New World A-Coming: Inside Black America* (Boston: Houghton Mifflin Co., 1943), p. 115.
[15] Claude McKay, *Harlem: Black Metropolis* (New York: E. P. Dutton, 1940), p. 191.

Especially bizarre was one Sufi Abdul Hamid. A gargantuan, booted, bearded figure, he customarily sported a turban, a robe, and sometimes a cape. On occasion he was attired in a Nazi-like uniform. His stage was a stepladder or soapbox, his theater the streets of Harlem. His Negro Industrial Clerical Alliance appealed mainly to the hopeless casualties of America's most serious Depression. The jobless Sufists included a small number of high school and college graduates. To this dispirited, impoverished audience Sufi preached the virtues of Islam. C. Eric Lincoln credits some of this country's first converts to that faith to his proselytizing zeal.[16]

He fulminated against white shopkeepers who bilked Harlem but who were unwilling to employ Negroes. Jewish merchants received the brunt of his invective. Among his slogans were "share the jobs" and "down with the Jews." No wonder, given the events unfolding in Germany, Sufi was labeled a "Harlem Hitler" and a "Black Hitler" by Jewish critics.[17] Apparently, he felt complimented by these characterizations. His career as a Jew-baiter ended abruptly after he was hauled into court for incitement of racial hatred. For the next few years before his death in an aircrash, Sufi resumed his earlier career as an Oriental cultist.[18]

Racial discrimination in employment also aroused the ire of Arthur L. Reid who, along with Ira Kemp and others, founded the Harlem Labor Union, Incorporated. Reid, a former lieutenant of Marcus Garvey's, urged his followers not to buy where they couldn't work. He advised them to buy black, to patronize Negro-owned businesses rather than those of alien merchants.[19] In enunciating his fervent advocacy of black economic power, Reid trotted out an assortment of anti-Jewish indictments. He leveled his charges against Jewish union leaders, against exploiting ghetto

[16] C. Eric Lincoln, *The Black Muslims in America* (Boston: Beacon Press, 1963), p. 169. Sufi claimed that he had been born in the Sudan. In actuality he was born in the American South.

[17] Ottley, *New World A-Coming*, p. 118; Wedlock; *The Reaction of Negro Publications and Organizations*, pp. 72–73, 132. By contrast a sympathetic account of Sufi's activities is found in McKay in his chapter entitled "Sufi Abdul Hamid and Organized Labor." McKay did not believe Sufi to be an anti-Semite. McKay, *Harlem: Black Metropolis*.

[18] Ottley, *New World A-Coming*, pp. 118–119.

[19] See Reid's obituary in *African Opinion* 8, nos. 1 & 2 (May–June 1967):13.

merchants, and against Bronx Jewish housewives who took advantage of Negro domestics.

High on the list of the most accessible, if undesirable "Negro jobs" were those in domestic service. Cooks, maids, and black cleaningwomen were commonplace in white homes. In Chicago at the beginning of World War II Drake and Cayton estimated that Negroes constituted almost 50 percent of all women engaged in domestic labor.[20] Nationwide 58 percent of the women working in private households were nonwhite.[21] Working conditions and wages were especially poor for those who did day's work, i.e., household labor negotiated ordinarily on a day to day basis with a variety of employers.

Even the circumstances under which housewives hired these scrubwomen were frequently shocking. The scandalous situation in New York City was popularly referred to as the "Bronx Slave Market." There the labor of Negro women was bought and sold in a fashion all too reminiscent of slavery in antebellum Dixie. After hearing countless grievances two black women journalists, Ella Baker and Marvel Cooke, exposed the circumstances of this lively trade. Simpson Avenue in the east Bronx illustrated the slave market at its worst.

Rain or shine, cold or hot, you will find them there—Negro women, old and young—sometimes bedraggled, sometimes neatly dressed—but with the invariable paper bundle, waiting expectantly for Bronx housewives to buy their strength and energy for an hour, two hours, or even for a day at the munificent rate of fifteen, twenty, twenty-five, or, if luck be with them, thirty cents an hour. If not the wives themselves, maybe their husbands, their sons or their brothers, under the subterfuge of work, offer worldly wise girls higher bids for their time.[22]

Pressed to the wall by economic necessity, the black women were scarcely in a position to negotiate effectively. All too often the housewives were unfeeling and unscrupulous, said Miss Baker and

[20] Drake and Cayton, *Black Metropolis,* I, 242.
[21] Department of Commerce, Bureau of Census, *Current Population Reports,* n.d., p. 57.
[22] Ella Baker and Marvel Cooke, "The Bronx Slave Market," *Crisis* 42, no. 11 (November 1935):330.

Miss Cooke, who accumulated their data firsthand by "selling" themselves on the market. They vividly described the fate of the typical "slave" hired by "Mrs. Simon Legree" to do manifold household drudgeries.

Under a rigid watch, she is permitted to scrub floors on her bended knees, to hang precariously from window sills, cleaning window after window, or to strain and sweat over steaming tubs of heavy blankets, spreads and furniture covers.

Fortunate, indeed, is she who gets the full hourly rate promised. Often, her day's slavery is rewarded with a single dollar bill or whatever her unscrupulous employer pleases to pay. More often, the clock is set back for an hour or more. Too often she is sent away without any pay at all.[23]

For the authors of this exposé, the real significance of the Bronx slave market was that it was the "economic battle front" in microcosm. It underscored the Negroes' lack of awareness of the potential benefits of collective action and it demonstrated the apathy of white-dominated labor unions where the well-being of black people was involved.

Just how many of the callous howsewives trading in the mart were Jewish was not made clear. But Jews were the only ethnic group explicitly named in the piece and the Bronx was characterized as a northern borough in New York City "known for its heavy Jewish population." The implication was that, by and large, the culprits were Jewish.

The Bronx was not unique. Unfavorable views of Jews were symptomatic of domestics in Chicago. Yet Drake and Cayton concluded that many of the servants in their study found Jewish employers less bigoted although more tight-fisted than their white Gentile counterparts. Of one hundred and fifty interviewed no less than two-thirds thought Jews more disposed to treat Negroes as equals but less inclined to pay on a level with other employers.[24] Not atypical was the complaint of a black "washwoman," a class earning on the average $2.50 per diem toward the end of the Depression:

[23] Ibid.
[24] Drake and Cayton, *Black Metropolis,* I, 244.

The Jewish woman that I work for tries to get a colored woman to do all of her work for as little as $2.00 a day and pay her own carfare.

She is expected to do all the washing, including the linen and towels as well as the clothes for the five members of the family. She is supposed to finish the work, that is, iron the entire wash—and then clean the house thoroughly—all for $2.00. Because there are some women who will do all of the work for that amount, this Jewish woman feels that a colored woman who demands more is silly to think that she can get it. She says that she doesn't understand why, if some colored people can get along on that amount, all can't do the same.[25]

That situations like this spawned anti-white and frequently anti-Semitic sentiments is scarcely surprising.

In May 1941 New York's inimitable Mayor LaGuardia initiated action to end the sidewalk hiring of houseworkers and the concomitant haggling and chiseling. With funds provided by the Social Security Board to the New York State Employment Service, the Simpson Street Day Work Office was ceremoniously opened. Informal indoor negotiations were to replace the outdoor flesh exchanges.[26] Whether working conditions and wages improved as a result is questionable. Lawrence D. Reddick writing in *The Negro Quarterly* a year later still cited the Bronx slave market as a source of anti-Semitism among Negroes.[27]

Tensions generated by this kind of unequal status contact have been reduced appreciably since World War II. Regrettably, they have not vanished altogether.[28] What has made the difference, how-

---

[25] Ibid., p. 249.

[26] *New York Times,* 2 May 1941.

[27] Lawrence D. Reddick, "Anti-Semitism Among Negroes," *Negro Quarterly* 1, no. 2 (Summer 1942):113.

[28] An article in the black nationalist monthly, *Liberator,* in 1967 contended that, "domestic service, today just as much as yesterday, is nothing but a euphemism for slave labor." Louise R. Moore "Maid in Westchester," *Liberator* 7, no. 1 (January 1967), pp. 18–19. Philip Roth's treatment of the Jewish housewife's relations with the Negro domestic is stereotyped but nonetheless rings true: "I'm the only one who's good to her. I'm the only one who gives her a whole can of tuna for lunch, and I'm not talking *dreck* either. I'm talking Chicken of the Sea, Alex. . . . Maybe I'm too good,' she whispers to me, meanwhile running scalding water over the dish from which the cleaning lady has just eaten her lunch, alone like a leper." *Portnoy's Complaint* (New York: Random House, 1967), p. 13. Portnoy's "rebellion" included sitting down and eating left over pot roast (not tuna) with the *shwartze* cleaning lady (p. 75).

ever, has been expanding job opportunities for black females. No longer are black high school graduates virtually restricted to the "whiskbroom, mop, and serving tray." They can and do become secretaries, clerks, saleswomen, etc. Others go on to higher education. Fair-employment practices and minimum-wage legislation have sometimes helped; wages have been hiked by the dwindling supply of domestics and the constantly rising demand for their labor.

Despite these changes, now as then, there are housewives, Jew and Gentile, who are slow to accept the full humanity and "adulthood" of their "girls." Frequently, the "girls" are many years older than their insensitive employers.

Contemporaneous with the Depression and its corrosive effect on Negroes was the emergence of Hitler's Third Reich. Nazi anti-Semitism was, of course, not restricted to Europe. In Detroit, relevant literature was distributed free in black sections by the notorious Jew-baiter, Father Coughlin.[29] Because of Hitler's much-vaunted theories of Nordic supremacy his career was bound to be scrutinized by the Negro press in this country. It reacted not only to the racist implications of Nazism but also to the meaning for black people of Hitler's persecution of the Jews.

A popular theme sounded in the Negro press was that oppression was no stranger to the Afro-American. Sympathy was extended to the Jew and efforts to assist him in hour of need were applauded. But what about the suffering of America's black population? Whence would come their relief? A *Crisis* editorial aptly titled "Charity Begins At Home," in commenting on the indignities visited upon Jews in Central Europe and our Negro citizens, found them amazingly alike. The Jews were disenfranchised; so were Negroes in the South. Both were discriminated against in education and employment. Jews were either excluded from beaches, playgrounds, and parks or were restricted to recreational facilities specifically designated for them. Jim Crowism humiliated Negroes in a similar fashion. Propaganda of the vilest variety calculated to incite hatred for Jews characterized the German educational system from kindergarten to university. In white America the school system

---

[29] Wedlock, *The Reaction of Negro Publications and Organizations*, p. 182.

buttressed society's pejorative image of the Negro. Finally, both Jews and Negroes were treated with great cruelty. But, whereas the plight of the former pricked the consciences of many Americans, those same Americans, including the president and the senate, were unmoved by the horrible oppression of black people on American soil.[30] Seen in retrospect, official concern for the lot of German Jews was probably overrated by the *Crisis* editorial; nonetheless the hypocrisy of America's governing elite's hand wringing (if not acting) on the Jewish question while turning a blind eye to the ongoing privations of black citizens is all too plain.

Other Negro publications made the same telling point. Shortly after Hitler came to power the *Philadelphia Tribune* recognized that it was hell to be a Jew in Germany. But, it opined, it was twice as terrible to be a black man in the United States.[31] A 1934 editorial entitled "Germany vs. America" published in the *Tribune* succinctly observed: "The persecution of the Jews in Germany by the Nazi Government is deplorable, stupid and outrageous. The persecution of colored Americans by Americans is cruel, relentless, and spirit breaking."[32]

In an editorial Baltimore's *Afro-American* called "The Nazis and Dixie" compared the old slave codes with the Nuremberg laws and other anti-Semitic measures. After enumerating some of the harsh disabilities imposed on German Jews, the editor remarked that such legislation was "designed to crush the spirit of the Jewish people and bring them down to the position our own people occupy in so many parts of the South." America below the Mason-Dixon line and Hitler's Germany were "mental brothers." The difference was that in this country the Constitution, in effect, compelled the South to resort to force and terrorism by proscribing Nuremberg-type laws.[33]

The same newspaper also scored the Führer for a speech in which he immodestly lauded German civilization. Tyrannizing Jews and using insulting invective in referring to Negroes was hardly

[30] *Crisis* 45, no. 4 (April 1968):113.
[31] See Wedlock, *Reaction of Negro Publications and Organizations,* p. 92, quoting from the *Philadelphia Tribune,* 12 October 1933.
[32] Ibid., p. 33, quoting from *Philadelphia Tribune,* 5 July 1934.
[33] *The Afro-American,* 22 February 1936.

evidence of an advanced culture, said the *Afro-American*. On the question of comparative cultural achievement it asserted:

Three thousand years ago when Africans were building pyramids and Jews temples, Germans were roaming the forest armed with clubs and drinking the blood of human sacrifices.

Civilization is not much over one thousand years old in Germany and it is plainly evident that what gentility it once had has departed, leaving the savage Hun in place of the well-meaning Herr.[34]

Hitler's talk reminded the *Afro-American* of a Klansman, and the force which for three and one half centuries had enslaved, lynched and hounded persons of African descent was called American Nazism.[35] Negrophobia in that troubled period in history was oftentimes called Hitlerism and the predicament in which blacks found themselves was proof of Nazism.[36] Kelly Miller writing in the *Washington Tribune* referred to the Führer as "the master Ku Kluxer of Germany."[37]

Miller, long associated with Howard University, was an esteemed essayist and one of America's leading black intellectuals for more than forty years until his death in 1939. Miller assigned Hitler the dubious distinction of being the "greatest demagogue of modern times." In an article in *Opportunity,* a monthly published by the National Urban League, Miller saw a striking analogy between the legal manifestations of race prejudice against the Negro in America and the Jew in Germany. "Between Hitler's treatment of the Jews and America's treatment of the Negro, you may pay your money and take your choice."[38] His editorial in a Norfolk Negro newspaper on "The Sad Plight of the Jews—Can It Happen Here?" took America to task for being smugly oblivious of her dismal record in relating to Indians and Negroes while it denounced Hitler. Of all peoples, Miller reflected, it was most incumbent upon the

34 Ibid., 11 April 1936.
35 See Wedlock, *Reaction of Negro Publications and Organizations*, p. 109, quoting from *The Afro-American,* 24 August 1935.
36 Ibid., p. 108.
37 Ibid., pp. 104–105, quoting from the *Washington Tribune,* 23 June 1933.
38 Kelly Miller, "Race Prejudice in Germany and America," *Opportunity* 14, no. 4 (April 1936):105.

black man to lament the quandary the Jew was in "lest it forbode the day when he, too, will be battered with the shocks of doom."[39] The tragedy of Hitlerism evoked many of the same thoughts from W. E. B. Du Bois. Few figures in black history enjoy more respect among Afro-Americans today than Du Bois who died in Ghana in 1963. This is true of militants and moderates alike. Born in Massachusetts in 1868, Du Bois was outstanding both as a scholar and as an articulate proponent of full citizenship rights for black Americans. He was a founder of the NAACP in 1910, an organization then regarded as dangerously radical. For more than twenty years Du Bois edited its organ, *The Crisis*.

With perhaps one exception the opinions about Jews which Du Bois expressed were virtually all sympathetic.[40] His initial exposure to anti-Semitism occurred during his student days in Berlin and as he traveled in Poland years before Hitler's ascent to power. But it was the Hitlerian persecution which elicited the most poignant comments from Du Bois' prolific pen.

Du Bois found Nazi racism loathsome. He thought that if Hitler were to lecture at white southern colleges "his race nonsense would fit beautifully."[41] What Germany was doing to the Jew, America had done to the Negro. No exact parallel existed between the two minorities. Whereas the Jews were not wanted in Germany, cheap Negro labor was lucrative and hence desirable in the South. Still, he speculated in an autobiography published in 1940 that, "We may be expelled from the United States as the Jew is being expelled from Germany."[42] Only the year before the notorious

---

[39] See Wedlock, *Reaction of Negro Publications and Organizations*, pp. 51–52, quoting from *Norfolk Journal and Guide*, 21 January 1939.

[40] A notable exception was contained in the youthful Du Bois' diary of his Atlantic crossing (1895). On that trip he met the Jewish aristocrats and the "low mean cheating Pöbel [mob]." He had not seen much of "the ordinary good hearted good intentioned man." Two Jews on the voyage he found congenial. As for the others, "there is in them all that slyness that lack of straight-forward openheartedness which goes straight against me." See Francis L. Broderick, *W. E. B. Du Bois: Negro Leader in a Time of Crisis* (Stanford: Stanford University Press, 1959), pp. 26–27.

[41] *Crisis* 40, no. 10 (October 1933):221.

[42] W. E. B. Du Bois, *Dusk of Dawn: An Essay Toward An Autobiography of a Race Concept* (New York: Schocken Books, 1968), p. 306.

Senator Bilbo of Mississippi had introduced legislation to resettle American Negroes in Africa.

The publicity accorded the plight of German Jewry contrasted sharply with the widespread complacency of white America on the Negro problem. Du Bois' anger about this was made sarcastically evident in his column, "As the Crow Flies," contained in *The Crisis* of September 1933. He "confessed" to being filled with "unholy glee" by Hitler and the Nordics. "When the only 'inferior' peoples were 'niggers' it was hard to get the attention of *The New York Times* for little matters of race, lynching and mobs. But now that the damned included the owner of the *Times,* moral indignation is perking up."[43] Du Bois was saying that Jews in particular should cry out against the oppression of Negroes. Crimes against one people were crimes against all humanity. During World War II, he conjectured about a special destiny for the Chosen People: "Suppose the Jews, instead of considering themselves a hopeless minority in the face of white Europe, should conceive themselves as part of the disinherited majority of men whom they would help to lead to power and self-realization; and at the same time imbue them with cultural tolerance and faith in humanity?"[44]

Given the Jewish contributions to German civilization, the disturbing lesson of Nazi racism for the Negro was abundantly clear. Shortly after Hitler assumed the chancellorship in March 1933 Du Bois wrote: "after all race prejudice has nothing to do with accomplishment or descent, with genius or ability. It is an ugly, dirty thing. It feeds on envy and hate."[45]

Speaking in 1952 on "The Negro and the Warsaw Ghetto," Du Bois commented that his three visits to Poland, and particularly the one in 1949 to the demolished Jewish ghetto in Warsaw, had deepened his own understanding of the black man's dilemma. Specifically, his conception of the battle against religious bigotry, racial segregation, and oppression by wealth had been enlarged. He had learned that the race problem "cut across lines of color and physique and belief and status and was a matter of cultural pat-

[43] *Crisis* 40, no. 9 (September 1933):197.
[44] "Book Department," *Annals of American Academy of Political and Social Sciences* 223 (September 1942):200.
[45] *Crisis* 40, no. 5 (May 1933):117.

terns, perverted teaching and human hate and prejudice, which reached all sorts of people and caused endless evil to all men."[46]

Somewhat less sympathetic to the Jews during the Hitler years was Marcus Mosiah Garvey, then in exile from the United States. Future historians may well view Garvey as the central figure in twentieth-century black history. He is already regarded as the patron saint of black nationalism and is honored in Africa, in London's Ladbroke Grove, in his native Jamaica, and in Harlem.

Like so many other black men Garvey entertained ambivalent feelings about Jews. At one and the same time he was mistrustful of them and held them up as a model to oppressed blacks. In the pages of the *Black Man,* a monthly magazine published by Garvey in London in the twilight of his checkered career, the paradox is obvious. Garvey felt that Hitler was making a fool of himself by persecuting Jews and attacking Judaism. Why? Because "Jewish finance is a powerful world factor. It can destroy organisations and nations."[47]

Even more caustic was Garvey's observation that most of the Jews' trouble in the world, but particularly in Germany "has been brought on by themselves in that their particular method of living is inconsistent with the broader principles that go to make all people homogeneous. The Jews like money. They have always been after money. They want nothing else but money."[48]

Garvey minced no words when Jewish interests appeared to conflict with those of Negroes anywhere in the world. That was the case in June 1939 when he heard that Neville Chamberlain, then British prime minister, was prepared to arrange for the settlement of Jewish refugees in British Guiana. No historical relationship existed between the wandering Jew and that colony. The planned introduction of Jews into Guiana, Garvey wrote, was "nothing else than an attempt to submerge and destroy the black population." While disclaiming any antipathy toward Jews as Jews, Garvey described them as a successful and cunning group. A Jew is always a Jew. His history has been one of selfishness. His greed has clouded

[46] W. E. B. Du Bois, "The Negro and the Warsaw Ghetto," *Jewish Life* 6, no. 7 (May 1952):14–15.

[47] *The Black Man* (London) 1, no. 8 (July 1935):9.

[48] Ibid., 2, no. 2 (July–August 1936):3.

his judgment.[49] Always the nationalist, Garvey's solution to the Jewish problem was to have the Jew establish and build a nation, but not in Guiana or the West Indies.

There were times when Garvey expressed sympathy for the Jews as he said he would for any persecuted people, and there were times when he saw them as brothers in adversity to the black man.[50] Many self-styled Garveyites have ignored this and have been more scornful of Jews than their mentor, for whom Jewish-Negro relations were of minor importance. The activities of Ira Reid have already been touched on. Another case in point is Carlos Cooks, a native of the Dominican Republic, who until his death in 1966, headed the neo-Garveyite African Nationalist Pioneer Movement with headquarters in New York. In 1942 Cooks, while addressing a Harlem crowd ostensibly about housing grievances, was heard to say about Hitler: "What he's trying to do, we're trying to do."[51]

It should be understood there is nothing inherently anti-Jewish about Garveyism or black nationalism and most nationalists are not anti-Semitic. If many of the highly publicized statements in recent years criticizing Jews have originated in those circles, it is probably because nationalism's greatest appeal is precisely to those black people whose contacts with Jews are of the unequal status, friction-generating variety.

In the 1930s and 1940s proponents of black nationalism were not the only ones whose perceptions of events in Germany were greatly influenced by the nature of Negro-Jewish encounters in America's urban North. There is a substantial corpus of journalistic impressions of the role of the Jew in the Third Reich and in this country. Many evinced unconcealed delight that the Jew was finally getting his comeuppance. Exemplifying this reaction was a column in the *Afro-American* in June 1933: "The Hebrews who get it in the neck are entitled to sympathy, but they, themselves, are not basically opposed to the Hitler principle. They, too, believe in hanging together and letting the devil take the hindmost. If you

[49] Ibid., 4, no. 1 (June 1939):5.
[50] Ibid., 1, no. 8 (July 1935):9; and 4, no. 1 (June 1939):3.
[51] Ottley, *New World A-Coming*, pp. 129, 334. Both Cooks and another erstwhile Garveyite, Harry Fredericks, were especially indebted to Hitler for turning whites against other whites.

doubt it, try to get a job as a clerk in one of those Pennsylvania Avenue department stores . . . there you will find Hitlerism in its most blatant form exercised by those who are being Hitlerized in Germany."[52]

In the same vein a *St. Louis Argus* editorial in July 1938 maintained that despite the fact that Jews were discriminated against here and abroad, "they, themselves are not free from using the same tactics and methods to persecute and discriminate against Negroes."[53]

J. A. Rogers, a lecturer, traveler, foreign correspondent, columnist, and historian of the Negro past, tended to put the onus for the Nazi nightmare on the Jews themselves. Rogers, whose literary works were required reading for Garveyites, explained his position in the *Philadelphia Tribune,* a major black newspaper of the day: "The Jew is accused of being an exploiter,—a charge which is, alas, but too true of a certain business element . . . the German opposition to the Jew is due largely to the fact that the Jew is powerful as a thinker, as a leader in advanced thought and as an exploiter of his fellowman."[54] It was his opinion that conditions were decidedly worse in the South for black men than for the Jews in Germany. Jews, Rogers contended, were capitalistic exploiters and leading Communists. On both scores they were odious.

George Schuyler, another Negro author who in the 1960s was closely identified with numerous conservative causes, was hesitant about extending sympathy to German Jewry in 1938: "I would be able to wail a lot louder and deeper if American Jews would give more concrete evidence of being touched by the plight of Negroes . . . Jewish-owned business is no more ready to hire Negroes in other than menial capacities than are Gentile-owned businesses. Jewish-owned and managed hotels and restaurants are quick to say 'We don't want to serve your people' as are those owned by Catholics and Protestants." He alluded to the deplorable Baltimore situation as symptomatic of the Pontius Pilate outlook of Jews. "If my Hebrew friends were only as quick to employ capable Negroes

---

[52] See Wedlock, *Reaction of Negro Publications and Organizations,* pp. 195–196, quoting from *The Afro-American,* 17 June 1933.
[53] Ibid., p. 78, quoting from the *St. Louis Argus,* 15 July 1938.
[54] Ibid., p. 149, quoting from the *Philadelphia Tribune,* 21 September 1933.

as they are other people and did not get so excited when a decent family moves in their districts," Schuyler wrote, "I could pray even harder for Hitler to let up on them."[55]

Hitler's undisguised anti-Negro feelings notwithstanding, there were a few black Americans who openly admired him. *Dynamite,* a short-lived Chicago tabloid that began publication in July 1936, voiced their thinking. Its owner and editor was one H. George Davenport, who combined careers as a sign painter and columnist. His aim was to disseminate facts "Negro Newspapers Are Afraid to Print." At first distributed free, *Dynamite* yearned for a Führer, a man of vision. "What America needs is a Hitler and what the Chicago Black Belt needs is a purge of the exploiting Jew."[56] Hitler had restored a tottering Germany to its place as a European power. Negroes also required someone to point the way.

No organ was more vicious in its Jew-baiting than *Dynamite.* "Scurrilous" was the epithet most commonly used by its contemporary critics, black and white. In its pages Jewish philanthropists were reviled and Jewish entrepreneurs derided. Local blacks who lacked the anti-Semitic crusading zeal of *Dynamite* were taunted about their exploitation. Referring to a citizens committee which had been formed to find work for jobless Negroes *Dynamite* said: "Now all you nice little Negroes, who are so much in love with your Jewish merchants can readily see that the very merchant you are always supporting does not want to see you prepare your son and daughter for jobs that call for better salaries, they wanted this committee to be a failure unless Jews control it."[57]

Dynamite further charged Jewish businessmen with making it impossible for black men to rent stores and thereby compete with them in Chicago. In addition, Negro consumers could not buy fish wholesale because Jews had cornered the market. Indeed, it was alleged, those same sharp business practices were used wherever Jews were involved. "It must be their religion," *Dynamite* pontificated, for such devious ways were peculiar to people of the Jewish faith.[58] Only by ceasing to trade with Jewish dealers could their

55 *Pittsburgh Courier,* 26 November 1938 and 3 December 1938.
56 Wedlock, *Reaction of Negro Publications and Organizations,* p. 77.
57 Ibid., pp. 171–172, quoting from *Dynamite,* 28 May 1938.
58 Ibid., p. 173, quoting from *Dynamite,* 25 June 1938.

chicanery be overcome. The ultimate solution would be their expulsion from the black community.[59] So vituperative were the repeated onslaughts against the Jews that the newspaper and its publisher were even investigated by the House Un-American Activities Committee or the Dies Committee as it was known in 1938.

A Negro scholar, Lawrence Reddick, tried to probe the psyche of Hitler's black fans. Given the Führer's utter contempt for Negroes, he concluded that his ghetto admirers were totally devoid of their rational faculties.[60]

By no means was antipathy toward Jews restricted to the unbalanced.[61] It was common, wrote Chandler Owen in 1941, to hear Negroes say, "Well, Hitler did one good thing: he put these Jews in their place."[62] By the early forties black writers while articulating widely divergent opinions about Jews were virtually all agreed that Negro anti-Semitism was definitely on the increase. Those who believe that Negro-Jewish frictions were novel in the late 1960s would be well advised to note the words of Ralph Bunche penned more than a quarter of a century ago: "It is common knowledge that many members of the Negro and Jewish communities of the country share mutual dislike, scorn, and mistrust."[63] James Q. Wilson

[59] Drake and Cayton, *Black Metropolis,* II; 432.
[60] Lawrence Reddick, "What Hitler Says About the Negro," *Opportunity* 17, no. 4 (April 1939):108–110.
[61] One study of racial stereotyping among black university students was reported to a professional association of psychologists in 1940. Working with a small sample (100) drawn from Negro colleges, mainly in the South, the author compared his results with a similar study done with an equal number of white Princetonians. A stereotype of the Jew was common to both groups. Choosing from some eighty-five adjectives, both characterized the Jew as "shrewd," "grasping," "sly," "mercenary," "aggressive," "persistent," "intelligent," "ambitious," and "progressive." While blacks added "deceitful" whites listed "talkative." See James A. Bayton, "The Racial Stereotypes of Negro College Students," *The Journal of Abnormal and Social Psychology* 36, no. 1 (January 1941):97–102.
[62] Chandler Owen, "Should the Negro Hate the Jew," *Chicago Defender* 8 November 1941. In association with A. Philip Randolph, Owen published the *Messenger* and organized the National Association for the Promotion of Labor Unionism among Negroes.
[63] See Bunche's Foreword to Wedlock, *Reactions of Negro Publications and Organizations,* p. 7. Claude McKay was one black writer who was inclined to minimize the anti-Semitism among Negroes. There seems to be general agreement that white anti-Semitism was more evident in the thirties and even the early forties.

in his study of *Negro Politics* originally published in 1960 wrote that "Negro anti-Semitism, which at one time was so prevalent that it formed one of the major themes of the Negro press, seems to have diminished, particularly among the better educated and more cosmopolitan Negroes."[64] Yet, the overt anti-Semitism in 1968 and 1969, hardly representative of the black community, caused hysteria as well as legitimate concern. With its proclivity for ferreting out the sensational, *Time* magazine thought it deserving of a cover story.[65] Jews old enough to know better regarded it as a new phenomenon, or at least one which had reached new heights. Earlier cases of black hostility to Jews had been overlooked for a few good reasons. One was that in the thirties and forties little notice was given to the Negro press by whites. A second was that Negroes were virtually without power to do anything in America and Jews in that era had more formidable anti-Semites to contend with in the white community.

It must not be forgotten that many Negro voices were raised in protest against the "rising tide" of Jew-baiting. Among the loudest and clearest in Harlem was that of Adam Clayton Powell, Jr. Powell succeeded his father as pastor of the mammoth Abyssinian Baptist Church in 1939—it had some eight thousand members— and was the first black Congressman to be elected by Harlem. In the 1960s his difficulties with the Internal Revenue Service, his playboy escapades, and personal peccadilloes captured the headlines and obscured his earlier substantial accomplishments. Those accomplishments actually antedate his first election to the House of Representatives in 1944. Kenneth Clark has written in his *Dark Ghetto* that in the 1930s "Powell became the symbol of the struggle for minimal Negro rights, his name a household word."[66] When Woolworth's on 125th Street declined to hire black girls as clerks, Powell took to the picket lines. He joined in the mass picketing of Harlem's Blumstein's. Between Powell and Sufi Abdul Hamid little love was lost, although ostensibly the two were agitating for the same "don't buy where you can't work" cause. When

---

[64] James Q. Wilson, *Negro Politics: The Search for Leadership* (New York: Free Press, 1960), p. 155.

[65] *Time,* 31 January 1969.

[66] Kenneth B. Clark, *Dark Ghetto: Dilemmas of Social Power* (New York: Harper & Row, 1967), p. 164.

Powell chided Sufi, the latter assailed Adam as an alcoholic fool.[67] "A professional anti-Semite" and a "black Hitler" were the terms Powell chose retrospectively to describe Sufi in his *Marching Blacks* published in 1945.[68]

In the dark days of the Depression when anti-Semitism was on the increase, Powell was instrumental in establishing a biracial committee which made a concerted effort to open up to Negroes theretofore unobtainable jobs. Using his column, the "Soap Box," in the *Amsterdam-News,* he spoke out on Negro-Jewish relations. No battle predicated on hatred could be won, he asserted on one occasion. Enmity could not be countered with enmity. Bigotry could not be destroyed with more bigotry.

Let us stop blaming the Jew for the wrongs perpetrated and blame those who are really at fault. Wherever the blame falls, let us not follow it up with hate. The fact is the Jew doesn't wrong us any more and probably much less than any other group. Maybe the corner grocer will short weigh you a couple of ounces, but so will Joe the vegetable man and Sam the ice man. Cheating is not confined to any one race. Whereas one group might cut the change a little bit or pad the bill, it is the so-called white Christian that is giving us the most hell right now.[69]

In *Marching Blacks* he described anti-Semitism as "a deadly virus of the American bloodstream," even deadlier than anti-Negroism in some regions.[70]

Powell also took up the cudgels in defense of European Jewry. He inveighed against Hitler, Mussolini, and their minions and called international fascism civilization's greatest danger. Nazi hatred of Jews he felt was unwarranted. Hitler was using German Jewry as a scapegoat. "By lampooning the Jew, he could make the lowest moron and the biggest degenerate in all Germany feel that, after all, he wasn't the lowest down, there were always the Jews."[71] Exactly the same psychology underlay prejudice toward Negroes in

[67] McKay, *Harlem: Black Metropolis,* p. 190.
[68] Adam Clayton Powell, Jr., *Marching Blacks: An Interpretive History of the Rise of the Black Common Man* (New York: Dial Press, 1945), pp. 75, 81.
[69] *Amsterdam-News,* 16 April 1938.
[70] Powell, *Marching Blacks,* p. 66.
[71] *Amsterdam-News,* 16 April 1938.

the American South, Powell opined: "He [the white southerner] wants the tobacco juice-stained moron of Tobacco Road to feel that there is always someone beneath him and so, he is taught that the Negro down the road is not his equal."[72]

Negroes, he argued, could not stand aloof. Neutrality and apathy were self-defeating. Prejudice in Germany, China, Spain, or Haiti, or wherever, imperiled America's "so-called free Negroes." In Powell's view the dilemma of Harlem's unemployed and the plight of the remaining Scottsboro victims and Hitler's persecution of German Jewry were inextricably intertwined.[73]

A. Philip Randolph, head of the Brotherhood of Sleeping Car Porters, made essentially the same point in June 1942, while addressing a Madison Square Garden audience: "no Negro is secure from intolerance and race prejudice so long as one Jew is a victim of anti-Semitism or a Catholic is victimized as Governor Alfred E. Smith was by religious bigotry during the Presidential campaign against Herbert Hoover, or a trade unionist is harassed by a tory open-shopper."[74]

In 1942, Ralph Bunche, chairman of the Department of Political Science at Harvard University, held both anti-Semitism among American blacks and irrational fear and dislike of Negroes on the part of Jews to be nonsensical examples of the pot calling the kettle black. For Afro-Americans anti-Jewish feeling was not just an unfortunate social phenomenon but a dangerous luxury. Bunche expressed a hope that Jewish and Negro leaders and organizations would labor to improve the strained relations between the two ethnic minorities. "In large measure," he maintained, "their problems—their grievances and their fears are cut to a common pattern."[75]

Chandler Owen who served as a consultant on Negro relations for the Office of War Information also wrote candidly in the face of growing anti-Semitism in the black ghettos. Owen ascribed that phenomenon to the mischief of Axis agents whose talk of Jewish

[72] Ibid.
[73] Ibid., 19 February 1938.
[74] Gunnar Myrdal, *An American Dilemma* (New York: McGraw-Hill Book Co., 1964), II, 852.
[75] Foreword to Wedlock, *Reactions of Negro Publications and Organizations*, pp. 8, 10.

control of commerce and industry was "echoed by stooges and light thinkers." Owen went so far as to say that Jewish capital invested in the ghetto had had a salutary effect there. Jews had a record of cooperation with Negroes superior to that of any other white group. In an article in the *Chicago Defender* Owen surveyed Jewish contributions to the welfare of the Negro.[76] He enumerated the interracial work done by Jewish foundations, Jewish activities in civil rights and Jewish benevolence in the field of entertainment. Owen found the receptivity to Negroes of Jewish labor unions, the International Ladies Garment Workers Union and the Amalgamated Clothing Workers of America, the fur workers, and cap makers especially praiseworthy. After looking at the record Owen's conclusion was that the facts "should generate a measure of gratitude, . . . and stimulate reasonable appreciation among Negroes as to their Jewish brethren." Owen's statement provided a much-needed balance to some of the aforementioned derogatory views, although he perhaps overstated the basic points he was making. In this light one can conclude that the record of Jewish labor leaders and members of the entertainment media was probably somewhat better than the record of white non-Jews in terms of their relationships with blacks. Yet the Jews as a group did not warrant as much praise as that accorded by Owen. Just as black people didn't want to be judged by their worst, Owen told his readers, they should refrain from generalizing about Jews based on their worst representatives.

Taken as a whole, the data about Negro-Jewish relations between the wars leads to the following broad conclusions: One, that the confrontations between first-generation American Jews and multitudes of transplanted southern Negroes in northern cities gave rise to a greater volume of criticism of Jews by blacks than that heard at any time before or since, including the late sixties. Two, that the Great Depression, severely worsening the already miserable position of the Negro, exacerbated tensions between Jews and Negroes who ordinarily met in a superior-subordinate relationship. Third, and perhaps most important, Hitler's rise to power accom-

---

[76] *Chicago Defender,* 8 November 1941; Many of the same points were made in Chandler Owen, "Negro Anti-Semitism: Cause and Cure," *The National Jewish Monthly,* September 1942, pp. 14–15. In this piece Owen blames, in part, American Fascist agencies, Axis agents, and Nazi propagandists, for Negro anti-Semitism.

panied by raucous anti-Semitism provided a point of departure for discussions of the Negro and the Jew in America by the Negro press. A tiny minority peddled raw anti-Semitism. Some emphasized the plight of the Jews in Germany to call attention to the way in which whites, including Jews, in America treated blacks. Others saw obvious parallels between Jewish suffering under Nazism and the predicament of black Americans. They deplored anti-Semitism. In sum, Negroes during that troubled era spoke not with one voice, but with many.

} 4 {

WELLSPRINGS OF
TENSION

THAT THE WELLSPRINGS OF IRRATIONAL PREJUDICE ARE NUMEROUS is obvious. Equally obvious is that whatever Jewish racism or black anti-Semitism exists in our society is to some degree explainable in psychological terms. Bigotry may well meet some psychological needs, if only in the short run. It may provide a target for the bigot's aggression, aggression which is ordinarily stifled socially. It may inflate his flagging self-esteem. It may assuage his sense of dissatisfaction with himself, a dissatisfaction which has often been the product of a society inclined to label black aspiration as insolence. "A poor man's snobbery," Jean-Paul Sartre felicitously dubbed anti-Semitism.[1]

Writing in 1942, Ralph Bunche observed:

Negroes are an oppressed frustrated people. Such a people hits always upon the simplest and most convenient explanation of its troubles. It pounces upon a scapegoat as a means of psychological escape. The Jew is handy. In Negro communities he has daily contact with Negroes in the conduct of his business. And it is safe to scorn the Jew. His powers

---

[1] Jean-Paul Sartre, *Anti-Semite and Jew,* trans. by George J. Becker (New York: Schocken Books, 1965), p. 26.

of retaliation are less great than those of the Gentile whites, for the Jew himself is a victim of race.[2]

Bunche also advanced the hypothesis that some blacks might derive solace from the knowledge that enmity toward Jews is not uncommon and that blacks are not alone in being despised.

Similarly, there are psychological causes of racial antipathy among Jews. Just as the Jew serves as a scapegoat for some blacks, Jews and other whites may project onto Negroes traits in themselves which are deemed undesirable. Tales of sexual immorality among blacks would fall into this category.[3] Repressed wishes are ascribed to other groups and individuals in this process. Another factor is the need on the part of somewhat insecure whites, particularly ethnic minorities including Jews, to conform to the attitudinal norm. A demeaning view of the Negro, held and expressed in common by Gentiles and Jews, may enable the latter to feel that for once they are really part of the "in" group. Religious distinctions between whites are thereby submerged. Writing insightfully more than twenty years ago about Negro-Jewish relations, Kenneth Clark observed "it is naive to assume that, because Negroes and Jews are each in their own way oppressed and insecure, this will necessarily lead to a feeling of kinship and understanding. . . . The common ground of insecurity itself may lead to an intensification of fear, suspicion and active hostility as each group competes in efforts to escape relegations to the lowest status."[4] No understanding of Negro-Jewish relations is possible without taking cognizance of these and many other psychological determinants of prejudice.[5]

---

[2] Foreword to Lunabelle Wedlock, *The Reaction of Negro Publications and Organizations to German Anti-Semitism* (Washington, D.C.: Howard University Press, 1942), p. 3.

[3] See Gerhard Saenger, *The Social Psychology of Prejudice: Achieving Intellectual Understanding and Cooperation in a Democracy* (New York: Harper & Brothers, 1953), chap. 8.

[4] Kenneth B. Clark, "Candor About Negro-Jewish Relations," *Commentary,* February 1948, p. 11.

[5] A wealth of relevant information can be found in Leonard Berkowitz, *Aggression: A Social Psychological Analysis* (New York: McGraw-Hill Book Co., 1962); Gordon W. Allport, *The Nature of Prejudice* (Garden City: Doubleday, Anchor Books, 1958); and Milton Rokeach, *The Open and Closed Mind* (New York: Basic Books, 1960).

However, they must not be separated from religious, historical, economic, and social determinants.

In perceiving one another both Negroes and Jews have been victims of their respective historical experiences in this country: Negroes as converts to Christianity and Jews as white men. Inevitably Jews were tainted by the racism that has pervaded white America's attitudes toward black people since the seventeenth century. There is no reason to expect that Jews should have remained immune to the racist mythology that has unremittingly poisoned black-white relations. Whatever their religious differences with the majority of Americans, Jews have had in common with fellow Caucasians an important characteristic—namely white skin. In color-conscious America, one's pigmentation has been incomparably more important than one's religious persuasion in determining social acceptability and vocational success.

As part of the dominant European culture Jews, by and large, imbibed the pejorative images of people of African descent. Those familiar images of the indolent, docile, uneducable, fetid, oversexed Negro have proven amazingly durable. They can be traced to a variety of factors. Xenophobia, in this case the fear and distaste for black strangers, different in customs, diet, religion, and most strikingly, in appearance, was perhaps paramount. The "moral" justification of the slave trade and slavery were based in large measure on the premise that Africans were childlike, inferior, savage beings. Rationalization of the oppression of blacks in the late nineteenth and twentieth centuries, while a bit more sophisticated, is really predicated on the same premise. In recent years it has become increasingly clear that our educational systems have always allowed white Americans, including many Jews as well as Gentiles, to believe that the "Negro problem" is not ascribable to enslavement, subjugation, and lack of equal opportunity.

Although most blacks have operated historically on the fringes of American society, they have been cut off, probably more than any other immigrant group, from their original culture. Assertions of an African identity so common in the last few years, e.g., studying Swahili and African history, wearing natural hairstyles, calling themselves Afro-Americans, are a reflection of this fact and of current black dissatisfaction with it. Negroes, who are American in a cultural if not a political or economic sense, have been overwhelmingly Christian. Naturally, they have been the beneficiaries of some time-honored Christian notions about Jews. On the other hand, there have been unique features of the Negro-Jewish relationship. Negroes, like the Hebrews of antiquity, were slaves. Consequently, in the antebellum era many Negroes identified with their Old Testament counterparts. This identification is mirrored in countless plantation spirituals.[6] Many spoke of a messianic Moses who would redeem the slaves from bondage. One spiritual ran as follows:

> Go down, Moses
> Way down in Egypt land
> Tell ole Pharoah
> Let my people go

Slave songs were replete with Old Testament names and places. References to Canaan-land were legion as were allusions to the Jordan.[7]

How meaningful in terms of black-Jewish relations today is this identification between the Negro bondsmen and the ancient Hebrews? Gary Marx's study cited one interviewee as saying: "They are Christ's chosen people and they are blessed." Marx has inferred from his data that "people who perceive Jews as the chosen people are less likely to be anti-Semitic than those who do not."[8] Among articulate blacks there is a minimum of identification between their own plight and that of the ancient followers of Abraham, Isaac, and Jacob. Social realities are infinitely more significant than religious traditions. Furthermore, many Christians, black and white alike, do not associate present-day Jews with the people of the Old Testament.

For almost two thousand years Christian hostility toward Jews has been based in part on "religious" grounds. Jews have been widely regarded in Christendom as a perfidious people because of

---

[6] Miles Mark Fisher, *Negro Slave Songs in the United States* (New York: Citadel Press, 1963).

[7] Canaan-land may actually have represented the nonslave North, and the Jordan may have stood for the Ohio River.

[8] Gary T. Marx, *Protest and Prejudice: A Study of Belief in the Black Community* (New York: Harper & Row, 1967), p. 149.

their explicit rejection of Christ. Beyond that, they have been charged with the crime of deicide; that is to say, they have been held responsible for the crucifixion of Jesus. Only in 1965 did the Roman Catholic Church, acting through Vatican Council II, exonerate the Jews.[9]

A number of crucial questions are raised by the foregoing. To what degree is black anti-Semitism qualitatively different from white Gentile anti-Semitism? To what extent is anti-Jewish feeling in the black community rooted in the traditional Christian hatred for the faithless Jew? More than one Jewish writer has believed Christian fundamentalism to be the central factor underlying black anti-Semitism. Professor Abraham G. Duker of Yeshiva University, speaking at a conference on Negro-Jewish relations in 1964, put great emphasis on the Christ-killer thesis which has been transmuted into folkways and stereotypes. He thought it probable that Negroes raised in the New Testament "absorbed anti-Jewish theological teachings and folklore."[10]

Judd Teller, writing in 1966, called the deicide notion "the first and primary source of Negro anti-Semitism." For Teller the Christian fundamentalism shared by the black man and the white cracker is the vehicle whereby the former asserts his equality within the white man's religion.[11]

A somewhat different interpretation was advanced by B. Z. Sobel and May L. Sobel, a sociologist and an historian respectively. The Sobels take due cognizance of the overwhelming preponderance of fundamentalist Protestantism in the black community and contend that there is a theological basis for anti-Jewishness in that community. What they believe, however, is that while the religious tradition should not be ignored in explaining Negro enmity to Jews it

---

[9] Implementation of the Vatican II resolution has varied from country to country and from diocese to diocese. While fewer parochial schools will foster the deicide idea in the future, American public schools will probably continue to assume that Christianity represents the fulfillment of Old Testament prophecy. Judaism therefore has lost its raison d'être. Many Jews object to this approach and rightly so.

[10] Abraham G. Duker, "On Negro-Jewish Relations—A Contribution to a Discussion," *A Symposium: Negro-Jewish Relations in the United States* (New York: Citadel Press, 1966), p. 23.

[11] Judd L. Teller, "Negroes and Jews: A Hard Look," *Conservative Judaism* 21, no. 1 (Fall 1966):17.

"has rather loomed and hovered in the background—there but not often verbalized."[12]

The reminiscences of Horace Mann Bond tend to undergird the Sobel thesis. Bond, an eminent Negro educator, was the dean of the school of education at Atlanta University. He is also the father of Julian Bond, the young civil-rights activist in the Georgia State Senate. A few years ago Bond recalled an incident that occurred when he was twelve, shortly after his family had moved to Atlanta in 1916.

I was walking along a street near my house, and had to pass a small grocery store located in our neighborhood. There was a small boy— perhaps six years old—looking through the picket fence that surrounded the store. As I passed he began to chant: "Nigger, Nigger, Nigger, Nigger." You may not believe it, but this was the first time I could remember anyone calling me a "Nigger." And my response still surprises me; I retorted to the boy, "You Christ-killer!" And the little boy burst into tears, and I have felt badly about it ever since.[13]

Dr. Bond was at a loss to explain how the term "Christ-killer" entered his vocabulary. To the best of his recollection he had not heard it at home. In retrospect Dr. Bond guessed that "the word I used hung immanent in the Atlanta air." The incident took place when the Leo Frank lynching was front-page news and back-fence gossip. "Somehow," Bond recalled, the epithet "had entered my mind, and remained like a knife, waiting only for opportunity for release. But of course the thought that Christ had been killed, and by the Jews, and that the little boy was such a one, may have had a more ancient basis in my twelve-year-old mind than I can now bring myself to admit."[14]

More than thirty years ago, Richard Wright, the renowned black

---

12 B. Z. Sobel and May L. Sobel, "Negroes and Jews: American Minority Groups In Conflict," *Judaism* 15, no. 1 (Winter 1966):5.

13 Horace Mann Bond, "Negro Attitudes Toward Jews," *A Symposium: Negro Jewish Relations in the United States* (New York: Citadel Press, 1966), pp. 3–4.

14 Ibid., p. 4; Baldwin has observed: "though the traditional Christian accusation that the Jews killed Christ is neither questioned nor doubted, the term 'Jew' actually operates in this initial context to include all infidels of white skin who have failed to accept the Savior." See James Baldwin, *Notes of a Native Son* (Boston: Beacon Press, 1955), p. 66.

novelist, in his autobiographical *Black Boy,* remembered his earliest childhood reactions to the neighborhood Jewish groceryman and to Jews in general.

I had never seen a Jew before and the proprietor of the corner grocery was a strange thing in my life. . . . All of us black people who lived in the neighborhood hated Jews, not because they exploited us, but because we had been taught at home and in Sunday school that Jews were "Christ-killers." With the Jews thus singled out for us, we made them fair game for ridicule.

We black children, seven, eight, and nine years of age—used to run to the Jew's store and shout:

> Jew, Jew, Jew
> What do you chew?

Or we would form a long line and weave back and forth in front of the door, singing

> Jew, Jew
> Two for five
> That's what keeps
> Jew alive

Or we would chant:

> Bloody Christ killers
> Never Trust a Jew
> Bloody Christ killers
> What won't a Jew do?[15]

Wright indicated that the entire repertoire of cruel anti-Jewish folk rhymes was generally approved of by the parents of the children. Distrust of Jews was bred in the children. It was an element in their cultural heritage.

From the available evidence it appears that there was a corpus of anti-Semitic ditties with which many Negroes as Christians were familiar.

But it is doubtful, as Lawrence Reddick pointed out in the early 1940s when he was curator of the Schomburg Collection of Negro Literature, that the rhymes had been translated into "active

---

[15] Richard Wright, *Black Boy: A Record of Childhood and Youth* (Cleveland and New York: World Publishing Co., 1950), pp. 75–77. Another reference to Jews in a Negro song was, "Virgin Mary had one son, the cruel Jews had him hung."

opinions."[16] Clearly today, the Christ-killer canard, while it has not vanished altogether, is not nearly as fashionable nor as important a factor in black dislike of Jews as it was earlier in this century. Louis Lomax and other blacks have concurred in this view.[17] Moreover, the black nationalists among whom vocal hostility toward Jews is more common are, in the main, either Muslim or secular. In large measure they are antagonistic to traditional Christianity. This is not to say that they have rejected all Christian teachings to which they have been exposed. It is possible that in their formative years anti-Semitic sentiments were internalized which cannot be shed by some black adults, even those whose rhetoric is distinctly unfriendly to Christianity. However, it is probably most accurate to assume that if classical anti-Semitism exists, it does so in the black community as a predisposition which is frequently aggravated by the nature of Negro-Jewish encounters, especially in the ghetto.[18]

At the heart of the confrontation between blacks and Jews is the structure of the ghetto itself. As has previously been noted Harlem, Watts, Roxbury, et al., are quite different from the Chinatowns and Little Italies in our major metropolitan centers. While the latter may have the trappings of ghettos, whatever economic value there is therein, and it is often considerable, accrues principally to the resident Chinese and Italians themselves. Not so with the black belts. They operate basically as colonies with much of the property

---

[16] Roi Ottley, *New World A-Coming: Inside Black America* (Boston: Houghton Mifflin Co., 1943), p. 128.

[17] Louis Lomax, *When the Word Is Given* (Cleveland and New York: World Publishing Co., 1963), p. 75.

[18] In October 1968 during the New York City school strike, according to the sworn statement of a striking teacher, "a sign appeared in the school window [PS 29 in the Bronx] held first by an adult and then by a child saying 'Christ Killers.'" A poem entitled "Jew-Land" which appeared in a Black Panther publication includes references to the crucifixion as well as other sources of anti-Jewish and anti-Israel feeling:

Jew-Land, On a summer afternoon
Really, Couldn't kill the Jews too soon

Now dig, the Jews have stolen all our bread
Their filthy women tricked our men into bed
So I won't rest until the Jews are dead

In Jew-Land, Nailing Rabbis to a cross
Really, Don't you think that would be boss

owned by whites and much of the wealth siphoned out of the ghetto.

The exact proportion of Jewish ownership of inner city stores and tenements varies somewhat from city to city. One significant determinant is the relative size of the Jewish community; another is whether substantial numbers of Jews formerly resided in the black neighborhoods. A supplementary report of the Kerner Commission has shown that in the black districts of fifteen large cities Jews own 39 percent of the stores.[19] In New York, Mayor Lindsay's Task Force Report on the Economic Redevelopment of Harlem estimated that whites owned 47 percent of all stores in central Harlem. Whites own 74 percent of food stores; 89 percent of furniture, hardware and appliance stores; 72 percent of apparel shops; and in excess of 60 percent of liquor and drug stores.[20] The report does not specifically assess the degree of Jewish ownership.

Under the direction of Naomi Levine, a political scientist and a consultant to the American Jewish Congress, a survey of a "typical" twenty-block area was carried out in the midst of Harlem.[21] One hundred and twenty-fifth street was omitted. The findings in a random sample showed that Negroes owned 58 percent of the stores. Excluding the Chinese and Puerto Rican-owned enterprises, non-Negroes owned 37 percent of the shops. Because of the reluctance of some store owners to disclose their religion, the number of Jewish-owned businesses was not precisely determined. The maximum percentage, according to Professor Levine, was thirty to

---

You know the Jews don't really want to fight
They're gonna say that we're just anti-Semite
But I don't care because the Jews are white.

In Jew-Land, Don't be a Tom on Israel's side
Really, Cause that's where Christ was crucified.

We're gonna burn their towns and that ain't all
We're gonna piss upon the Wailing Wall.
See *Black Power* 1, no. 7 (June 1967).

[19] *Supplementary Studies for the National Advisory Commission on Civil Disorders* (Washington, D.C.: U.S. Government Printing Office, 1968), p. 126.
[20] *Mayor's Task Force Report on the Economic Redevelopment of Harlem,* 15 January 1968, table IV–3.
[21] Naomi Levine, "Who Owns the Stores in Harlem," *Congress Bi-Weekly,* 16 September 1968, pp. 10–12.

thirty-five and she believed her sample to be representative of the entire Harlem community. Professor Levine did concede that the most visible, the largest, and most lucrative stores on 125th street were owned by whites. Her failure to include Harlem's preeminent commercial thoroughfare in the survey was sarcastically commented on in a letter to the editor of the *Amsterdam-News:* "When the American Jewish Congress gets around to doing a survey on crime in Harlem, I hope, that time, they do include the businesses on 125th St."[22]

Despite the serious omission, Professor Levine's results substantiated a recent study previously conducted by Detroit's Jewish Community Council. It concluded that Jewish merchants comprised 9.5 percent of the total number of merchants in the area investigated as compared with 15 percent before that city's destructive riot. To quote the Detroit report: "it is apparent that the number of Jewish merchants in the ghetto has been overinflated."[23] Similar misconceptions are rife. And the fact that Negro ownership, though growing, is for the most part still confined to beauty parlors, funeral homes, small "soul food" shops etc., while the bigger, more glamorous establishments are mainly in the hands of whites and sometimes bear Jewish-sounding surnames, reinforces the idea that Harlem is a colony exploited solely by whites, mostly Jews.

There is no gainsaying the fact that the ghetto dweller is taken advantage of day in and day out. Thievery of the poor takes a multitude of forms and constitutes as great a social problem as thievery by the poor. Criminally imaginative merchants and salesmen delude the poverty-stricken with garish, shoddy, outrageously priced merchandise. Secondhand goods are routinely sold as new. For the staples of life the poor frequently pay more than middle-class consumers. Intimidation of the unsuspecting by callous storekeepers is common in the slums as is the widespread use of deceptive and misleading interest rates. The consequences for the poor are never-ending indebtedness and, not surprisingly, hostility toward whites.

Obviously, unethical business practices to which governments, federal, state, and local have so long turned a blind eye, urgently require remedial action. But unfortunately it is not always a simple

[22] *Amsterdam-News,* 25 January 1969.
[23] Quoted in Levine, "Who Owns the Stores in Harlem," p. 11.

matter to ascertain what is a fair price or a reasonable rate of interest. Insurance premiums are higher in the inner cities, the more so since the urban turmoil which began in the summer of 1964. This is reflected in retail prices. Then there is the question of capitalization with which relatively few in the ghetto are familiar. Addressing himself to this point in a speech in 1968, Bayard Rustin commented:

The fact is, if you walk up 125th Street you will see what they say you will see—a television set that sells in department stores for $79.50 costs $132 in Harlem. But the ghetto dweller does not calculate that the department store is able to sell the TV set at $79.50 because he has made a considerable down payment, and is required to finish payments within one year; while in the ghetto he is often given with no down payment, three or four years in which to pay. He often does not understand that as the length of time for payment is increased, the interest is increased. He does not always understand that only such long-term capitalization makes it possible for him to have a TV set at all.

Many people are kept alive for three and four weeks at a time by local businessmen who let them pile up the debt until they hit the numbers or something and can pay for what they bought. But if you hit the numbers once in a year and have to give most of the money to the groceryman for things you have already eaten, when there are still more things you need, you hate him for taking your money even though you know it belongs to him.[24]

Rustin's objective was to put slum business practices in their proper social and economic context. It was definitely not to pooh-pooh the mercantile turpitude which is rampant in our black ghettos. To be sure the guilty are black as well as white, Gentile as well as Jew. However, Jews have often been seen as the prime malefactors.

Frequently Jews are associated, almost reflexively, with money, parasitism, and oppression. The pawnbroker's sign, symbolic of the black man's despair is colloquially referred to as "Jew's balls." Cadillacs in ghetto argot are called "Jew canoes."

Claude Brown in his autobiographical bestseller, *Manchild in the Promised Land,* captured what may be the prevailing image of

[24] Bayard Rustin, "The Anatomy of Frustration" (Address delivered at the 55th National Commission Meeting of the Anti-Defamation League of B'nai B'rith, 6 May 1968, New York City).

"Goldberg" as one who's "got all the money in the world" and the one who has Harlem in his pocket. These images confirm Brown's childhood distinctions between a "cracker" and a Jew: "white people is all mean and stingy. If one-a dem is more stingy than he is mean, he's a Jew, and if he is more mean than he is stingy, then he's a cracker."[25]

While not all or necessarily even most of those whites who have economically suffocated or spiritually ravaged urban Negroes have been Jews, when black Americans have encountered Jews they have ordinarily done so as dependents. The consequences were predictable.

The brilliant novelist, James Baldwin, in a poignant exposition of Negro anti-Semitism remembers his own upbringing, its attendant frustrations and anguish and the attitudes that were being shaped.

When we were growing up in Harlem our demoralizing series of land-lords were Jewish, and we hated them. We hated them because they were terrible landlords, and did not take care of the building. . . . Our parents were lashed down to futureless jobs, in order to pay the outrageous rent. We knew that the landlord treated us this way only because we were colored, and he knew we could not move out.

The grocer was a Jew, and being in debt to him was very much like being in debt to the company store. The butcher was a Jew and, yes, we certainly paid more for bad cuts of meat than other New York citizens and we very often carried insults home, along with the meat. We bought our clothes from a Jew and sometimes, our secondhand shoes, and the pawnbroker was a Jew—perhaps we hated him most of all. The merchants along 125th Street were Jewish—at least many of them were. . . .

Not all of these white people were cruel—on the contrary I remember some who were certainly as thoughtful as the bleak circumstances allowed—but all of them were exploiting us, and that was why we hated them.[26]

Baldwin's youthful perceptions are shared today by some indi-

25 Claude Brown, *Manchild in the Promised Land* (New York: New American Library, 1966), pp. 295, 337.

26 James Baldwin, "Negroes Are Anti-Semitic Because They're Anti-White," *New York Times Magazine,* 9 April 1967, p. 27.

viduals in the black zones of our cities and they are much less favorably disposed to Jews than he. For them Jews are above all else merchants who sell poor grade meats and tawdry merchandise at high prices, and absentee slumlords who charge excessive rents for unliveable housing. "It was . . . the exploitation by Jewish landlords and merchants which first created black resentment towards Jews—not Judaism," Stokely Carmichael wrote bluntly in 1966.[27]

A column in *Nite Life,* a Philadelphia publication received in many bars in that city, tersely identified the Jew as "the rent man, the grocery store owner, the dollar down and dollar when I catch you man."[28] *Nite Life* has also carried an open letter to various Jewish agencies developing this same image of the exploiter. The author of the letter was Cecil Moore, an ex-Marine, an attorney, and a civil rights activist. To eliminate the causes of anti-Semitism, Moore recommended that the agencies do the following:

Rid us of those Jews who sell black people rotten and maggot ridden meat, stale bread and sour milk for fresh bread and milk. Rid us of those Jews who charge us for three pounds of meat when there are only two. Rid us of those Jews who add ten-fifteen cents to every bill. Rid us of those Jews who sell us shoes with cardboard soles. . . . Rid us of those Jews who put six families in a one family house. Rid us of those Jews who charge fifteen to twenty dollars a week for a two and one half room apartment; the highest rent paid for roaches, rats and garbage filled hallways. Rid us of those Jews who levy and evict black people for being one day late in their rent. . . . Rid us of those Jews who refuse to employ Negroes in neighborhood stores.[29]

Can it be assumed that the above sentiments are widely held by blacks? In an attitudinal study carried out by Selznick and Steinberg under the auspices of the Anti-Defamation League, the au-

[27] Stokely Carmichael, *Power and Racism: What We Want* (Boston: New England Free Press, n.d.), p. 4.

[28] *Nite Life,* 10 January 1967.

[29] Ibid., 19 December 1967. Interesting in the light of the discussion of black nationalism and the Middle East conflict (chap. 5) is Moore's plea to "rid us of those Jews who claim draft deferments, raising the quota of our boys to die in Vietnam, but yet can raise 10 million dollars to send to Israel and give up their draft deferments to go to Israel."

thors concluded that Negro hostility toward Jews was greatest in the "economic sphere."[30] In other spheres, the noneconomic ones, there were no significant differences between white and Negro attitudes about Jews. However, on the whole Negroes were less likely than whites to translate negative feelings into actual discriminatory behavior.

By and large ghetto Negroes encounter the elderly, less-educated, more prejudiced Jews. For poor, unskilled, uneducated blacks, who meet these Jews in the least propitious of conditions, the stories they have heard about Jews being "unethical, untrustworthy and indifferent to the fate of others" are frequently confirmed by their own experiences.[31]

Selznick and Steinberg also point out that the participation of Jewish businessmen in an economic system which exploits Negroes, creates a real source for negative Negro feelings toward Jews. Generally such feelings toward a source of frustration should not be classified as prejudice. These feelings can and sometimes do "spill over into the realm of prejudice" when "the behavior of Jewish businessmen is perceived as somehow derived from their Jewishness, or when resentment against Jewish businessmen is directed against Jews generally."[32]

In this connection the reader should be conversant and cog-

---

[30] Gertrude J. Selznick and Stephen Steinberg, *The Tenacity of Prejudice* (New York: Harper & Row, 1969). This book and the Marx volume are among a five-volume series based on the University of California Five-Year Study of Anti-Semitism in the United States, conducted by the Survey Research Center in Berkeley. The survey data for the two studies were accumulated by the California Survey Research Center and the National Opinion Research Center at the University of Chicago respectively.

[31] Ibid., pp. 126–127. However, among the respondents interviewed in the Marx study in 1964, 34 percent of the Negroes said it "is better to work for a Jew" than for a non-Jewish white; 19 percent said they would prefer to work for a non-Jew. (The remaining 47 percent replied "about the same" or "don't know.") Twenty percent said that Jewish store owners were better than other white store owners and only 7 percent said that Jewish store owners were worse (68 percent replied "about the same" and 5 percent "Don't know"). Asked whether Jewish landlords were better than other white landlords, 24 percent said they were, 7 percent said they were not, and 69 percent replied "about the same" or "don't know." Marx, *Protest and Prejudice* (1969 paperback ed.), p. 137.

[32] Selznick and Steinberg, *The Tenacity of Prejudice*, p. 131.

nizant with facts that emerge from the Marx study previously cited
—that although Negroes were prone to negative stereotyping of
Jewish commercial behavior, at least 75 percent of the black respondents in each city studied did not feel that they had ever been
unfairly treated by a Jewish businessman. In addition, the majority
in every sample believed Jews were more liberal than other whites
in extending credit and more flexible in dealing with those who
were lax in making credit payments.[33]

Although some black critics have set the Jew apart from whites
in general, the Chinese on the West coast, the Italians and a number of ethnic minorities from Eastern Europe have been similarly
castigated. In New Orleans, for example, Drake and Cayton have
observed that the white merchants who were most visible in the
black neighborhoods were Italians. There the "dagos" received the
brunt of the black criticism.[34] Italian-Negro relations in Newark
have often been acrimonious in recent years as have Irish-black
relations in Boston. Unease, envy, and tension have even marked
contacts between Negroes from the rural South and the West Indian immigrant population which burgeoned after World War I.
By and large, the Caribbean Negroes were better educated and
boasted more marketable vocational skills. They were conspicuous
in the black professional classes, and, significantly, they were responsible for a large proportion of the black-controlled businesses.[35] Their commercial success was variously ascribed to their
frugality, their craftiness, their pushiness, and their clannishness.
Sometimes, for obvious reasons, these foreign-born Negroes have
been called "the Jews of the race."[36]

In view of the foregoing, to what degree, one may logically ask,
is black rage in the ghetto directed against Jews per se rather than
against any who bilk the oppressed populace? West Indians,
though frequently of mixed descent, were clearly not white and
customarily lived in close proximity to the American black. There-

[33] Marx, *Protest and Prejudice*, pp. 160, 163.
[34] St. Clair Drake and Horace R. Cayton, *Black Metropolis: A Study of
Negro Life in a Northern City* (New York and Evanston: Harper &
Row, 1962), II, 432.
[35] Ottley, *New World A-Coming*, p. 46.
[36] Gilbert Osofsky, *Harlem: The Making of a Ghetto* (New York: Harper
& Row, 1968), p. 133.

fore they would not be subject to the kind of observation noted by James Baldwin: "It is bitter to watch the Jewish storekeeper locking up his store for the night and going home. Going, with your money in his pocket, to a clean neighborhood, miles from you, which you will not be allowed to enter."[37]

The civil disorders which have occurred since 1964 in many American cities provide some data, albeit inconclusive, relevant to anti-Semitism. After the rioting which occurred in the aftermath of the tragic assassination of Martin Luther King, Jr., the American Jewish Committee surveyed some thirteen major cities to ascertain the status of Jewish enterprises in the ghettos and the effect of the disturbances on them. Most of the urban reports did *not* endorse the thesis that Jews were particular targets of violence. Apparently, the burning of Jewish property was part of the general pattern of destruction of white-owned businesses.[38]

A study of the 1964 conflagration in Philadelphia has yielded the impression that "anti-Semitism was not a primary factor in the rioting." Jews were the principal commercial representatives of the white community in the riot area, but whatever pent-up fury was released was aimed at them as Caucasians and shopkeepers rather than as Jews. Anti-white remarks abounded, but Lenora E. Berson, author of this *Case Study of a Riot,* has declared that anti-Jewish epithets were not heard. Nor is there any reason to believe "that the results would have been appreciably different had the majority of the white merchants been of Italian, Swedish or German background."[39]

Nevertheless, partly because of recent chaos, partly because of the often reiterated demands by blacks for control of their own

[37] Baldwin, "Negroes Are Anti-Semitic Because They're Anti-White," p. 135.

[38] Bertram H. Gold, *Jews and the Urban Crisis* (New York: American Jewish Committee, Institute of Human Relations, 1968), pp. 14–15. Gold is Executive Vice-President of the American Jewish Committee.

[39] Lenora E. Berson, *Case Study of a Riot* (New York: American Jewish Committee, Institute of Human Relations, 1966), p. 46. In 1949 one scholar wrote of the 1935 Harlem riot: "A definite feeling of anti-Semitism was manifested during this riot and has been generally present during riots, among Northern Negroes at least, ever since." See Arnold Rose, *The Negro's Morale: Group Identification and Protest* (Minneapolis: University of Minnesota Press, 1949), pp. 52–53.

neighborhoods, Jewish and other white businessmen in the inner cities are reassessing their position. A survey of Boston's black ghettos involving some three hundred merchants, four-fifths of whom are Jewish, disclosed that as of January 1969 25 percent had liquidated their operations and an additional 50 percent intended to follow suit. The remainder were uncertain about their future.[40]

Given the current state of race relations in our decaying inner cities, perhaps there is no future there for Jewish and other white merchants. Back in June 1966 Max Geltman, writing in the *National Review,* suggested that Jewish shopkeepers in volatile neighborhoods train local blacks with a view to selling their businesses to their trainees at a fair price. Geltman's suggestion was based on the conviction that the Watts riot was marked by anti-Semitism —he quotes the Yiddish-language *Daily Foreword* to the effect that the Watts outburst was a pogrom—and he argues that only indigenous ownership can prevent a repetition of the same elsewhere.[41]

An article by Judd Teller published a few months later also advocated that Jews remove themselves from the ghetto. Teller, a well-known writer on Jewish subjects, favored the relocation by the Jewish community of many thousands of Jewish families who are involved in inner city businesses, mostly operating small concerns. As for the slum lord of the Jewish faith, Teller believed that the "Jewish community should force his removal by barring him from all office, national and local, in Jewish life." The pernicious myth that Jewish wealth is based on Negro poverty will thereby be demolished and Negro-Jewish tensions reduced.[42] The *Herald-Dispatch,* a Los Angeles black nationalist publication, said that the Teller piece should be on everyone's Christmas reading list. Moreover, it asked the "racist-crackpots" to follow Teller's advice and "remove yourselves from our community, and our country."[43] The

---

[40] Sol and Shirley Kolack, "Who Will Control Ghetto Businesses?" *National Jewish Monthly,* July-August 1969, p. 7.

[41] Max Geltman, "The Negro-Jewish Confrontation," *National Review,* 28 June 1966, pp. 621, 623.

[42] Teller, "Negroes and Jews: A Hard Look," pp. 18–19.

[43] *Herald-Dispatch,* 15 December 1966.

article evoked considerably less enthusiasm in the Jewish community where organizationally, at least, no effort has been made to implement Teller's recommendations.

Wholesale withdrawal of white businessmen from the black ghettos may be a drastic step. It may represent acquiescence to a policy of racial apartheid. Ideally, white merchants should be free to engage in lawful and ethical commerce in black areas and Negro merchants should have the opportunity to operate businesses in predominantly white neighborhoods. Regrettably, the social reality does not coincide with the ideal. The black-owned store functioning beyond the boundaries of the black district is a rarity and is likely to remain so in the foreseeable future. This being the case, black demands for economic control of their own neighborhoods will continue to be heard.

Transferring control of the ghetto economy is not easily accomplished. The major impediment is the lack of black capital. Despite the publicity about President Nixon's black capitalism, government support of black entrepreneurship has been minimal. This suggests an alternative policy to the outright uprooting of Jewish and other white shopkeepers. Perhaps Jewish social action organizations and Jewish philanthropies should provide capital to enable Negroes to purchase the businesses of Jews who desire to terminate their activities in the black communities and relocate elsewhere.[44] Using their vast resources these same agencies might also foster integrated enterprises: black businessmen could associate themselves with Jewish entrepreneurs both inside and outside the ghetto. Jewish skills and, more importantly, Jewish money could be made available to finance various business ventures, especially cooperatives in the black enclaves.

A praiseworthy example has been set by one Jewish "builder-benefactor," Bernard J. Rosen. He has sponsored and built, largely

[44] As a short-range program, Bertran Gold has recommended help for the marginal Jewish businessman and the owners of "Mom and Pop" stores to leave them. He has also advocated a program to assist blacks to purchase Jewish ghetto businesses and to train them to operate those businesses. In a speech delivered in September 1968 Jacques Torczyner, President of the Zionist Organization of America, criticized Jewish groups for not resettling Jewish merchants who lost their businesses in ghetto riots. *New York Times,* 13 September 1968.

with black workmen, a middle-income cooperative housing complex in Harlem. Rosen, who has been described as a "former Harlem boy," also helped to organize and arrange the financing for a supermarket cooperative. In 1969 and 1970 the American Jewish Congress and the Interracial Council for Business Opportunity have sponsored a program, "Project Transfer," facilitating the orderly purchase by blacks of profit-making, white-owned businesses in the ghetto. Some of the sellers are elderly Jews who are close to retirement age. An important feature of the project permits a future black proprietor to work as a salaried employee of the business before actually buying it. What Rosen did as an individual and the American Jewish Congress did as an organization can and should be replicated by other concerned individuals and agencies.

Dealing with avaricious absentee landlords is a thornier problem. This is not because the relative affluence of American Jewry is dependent upon investments in the ghetto. The problem is how to strike a responsive chord in the conscience of persons who are all too often devoid of consciences. One interesting pilot project has been attempted in the Boston area where disputes between Jewish landlords and black tenants have been submitted for adjudication to the *Bet Din,* the rabbinical court of justice. Tenant complaints are investigated by a board of arbitration which reports its findings to the *Bet Din.* Landlords and tenants are represented on the board whose decisions are legally binding on both. According to the agreements entered into, tenants may not be arbitrarily and summarily evicted, fines may be levied on landlords, rents may be held in escrow for repairs, and a tenant's council may be given an option to purchase a building which is for sale. The procedure of the *Bet Din* has, in the words of a Boston radio station, served as a "meaningful bridge between the rich and the poor, the powerful and the impotent."[45] However, the only people who potentially may be affected by the *Bet Din*'s judgments are a relatively small number of orthodox Jews, and it is too early at this juncture to assess the results of the *Bet Din*'s interest in landlord-tenant relations.

[45] Yehudy Lindeman, "Urban Crisis and Jewish Law," *Hadassah* Magazine, March 1969, p. 29.

What can safely be assumed is that the Boston *Bet Din*'s direct involvement will yield more social dividends than mere rabbinical sermons or homilies from Jewish agencies imploring absentee landlords to act justly. These sermons are requested by some Negroes who believe somewhat naively that they will be efficacious. They should be forthcoming. But ethically illiterate persons, Jew and Gentile, black and white, are not likely to be moved by such pleas.

}5{

BLACK NATIONALISM
AND THE ARAB-
ISRAELI CONFLICT

IN THE LAST FEW YEARS MUCH ATTENTION HAS BEEN FOCUSED ON anti-Zionist utterances which have emanated from the black ghettos. Some militants have stridently upbraided the Jewish state and proclaimed their racial solidarity with the Arab world. However, only a small minority of black Americans have assumed this position. In this light, Eric Hoffer's statement to the effect that if Israel had been liquidated in the June 1967 war "every Negro leader" would have been relieved, is absurd.[1] The majority of black nationalists today are not vocally anti-Zionist, although those in the black community who are outspokenly pro-Arab are most likely to be nationalists.

Prior to 1947 Zionism was of little interest to the American Negro. When it was discussed, the movement was usually held up as a paradigm to be studied and emulated by New World Negroes.

Statements of W. E. B. DuBois and Marcus Garvey, two of the most important black personalities of the twentieth century, are cases in point. Just after World War I DuBois, in explaining his Pan-African philosophy and in differentiating it from Garvey's back-to-Africanism, wrote:

The African movement means to us what the Zionist movement must mean to the Jews, the centralization of race effort and the recognition of a racial fount. To help bear the burden of Africa does not mean any

[1] Eric Hoffer. "The Reason for Negro Hostility Towards Jews," *San Francisco Examiner,* 18 November 1968.

lessening of effort in our own problems at home. Rather it means increased interest. For any ebullition of action and feeling that results in an amelioration of the lot of Africa tends to ameliorate the conditions of colored peoples throughout the world. And no man liveth unto himself.[2]

Garvey, in exile in London in the 1930s, observed that of all minority groups the black man and the Jew seemed to be the only ones devoid of a head or body which the world recognized as such. Jews through the Zionist movement had provided Negroes with an object lesson.[3] Partitioning Palestine for a Jewish homeland might actually aid the Negro to procure a country of his own. After all, his right to a state in Africa was actually greater than

[2] *Crisis* 17, no. 4 (February 1919):166. By no means was Du Bois the only Pan-Africanist to see Jews and Negroes as kindred people. Edward Wilmot Blyden was another. Born in St. Thomas, Virgin Islands, in 1832 he was to visit the United States eight times during his long and multifaceted career. Seemingly a homo universale Blyden, who emigrated to West Africa, was an editor, a prodigious writer of books and pamphlets, a professor of classics, the Liberian Secretary of State, Liberian Ambassador to the Court of St. James, and President of Liberia College. Perhaps most importantly, he was a Pan-Negro patriot. In the informed opinion of a biographer, Hollis Lynch, "Blyden was easily the most learned and articulate champion of Africa and the Negro race in his time." Long an apostle of Negro repatriation to Africa, Blyden who once journeyed to Palestine (1866), called Zionism "that marvellous movement." Jews and Afro-Americans, he believed, were specially qualified to be spiritual leaders of a materialistic world by virtue of their heritage of suffering and sorrow. With this objective in mind, in 1898 he invited the Jews to establish themselves in Africa. See Hollis Lynch, *Edward Wilmot Blyden, Pan-Negro Patriot, 1822–1912* (London: Oxford University Press, 1967).

One who idolized Blyden was George Padmore. Padmore, born Malcolm Nurse in Trinidad in 1902 or 1903, attended a number of American universities in the twenties. After many years as a communist he renounced that philosophy and became an indefatigable champion of Pan-Africanism. Padmore's last years before his untimely passing in 1959 were spent as an advisor to Kwame Nkrumah in Ghana. Padmore, whose "wife" was an English Jewess, is reported to have leaned towards Israel in its altercation with the Arab world. He visited the Jewish state and was impressed by the help given to Israel by worldwide Jewry. See James Hooker, *Black Revolutionary: George Padmore's Path from Communism to Pan-Africanism* (New York: Frederick A. Praeger, 1967), p. 135.

[3] *The Black Man* 4, no. 1 (June 1939):3, and 2, no. 2 (July-August 1936):3.

that of the Jew in the Holy Land. But, Garvey wrote, it was imperative that blacks earnestly support his Universal Negro Improvement Association as the Jews backed Zionism.[4] Aware of the similarity between the Zionists' notion of the ingathering of the exiles and his own back-to-Africanism—he once referred to his adherents as Zionists—Garvey in 1937 wished the Jews good luck.

When the Palestine question came before the United Nations in 1947 it received some space in the Negro press. But then as now there was no unanimity of opinion among black Americans. For example, columnist George Schuyler in the *Pittsburgh Courier* called upon Negroes to follow the model of Zionism. At the same time he took Palestinian Jews to task for their "imperialistic spirit" and "Hitler-like" methods. Jews, Schuyler argued, had "no more claim on Palestine than the Alpha Kappa Alpha." It was the "Arab aborigines" tarbrushed with Negro blood who were truly entitled to the land. The Bible, which he called the "Jewish Mein Kampf," provided no justification whatsoever for Zionism.[5] Procuring the Holy Land was only the immediate objective of the Zionists, he informed his readers. Their long-range goal was to once again build a great political state and "to become one of the richest and most powerful groups in the world today."[6] Such strong sentiments were rarely expressed by the Negro press and, as far as can be determined, virtually never by Negro leaders.

It is significant that in March 1948 a long editorial in the same *Pittsburgh Courier* argued strongly for the legitimacy of a Jewish state. Entitled "Persecution and Doubletalk," the editorial demanded that "the lust for Arabian oil" not be allowed to interfere with the United Nations' pledge to partition Palestine. "Not only do the Jews have the legal right to a part of Palestine based on

4 Ibid., 2, no. 7 (August 1937):2. Garvey did once declare that an injustice had been done to the Arabs in Palestine. That was in the *Black Man* in June 1939 and formed part of an attack on Prime Minister Neville Chamberlain's reported project to introduce Jewish refugees into British Guiana.

5 *Pittsburgh Courier*, 24 May 1947.

6 Ibid., 27 December 1947. In the *Courier* of 27 March 1948 Schuyler denied the charge made by several "Zionist fanatics" that he was anti-Semitic and added that Arabs are "far more Semitic than most of the Zionists now in Palestine or abroad."

years of international commitments," the editorial stated, "they also deserve the heartfelt sympathy and support of everyone who hates cruelty and tyranny."[7]

In the 1950s there was not much comment about Israel in the Negro press. Even during and after the Suez campaign of 1956 in which Israel joined in the Anglo-French invasion of Egypt there was very little animosity toward Israel.[8]

Criticism of the invasion was directed in the main against British and French imperialism and was related to their colonial policies in sub-Saharan Africa. One editorial in the *Afro-American* coupled British bloodletting in Port Said and Kenya. There was no mention whatsoever of Israel. Referring to the furor in the United States and the United Nations over the Russian intervention in Hungary the editor inquired: "Are the Hungarians, because they are white entitled to any more self-determination and freedom than East Africans and Egyptians who happen to be colored?"[9] An unsigned article in the same newspaper flagellated the British and the French for the "high handed manner" in which they attempted to reassert their authority over the Suez Canal. Israel was judged guilty of "bare aggression," but was assigned a secondary role. In fact the Jewish state, in the opinion of the *Afro-American,* was allowing itself to be used as a pawn by the old imperial powers. The crux of the problem was that France and England could not accept the fact that the era of colonialism had ended.[10]

Editorial comment in the *Norfolk Journal and Guide* was clearly sympathetic to Israel, "this little democracy—the only one in the Middle East." While Britain and France attacked "to save their tottering empires," Israel acted in self-defense. "When the little Zionist nation struck, it was a blow of desperation, for the Arab nations were mobilizing armed forces for a push against Israel."[11]

One minor instance of Negro-Jewish friction in the wake of the

[7] Ibid., 13 March 1948.
[8] Writing on this point in the Communist party paper, the *Daily Worker,* an Afro-American, Abner Berry, noted that he could not find any evidence in the Negro press or statements by Negro leaders of hostility toward Israel after the 1956 war. *Daily Worker,* 2 April 1957.
[9] *The Afro-American,* 1 December 1956.
[10] Ibid., 10 November 1956.
[11] *Norfolk Journal and Guide,* 10 November 1956.

Suez crisis was reflected in a *Pittsburgh Courier* editorial. "Despite the provocations suffered by Israel," the *Courier* cautiously observed, "there are many persons of integrity who question the wisdom of Israel's attack (or counterattack) on Egypt." The overriding issue, however, was freedom of the press in America. Unidentified Jewish groups were accused of trying to thwart free discussion of the Middle East problem. The editor was distressed because the anti-Zionist opinions of some of the *Courier's* columnists were being confused with the newspaper's official policy. Jews were also counseled to avoid "imputing anti-Semitism to individuals who might differ strongly with them about Israel."[12]

A sizeable segment of the Negro press editorially ignored events occurring in Egypt in the fall of 1956. For example, the *Chicago Defender* gave the issue a wide berth, limiting itself to commentary on Ralph Bunche as the United Nation's experienced peacemaker in the troubled region.[13]

Until the 1960s, except for the Black Muslims, even black nationalists did not evince much concern for the Middle East. The battle for equal rights absorbed most of their energies. While there was a growing consciousness of the striving toward political and economic independence by colonial peoples, there was not, by and large, a sense of immediate identification with the Third World.

[12] *Pittsburgh Courier,* 29 December 1956. True to form, George Schuyler had written that the "unabashed aggression" against Egypt proved not only the uselessness of the United Nations but "why Israel was set up against the wishes of Palestine's inhabitants (most of whom were chased into the desert and their bank accounts sequestered)." See *Pittsburgh Courier,* 10 November 1956. J. A. Rogers called the invasion "asinine," and said that anti-Semitism had increased throughout the world because of Israel. He asked whether the United States could trust France, Britain, and Israel after their joint aggression. See *Pittsburgh Courier,* 24 November 1956. Other columnists in the same newspaper were sympathetic to Israel. For example, the distinguished scholar, Horace R. Cayton, wrote: "The fact of the matter is that Israel is fighting for her life. Egypt and the rest of the Arab countries have openly avowed their purpose of destroying the country." *Pittsburgh Courier,* 10 November 1956. Foreshadowing recent black nationalist identification with the Arab world are Cayton's observations about Nasser's effect on some Negroes in the fall of 1956: "A brilliant and talented Negro painter . . . greeted Nasser's seizure of the Canal with the same enthusiasm he had for the Montgomery bus strike. And this was not an unsophisticated man politically." *Pittsburgh Courier,* 24 November 1956.

[13] *Chicago Defender,* 10 November 1956. Perhaps coincidentally the No-

What interest there was centered naturally on sub-Saharan Africa. Before the time of Frantz Fanon, who more than any other writer, focused on the common bonds of oppressed peoples around the world, there was little empathy with the Arab cause.

As already indicated, the Nation of Islam (or Black Muslims as the organization is commonly called) is the only major exception. Scholars have traced the Muslim movement to Noble Drew Ali, founder in 1913 of a Moorish-American Science Temple. Ali claimed that Morocco was the original homeland of the American Negroes, hence they were really Moors.[14] Upon his mysterious death the Islamic prophet was succeeded by W. D. Fard. Fard's background is obscure, but C. Eric Lincoln has written that when he arrived in Detroit in 1930, the black community believed him to be an Arab.[15] According to one legend Fard was actually a Palestinian. Another had it that his father had been a Syrian of the Islamic faith.[16] A third listed his place of birth as the holy city of Mecca.[17] After Fard's strange disappearance in 1934, Georgia-born Robert Poole became leader of the Muslims, the black nationalist sect which he has fashioned and nurtured to this day. Poole is, of course, Elijah Muhammad.

It is only logical, given the antecedents and the nature of the movement, that the Muslims should identify with the Arab world. With that world they share a corpus of religious belief, despite

---

vember 1956 issue of *Crisis* contained a report on Israel by Hubert Delany, a retired justice of the Domestic Relations Court in New York City who had visited Israel as a consultant on questions relating to juvenile delinquency. Delany's piece talked of the Israeli struggle as an "anti-colonial movement." The author commented also that he had found "no evidence in Israel of a concept of 'inferior races.' "

[14] E. U. Essien-Udom, *Black Nationalism: A Search for an Identity in America* (New York: Dell Publishing Co., 1964), p. 46.

[15] C. Eric Lincoln, *The Black Muslims in America* (Boston: Beacon Press, 1963), p. 10.

[16] Ibid., p. 12.

[17] Essien-Udom, *Black Nationalism,* p. 35. It has even been speculated, quite inaccurately, that W. D. Fard and Arnold Ford, musical director at Garvey's New York headquarters, were one and the same. Ford was a black Jew who, it was believed, tired of Judaism in the 1930s had resettled in Africa where he embraced Islam. Perhaps instead he went to Detroit where he founded the Nation of Islam. See Howard Brotz, *The Black Jews of Harlem: Negro Nationalism and the Dilemmas of Negro Leadership* (Glencoe: The Free Press, 1964), pp. 11–12.

some disparate practices. In common they use Arabic for religious worship. Shared also is a distasteful historical experience with fair-skinned Westerners. Lastly, there is a common psychological plight: they both sense an oppression by powerful and often uncontrollable forces, either white or financed by whites. The American black man has long felt the imprint of the white man's boot; the Arab perceives that his brother has been dispossessed from his lands by an expansionist Israel. Although the historic explanation for their respective conditions differ, in numerous respects, many Afro-Americans and Arabs have a natural bond in that they see white America (and its Zionist counterpart) as their common oppressor.

Muslim thinking about Zionism has been communicated through many channels. The *Los Angeles Herald-Dispatch* which C. Eric Lincoln in 1960 called "the official Muslim organ," has been particularly plain-spoken.[18] Beginning in the early fifties the paper was published by Sanford Alexander, a black nationalist and disciple of Garvey. Afterwards its editor was his wife, Mrs. Pat Alexander.

In 1959 there was a sharp exchange between the *Herald-Dispatch* and Associate Justice Thurgood Marshall. Speaking at Princeton in that year Marshall, then chief counsel for the NAACP, condemned the Muslims as "run by a bunch of thugs organized from prisons and jails" and alleged that they were supported by "Nasser or some Arab group." The *Herald-Dispatch*'s rejoinder was that knowingly or unknowingly Marshall had espoused Zionism. His Princeton statement about the Muslims was "Zionist ideology at its ugliest." The *Dispatch* went on to say that the Zionists, "subtle, successful and insidious . . . have injected their poison into the ugly American, the Uncle Tom."[19] This last category also included Ralph Bunche, who won the Nobel Peace Prize in 1950 for his role as United Nations mediator in the Palestine dispute.[20]

The *Dispatch* spoke out against Jewish practices in general as well as Zionism. In a January 1960 issue, the *Dispatch* explained

---

[18] Lincoln, *The Black Muslims in America,* p. 129.
[19] Ibid., pp. 148–149, quoting from the *Dispatch,* 30 January 1960.
[20] *Playboy,* interview with Malcolm X, May 1963, pp. 53ff.

that Jews engaged in trade in black ghettos had had "an excellent opportunity to study the habits and weaknesses of the Negro." Moreover "by 1940 the Negro was almost entirely dependent upon the Jews and had accepted the thinking and ideology of the Jewish people. In the late '30's and by the early '50's the Jews had finally gained control of the N.A.A.C.P. . . . Our main task . . . in 1960 is to rid ourselves of this phony Jewish leadership."[21]

In August of the same year the destruction of the Jews was justified by the *Dispatch* because "white Christians and Jews are the guilty race, they have persecuted and killed the Prophets of Islam and their followers (the Muslims or black people in general)."[22] Seven years later the *Dispatch*'s message was unchanged. "If the Jews run the U.S. today, you white people gave them the power to do so, not we Negroes." Mrs. Alexander accused the Jews of attempting to murder her and lashed out at the "Zionist controlled Rockefeller and Ford Foundations."[23] With considerable imagination the *Dispatch*, in 1966, attacked the Anti-Defamation League of B'nai B'rith as a "Zionist-Communist Front Gestapo."[24]

In the cause of anti-Semitism and anti-Zionism the Alexanders have not been above joining forces with the radical right. For example, they assisted in the preparation of a booklet, *Muslims Black Metropolis* by one Alfred Q. Jarette, which contained an editorial originally published in *Right, The Journal of Forward Looking American Nationalism*. Elijah Muhammad was hailed for his support of the Arabs "in their just war against the bandit state of Israel." Zionism was "the poisoner of all peoples," was behind the NAACP, "the extreme left-wing organization," and was bent on crushing the Muslims. In addition, Zionist opposition and trickery allegedly caused the failure of Garveyism, an unsupported and unsupportable charge which has been repeated elsewhere.[25]

Muslim views on Zionists and Jews were perhaps articulated

[21] Lincoln, *The Black Muslims in America*, p. 149, quoting from the *Dispatch*, 16 January 1960.
[22] *Los Angeles Herald-Dispatch*, 6 August 1960.
[23] Ibid., 12 January 1967.
[24] Ibid., 29 September 1966.
[25] Alfred Q. Jarette, *Muslims Black Metropolis* (Los Angeles: Great Western Book Publishing Co., 1962). *Right*, a newsletter published in

best by the late Malcolm X. Just a few years have elapsed since his violent death. Born in Omaha in 1925, Malcolm was the son of a Baptist minister who served as an organizer for Garvey's UNIA, and who was slain at the hands of white racists. Malcolm's turbulent life led him into underworld crime, but he emerged after having been converted in prison to the Black Muslim movement.

Interviewed by C. Eric Lincoln, Malcolm voiced resentment at "the Jews who with the help of Christians in America and Europe drove our Muslim brothers (i.e., the Arabs) out of their home-land, where they had been settled for centuries and took over the land for themselves."[26] The religious and linguistic reasons for black Muslim identification with Arabs have already been alluded to. Malcolm appears to have had a particular affinity for Egypt as a revoluntionary state.[27] Nasser's seizure of the Suez Canal he thought significant because for the first time the waterway was "under the complete jurisdiction of an *African* nation" [italics added].[28] Cairo he found unusually congenial. "More so than any other city on the African continent, the people of Cairo look like American Negroes—in the sense that we have all complexions, we range in America from the darkest black to the lightest light and here in Cairo it is the same thing; throughout Egypt it is the same thing."[29] The object of Malcolm's admiration, Nasser's Egypt, the Arab world's most prestigious and populous country, has been Israel's main antagonist in the Middle Eastern cockpit.

For Malcolm there were local as well as international implications of Israel's creation and maintenance. To perpetuate Israel, its military, and "its continued aggression against our brothers in the East," Malcolm told C. Eric Lincoln that "the Jews sap the very lifeblood of the so-called Negroes."[30] Christian assistance to Zionism was predicated on the expectation of promoting Jewish emigration to Israel. Jewish businesses could then be taken over.

---

the San Francisco area, has been described by Benjamin Epstein and Arnold Forster of the Anti-Defamation League as "racist and anti-Jewish."

[26] Lincoln, *The Black Muslims in America*, p. 166.
[27] George Breitman, ed. *Malcolm X Speaks* (New York: Grove Press, 1965), pp. 126–127.
[28] Ibid., p. 123.
[29] Ibid., p. 83.
[30] Lincoln, *The Black Muslims in America*, p. 166.

But the "American Jews aren't going anywhere," Malcolm disclosed. "Israel is just an international poor house which is maintained by money sucked from the poor suckers in America."[31] An unidentified militant black in Watts put it this way: "You know them trees you got planted all over Israel from the Jews in Los Angeles, well they should have our names on them, not the Jews' names. The money for them trees came out of my back, out of the back of every black brother in the ghetto!"[32] According to this thesis, ghetto merchants and slum landlords use their ill-gotten gains to sustain a Zionist state. As a consequence "colored people" thousands of miles apart suffer a common fate: exploitation by parasitic Jews.

Clearly, the ghetto situation and the Middle Eastern quandary cannot be separated in analyzing black nationalist antipathy to Jews. In his autobiography Malcolm asserted that "in every black ghetto, Jews own the major businesses. Every night the owners of those businesses go home with that black community's money, which helps the ghetto to stay poor."[33] In a speech given in 1965 he talked of absentee landlords who "usually live around the Grand Concourse [Bronx]," a thoroughfare heavily populated by Jews.[34] On an earlier occasion, before his split with Elijah Muhammad, Malcolm had denied that his movement was hostile toward Jews qua Jews. Such tensions as existed were between the Muslims and those who exploited, oppressed, and degraded black people, be they Jews or Christians.

Malcolm credited Jews with being among whites the most active and most vocal financiers of the Negro civil rights movement. But Jews were also hypocritical. In the north he said they were the quickest to segregate themselves; they were in the vanguard of the white exodus to suburbia to avoid integrated neighborhoods.[35] He

---

[31] Ibid.

[32] Paul Jacobs, "Watts vs. Israel," *Commonweal,* 1 March 1968, p. 649.

[33] Malcolm X, *The Autobiography of Malcolm X* (New York: Grove Press, 1966), p. 283.

[34] Breitman, ed., *Malcolm X Speaks,* pp. 204–205.

[35] Malcolm X, *Autobiography,* pp. 372–373. While in prison, Malcolm disagreed with his older brother's belief that all whites were devils and told his brother that "Jews were different and that I had known good ones who hustled with me. I knew them, men and women and liked them." Essien-Udom, *Black Nationalism,* p. 115.

felt Irish Catholics and Italians were somewhat less resistant to residential desegregation, an opinion which would surely elicit loud dissent today in the black communities of Boston and Newark. Malcolm also greatly exaggerated the potentially positive influence of Jewish capital when he wrote: "Look at everything the black man is trying to 'integrate' into for instance; if Jews are not the actual owners, or are not in controlling positions, then they have major stockholdings or they are otherwise in powerful leverage positions—and do they really exert these influences? No!"[36]

As has been the case in the twentieth century with many black leaders, both separatists and integrationists, Malcolm had mixed feelings about Jews. Once when speaking at a Nigerian university, he solicited the assistance of independent African states in bringing the cause of the Afro-American before the United Nations. He said on that occasion: "just as the American Jew is in political, economic and cultural harmony with world Jewry," he was persuaded, "it was time for all Afro-Americans to join the world's Pan-Africanists."[37] The statement is reminiscent of DuBois' comparison of Zionism and Pan-Africanism more than four decades earlier. At a press conference held in May 1964 Malcolm told newsmen: "If black men become involved in a philosophical, cultural and psychological migration back to Africa, they will benefit greatly in this country." The benefits would be similar to those which diaspora Jewry had derived from their links to Israel.[38] Malcolm was distressed, and rightly so, by the inability of blacks in one area of the world to give aid and comfort to needy blacks in another area. Because of his powerlessness, the black man's dilemma had been compartmentalized. In stark contrast, world Jewry had successfully internationalized the Jewish problem.

In 1964 Malcolm attended an Organization of African Unity (OAU) conference as an observer. As such he was allowed to

---

[36] Ibid.
[37] Ibid., p. 350.
[38] George Breitman, *The Last Year of Malcolm X: The Evolution of a Revolutionary* (New York: Merit Publishers, 1967), p. 63. Though ardently anti-Zionist, Harold Cruse believes that black intellectuals must learn the techniques developed by Zionists to survive. He admires the ability of the Zionist movement to mobilize political power by using its intellectuals as propagandists. Harold Cruse, *The Crisis of the Negro Intellectual* (New York: William Morrow & Co., 1967), pp. 490–491.

submit a memo to that body. The predicament of twenty-two million American blacks had to be brought to the attention of the United Nations by "their elder brothers," the Africans, Malcolm stated.

If the United States Supreme Court justice, Arthur Goldberg, a few weeks ago, could find legal grounds to threaten to bring Russia before the United Nations and charge her with violating the human rights of less than three million Russian Jews, what makes our African brothers hesitate to bring the United States government before the United Nations and charge her with violating the human rights of 22 million African-Americans?[39]

It can be noted parenthetically, that Malcolm wanted Justice Goldberg himself to raise the matter in the same forum. While it was unrealistic for Malcolm to have expected any American representative at the United Nations to take such action, the mistreatment of ethnic and racial minorities within a country's borders is *not* exclusively a domestic matter. United Nations concern with apartheid in South Africa and with Portuguese colonial policy in Angola and Mozambique are two examples. Actually, as good a case can be made for international affirmation of American Negro rights as the rights of Russian Jewry.

That the black man in America is seeking identity as well as power is obvious. For Malcolm the Jews' assimilationist experience in pre-Nazi Germany contained a moral for Afro-Americans concerned with developing a racial identity. Jewish cultural contributions had been enormously impressive. "Every culture in Germany was led by the Jew. . . . But those Jews made a fatal mistake—assimilating." Specifically, their error had been intermarrying, changing their names, converting to other faiths—in short, trying to become Germans. If assimilationism born of a diluted ethnic identity was self-defeating, even tragic for German Jews, then integration was equally disastrous for American blacks.[40] Even while sharply criticizing the Zionists' "usurpation" of Arab Palestine to erect a Jewish state, Malcolm's black nationalism prompted him to observe that the establishment of one's own nation is the only thing every race respects.

[39] Breitman, ed., *Malcolm X Speaks,* p. 75.
[40] Malcolm X, *Autobiography,* pp. 277–278.

Malcolm also used the Nazi holocaust to remind Negroes of their own vulnerability. Less than twenty-four hours after his own home in Queens had been bombed, Malcolm was speaking in Detroit. He warned his listeners: "if you don't wake up . . . I tell you, they'll be building gas chambers and gas ovens pretty soon— I don't mean those kind you've got at home in your kitchen . . . you'll be in one of them, just like the Jews ended up in gas ovens over there in Germany. You're in a society that's just as capable of building gas ovens for black people as Hitler's society was."[41]

Jewish history could be utilized to discredit integrationist tactics. In a 1963 *Playboy* interview Malcolm explained the success of American Jews by pointing out that, "The Jew never went sitting-in and crawling-in and sliding-in and freedom-riding, like he teaches and helps Negroes to do. The Jew stood up and stood together, and they used their ultimate power, the economic weapon. That's exactly what the Honorable Elijah Muhammad is trying to teach black men to do. The Jews pooled their money and bought the hotels that barred them."[42]

It is impossible to know to what extent Malcolm's ideas about whites in general and Jews in particular were changing in the months before his tragic assassination. During his trip to Mecca he felt that he had found something he had been unable to find in America: the brotherhood of all races and colors coming together as one. In January 1965, one month before his death, he told a Canadian television audience in response to a question about intermarriage and integration: "I believe in recognizing every human being as a human being—neither white, black, brown, or red."[43]

Muhammad Speaks, a weekly published in Chicago, serves as the official voice of the Muslims. Its biases on the Arab-Israeli altercation are never hidden. The paper feels that the side of the white West is adequately covered by the popular media. Therefore its announced policy is to present the outlook of "black Africa." In keeping with this policy the 16 June 1967 issue carried a picture of a dark Sudanese commando and some Egyptians. The

---

[41] Breitman, ed., *Malcolm X Speaks,* p. 168.
[42] *Playboy,* interview with Malcolm X, May 1963, pp. 53ff.
[43] Malcolm X, *Autobiography,* p. 424.

caption explained that the Arab struggle is interwoven with other liberation movements, especially in Africa. Indeed, Africa is revealed to be the locus of the conflict over Palestine. "Although Israel claims that the war in northeast Africa has been won it is evident that the larger struggle has not yet fully begun as black Africans, such as this Sudanese commando undergo training with UAR troops for the day when the battle for the liberation of the whole of Africa commences."[44]

The same idea was elaborated on in a report on the position taken by a Chicago-based black organization, the African-American Heritage Association: "Egypt is also in Africa, and Egypt under Nasser is one of the key countries essential to and supporting African continental unity against Western racist, imperialist powers."[45] To weaken Egypt was, in effect, to weaken Africa and to strengthen a racist and neocolonialist America.

Israel is seen as an extension of Europe, a tool of Western imperialism. Egypt, a member of the OAU, is viewed as an "African nation" which threw off the colonialist yoke and is trying to assist others to do likewise. As proof, a Tanzanian quoted by *Muhammad Speaks* commented that "Nasser not Israel fought to protect Lumumba."[46]

A report on the United Nations in a late June 1967 issue of the Muslim organ tied the Israeli military victory to the future of black countries close to the Republic of South Africa. "The sudden, successful onslaught against Arab nations by Israel—with West-supplied arms, munitions, aircraft and training—has created further consternation among southern independent African nations concerning plans of fascist South Africa."[47]

There is no evidence that South African foreign policy vis-à-vis its black neighbors was in any way influenced by the June war. Bracketing Israel and white-supremacist South Africa can only make the name of the Jewish state anathema to the nonwhite world. Totally ignored in the *Muhammad Speaks* article was the fact that

[44] *Muhammad Speaks* (Chicago), 16 June 1967.
[45] Ibid.
[46] Ibid., 23 June 1967.
[47] Ibid.

since 1961 Israel has consistently cast her vote against South Africa on the issue of apartheid in the General Assembly.

Articles in *Muhammad Speaks* repeatedly used loaded phrases such as "Israeli persecutors" and "Israeli occupation of Palestine." One spoke of the "Nazi-like tactics exercised by the Zionists against the defenseless civilian population in the occupied Arab lands."[48]

Few pro-Arab black nationalists missed the opportunity to expose sinister Zionist intentions presented by the Six Day War. The Middle East crisis was covered in inordinately gory and sensational fashion by the October 1967 *News-Gram* published by the Islamic Press International in New York City. Both the front and back covers of the periodical showed horrible pictures of "Arabs permanently disfigured by Israeli napalm bombs—for the 'crime' of simply defending their Homelands." One article detailed the United Nations' "Historic 19 Year Mistake."[49] Another provided a "first-person, eye-witness account" of Israeli terrorism allegedly perpetrated on the Arab population of Old Jerusalem.[50]

A few articles globalized the dilemma of black people in such a way as to excoriate Jews. Miss Sudia Masoud, the Afro-American publisher and editor of the *News-Gram,* dealt not only with Zionist readiness "to ply every advantage of the premeditated mass murder of untold thousands of Muslim Arabs, in their own homelands," but wtih alleged Zionist schemes to undermine African independence.[51] Their instrument was to be "the powerful Zionist labor unions" in the United States working through their Negro stooges. Another weapon of the wily Zionists is the rewriting of Africa's past so long distorted by historians. Burgeoning interest in African history is seen as an integral part of a Zionist conspiracy to deprive black youngsters of an appreciation of Arab and Islamic contributions to the history.

Supposedly, Zionist expansionist designs include Africa. These designs can be foiled only through unity in the African-Asian-Arab world. For members of the darker races the terrible alternative was

[48] Ibid., 7 June 1968.
[49] *Islamic Press International News-Gram,* October 1967, p. 4.
[50] Ibid., p. 11.
[51] Ibid., pp. 18–19.

to become "pawns in the dream of Zionism for world power and dominance."[52]

A piece on "Chicago's Black Power Conference" underscored the cultural bonds between Arabs and black Americans.

Many black people are comfortable regarding themselves as a part of the Arab culture. Learning about Arab food, Arab dress and any and all things Arabic has become a serious business with many hundreds of thousands of black people.

Moreover, the Arab culture is an African culture. Call it Middle East if you will. The fact is that most of the Arab world is the African world.[53]

Without chastising Negroes who backed Israel in the June war, the issue would have been incomplete. These Negroes—that is, black men with slave mentalities—mirrored the thinking of the "master." It is he who masterminds Negro organizations. He creates slums and collects exorbitant rents.[54]

Taking all of the articles together, a naive reader might well accept the notion of a worldwide Jewish conspiracy extending from the ghettos of the United States where Afro-Americans are subjugated by Jews to the Levant where Israeli imperialists are stealing Arab territory. And Zionist aggression in the Middle East portends a like fate for the African motherland.

African Opinion, an obscure bimonthly which serves as a forum for back-to-Africanism, added to the swelling chorus of black nationalist denunciation of Israel. A philippic delivered by Jamil M. Baroody, Saudi Arabian delegate to the United Nations, was prominently featured.[55] In addition, a column entitled "World Foundation Disturbed in Jerusalem" reiterated the familiar Arab objection to the United Nation's action in first establishing Israel. Failure on the part of the United Nations to compel Israel to return Arab land conquered in June 1967, it was suggested, would hurt the cause of black Africans in Rhodesia who were also victimized by white aliens. However unwarranted such analogies may be, they

[52] Ibid., p. 19.
[53] Ibid., p. 17.
[54] Ibid., p. 8.
[55] *African Opinion* 8, nos. 3, 4 (August and September 1967):2–3, 14–15.

are reflective of an overall approach to the enduring Middle East dilemma which requires understanding.[56] Three months after the lightning Israeli victory, the New Politics Convention met in Chicago. In exchange for their participation in the convention the Black Caucus, dominated by nationalists, demanded that the white new leftists agree to some thirteen resolutions. One of those assailed the "imperialist Zionist war." The resolution concomitantly noted that the condemnation of Israel "does not imply anti-Semitism."[57]

While traveling in the Arab world in September 1967 Stokely Carmichael, a leading exponent of black power, lashed out at "Zionist aggression." In Syria he accused "high officials" in America of being in league with Zionism and, according to the Damascus radio, he pledged military aid by American blacks to the Arabs. Eleven months later, in his keynote address to an Arab students' convention in Michigan, Stokely informed his audience that militant Afro-Americans were ready to fight and die if necessary to aid the Arabs in freeing Palestine.[58] He employed such phrases as the "trickery of Zionism" and the "evil of Zionism," called the United States the "greatest de-humanizer in the world," and argued that "Israel is nothing but a finger of the United States of America." A further point was that the "aggression [Israel's] of June 6th was for several reasons; one of them was to destroy the revolutionary governments of the Arab world." Also meaningful in Stokely's Michi-

---

[56] Ibid., p. 10; The reasoning of the critics of Israel is that if the Zionist state can defy the United Nations with impunity, Rhodesia and South Africa can do likewise. Significantly El Fatah recently informed delegates to the Pan-African Cultural Festival in Algeria that Dr. Hendrick F. Verwoerd of South Africa (assassinated in 1966) and Ian Smith of Rhodesia "are the same as Ben-Gurion and Dayan." See the *New York Times,* 2 August 1969.

[57] Abdeen Jabara, "The American Left and the June Conflict," *The Arab World* 14, nos. 10–11 (Special Issue n.d.):76; Walter Goodman, "When Black Power Runs the New Left," *New York Times Magazine,* 24 September 1967. Many Jews and their sympathizers walked out of the convention. The resolution was subsequently scored by Jacques Torczyner, president of the Zionist Organization of America and Mrs. Mortimer Jacobson, president of Hadassah, The Women's Zionist Organization. See the *New York Times,* 13 September 1968 and 18 September 1967.

[58] *New York Herald Tribune* (Paris), 22 September 1967; *National Guardian,* 16 September 1967; *Ann Arbor News,* 27 August 1968.

gan speech was his statement that "the same Zionists that exploit the Arabs also exploit us in this country. That is a fact. And that is not anti-Semitic."

Best publicized of all the anti-Zionist assaults unleashed by the June war was the statement issued by the Student Non-Violent Coordinating Committee (SNCC).[59] The expressed purpose of the SNCC newsletter was to shed light on "the Palestine problem." It explained that Afro-Americans are an integral part of the Third World and as such had to appreciate what their brothers were doing in their native lands. To this end photographs of "Gaza Massacres 1956" were reproduced with the following provocative caption: "Zionists lined up Arab victims and shot them in the back in cold blood. This is the Gaza Strip, Palestine, not Dachau, Germany." Another photograph showed "Zionist Jewish Terrorists." Two rough sketches accompanied the text. One was of Moshe Dayan who was portrayed with dollar signs on his epaulets. The second depicted Nasser and Muhammad Ali [Cassius Clay] each with a noose around his neck. Holding the rope was a hand marked with a Shield of David and a dollar sign. An arm labeled "Third World Liberation Movement" holding a scimitar was poised to cut the rope.

Some thirty-two "points of information" about the Palestine issue were offered for the readers' edification as answers to the question, "Do you know?" Among these were:

That the Zionists conquered the Arab homes and land through terror, force, and massacres? That they wiped out over 30 Arab villages before and after they took control of the area they now call "Israel" . . .

Israel was Planted At the Crossroads of Asia And Africa Without The Free Approval Of Any Middle-Eastern, Asian Or African Country![60]

That Israel segregates those few Arabs who remained in their homeland, that more than 90 per-cent of these Arabs live in "Security-

---

[59] *SNCC Newsletter,* June–July 1967.

[60] In point of fact, there were no sub-Saharan nations in the United Nations at the time except South Africa, Liberia, and Ethiopia. White-supremacist South Africa voted with the majority as did Liberia. Ethiopia abstained. SNCC's contention was that the Liberian vote for partition was controlled by the United States. "Uncle Sam" also determined the Filipino vote in favor of the United Nations resolution according to SNCC.

Zones" under Martial Law, are not allowed to travel freely within Israel, and are the victims of discrimination in education, jobs etc.

That dark skinned Jews from the Middle East and North Africa are also second-class citizens in Israel, that the color line puts them in inferior positions to the white European Jews?

That the U.S. Government has worked along with Zionist groups to support Israel so that America may have a toehold in that strategic Middle-East location, thereby helping white Aemerica [sic] to control and exploit the rich Arab nations?

That several American and European Jews, who are not Zionists and cannot support the horrors committed by Zionists in the name of Judaism, have spoken out and condemned the Zionist distortions of the Jewish religion; but their opinions are never printed in the Zionist controlled press or other communications media?[61]

That the famous European Jews, the Rothschilds, who have long controlled the wealth of many European nations, were involved in the original conspiracy with the British to create the "State of Israel" and are still among Israel's chief supporters. That The Rothschilds Also Control Much Of Africa's Mineral Wealth.

From its founding in 1960 SNCC had attracted much Jewish support. Jews were disproportionately represented in the ranks of the "new abolitionists," whose ideal was that of philosophical pacifism. SNCC members worked tirelessly for racial justice, often at great personal risk. However, disillusionment with the glacial slowness of achieving dignity and equality for black Americans, and the marked indifference of the substantial majority of white Americans, led SNCC to question its initial commitment to solely nonviolent means to achieve its ends.[62]

[61] One could argue that in view of its tiny following, the Anti-Zionist American Council for Judaism receives more space in the supposedly pro-Israeli *New York Times* than its numbers merit. In a recent publication the Council demanded of fellow Jews "that they devote at the very least the same energy and finances which they raise on behalf of Israel in assisting the Negro community to attain its full rights." Michael Selzer, *Israel as a Factor in Jewish-Gentile Relations in America: Observations in the Aftermath of the June 1967 War* (New York: American Council for Judaism, 1968), p. 26.

[62] In July 1969 SNCC officially deleted "non-violent" from its name. Henceforth it will be the "Student National Coordinating Committee." H. Rap Brown explained that the organization would have no connection to the "concept of nonviolence as a solution to the problems of oppressed people." See *New York Times*, 23 July, 1969.

When the anti-Zionist polemic appeared, Jewish withdrawal from SNCC which had already begun, was sharply accelerated. Such noted Jewish figures as Theodore Bikel, folk singer and actor, and Harry Golden, humorist and social critic, discerned anti-Semitic overtones in SNCC and resigned from the organization. Financial contributions to SNCC by American Jews also declined sharply. B'nai B'rith's Anti-Defamation League described SNCC as racist and anti-Jewish as well as anti-Zionist. The League asserted that the newsletter parroted anti-Israeli diatribes produced by the Palestine Arab Delegation and the Palestine Liberation Organization. The latter was then led by the vitriolic Ahmed Shukairy.[63]

Both the illustrative material and the text of the newsletter seem to have been borrowed from Arab propaganda sources. Ralph Featherstone, SNCC program director, admitted that Arab embassies had furnished some data. SNCC, he steadfastly maintained, was not anti-Semitic. Not Jews per se, only oppressors, in which category he put Israel and "those Jews in the little Jew shops" in the ghettos, deserved severe condemnation.[64] H. Rap Brown, successor to Stokely Carmichael as SNCC chairman, contended that "we are not anti-Jewish and we are not anti-Semitic. We just don't think Zionist leaders in Israel have a right to that land."[65] Especially ironic is the fact that the SNCC creed closely paralleled an onslaught on Israel featured in *Thunderbolt,* the official organ of the white supremacist National States Rights Party.

Virtually without exception Jewish spokesmen rejected the disclaimer of anti-Semitism. The reaction of Rabbi Israel Miller, head of the American Zionist Council, was representative of Jewish feeling. He saw the SNCC publication as an example of "crude and unadulterated anti-Semitism."[66] Many black public figures agreed. Bayard Rustin, organizer of the 1963 march on Washington, and

---

[63] *New York Times,* 23 October 1967; Jerome Bakst, "Negro Radicalism Turns Antisemitic—SNCC's Volte Face," *Wiener Library Bulletin,* Winter 1967–1968.

[64] *New York Times,* 15 August 1967. Featherstone, who had been an organizer in the voter registration campaigns in the South in the early 1960s, was killed in Maryland in March 1970 when an explosion destroyed the car he was driving.

[65] Ibid., 19 August 1967.

[66] Ibid., 16 August 1967.

A. Philip Randolph were both "appalled and distressed by the anti-Semitic article." Whitney M. Young, Jr., executive director of the National Urban League, was struck by the similarity of American Nazi Party and SNCC views on the thorny problem of the Middle East.[67]

Undoubtedly, SNCC's analysis was one-sided and superficial. Unquestionably, many of its statements were inaccurate and misleading. But was it really anti-Jewish as well as anti-Zionist? Because of their tragic history, Jews are acutely sensitive about direct assaults on the State of Israel. This sensitivity has been heightened in recent years because anti-Semitism is often paraded in the guise of anti-Zionism. Certainly, all sympathy for the Arabs is not veiled anti-Semitism. Still, a content analysis of the SNCC pronouncements strongly suggests anti-Semitic along with anti-Zionist sentiment. What, one may legitimately ask, has Cassius Clay, the erstwhile heavyweight boxing champion, to do with the relative merits of the Arab and Israeli cases? Why the dollar signs on the hand holding the rope choking Clay and Nasser? Why the dollar signs on Dayan's shoulders?[68] References to the Rothschilds, associated as they are with myths about worldwide Jewish financial domination, also raise nagging doubts about SNCC's intent.

In the process of lambasting Israel, strong anti-Semitic feelings have sometimes surfaced. At the time of the Six Day War, mimeographed notices affixed to telephone poles in Queens, New York, implored black people to support their brothers and sisters in Egypt by not patronizing Jewish merchants at home. "R.A.M. [Revolutionary Action Movement]—The Black Guards" claimed authorship of the notices.[69]

On 22 March 1968, a handbill signed "The Arabs" was distributed in racially tense Newark. It read as follows: "This Black Man You Call 'nigger' is Hamitic Arab and The Arab World Will Protect Its Kin. . . . If Black Men Are Further Abused in This

[67] Ibid.

[68] For some the dollar signs on Dayan reflect American support for Israel. Others see them as an anti-Semitic equation of Jews and money.

[69] *ADL Bulletin,* September 1967, p. 3. This is published by the Anti-Defamation League of B'nai B'rith.

America The Arab American Will Declare An All-Out War Against The Zionist Jew In This america [sic]."[70]

In the midst of New York City's recent emotion-searing school crisis leaflets surreptitiously placed in teachers' mailboxes in JHS 271 and PS 144 (Brooklyn) declared that "African American History and Culture" could not possibly be taught by the "Middle East Murderers of Colored People." Unwillingness to allow the black community to administer its own schools and control its own neighborhoods would mean that "Your Relatives in the Middle East Will Find Themselves Giving Benefits To Raise Money to Help You Get Out From The Terrible Weight Of An Enraged Black Community." It is significant to note that this vicious leaflet was anonymous.[71]

Another flyer issued by Jesse Gray, chairman of the Tenants Right Party in Harlem, baldly stated: "Zionists kill black people in their own land in the Middle East. They run the people out of their own communities. Now, here, Shanker is trying to use the same tactics and throw us out of our own community." Albert Shanker and the United Federation of Teachers of which he is president were then labeled "Racist, Ruthless Zionist Bandits."[72]

Suspicion of anti-Jewishness has been aroused by the confusion between Zionist and Jew. Most Jews, here and abroad, are pro-Zionist. Some are not. Almost all Zionists are Jews. A few are not. Unfortunately, the designations are used interchangeably. How else can one explain an allusion to Albert Shanker as a Zionist bandit? How else can one fathom the following ludicrous assertion contained in an *Amsterdam-News* gossip column: "Charles Kenyatta says the Cosa Nostra, Zionists and their black stooges are flooding Harlem with dope."[73] By this logic, all Jews are ipso facto Zion-

---

[70] *Subversive Influences In Riots, Looting, and Burning: Part 4 (Newark, N.J.) Hearings Before The Committee On Un-American Activities—House of Representatives, April 23 and 24, 1968.* (Washington, D.C.: U.S. Government Printing Office, 1968), p. 1927.

[71] There is no evidence that the Ocean Hill-Brownsville Governing Board was in any way responsible for this leaflet which was widely distributed by the United Federation of Teachers.

[72] Gray was not affiliated with the Ocean Hill-Brownsville Governing Board. The leaflet began "Shanker: This Is Not Egypt—You Ain't Coming In Here."

[73] *Amsterdam-News,* 9 November 1968.

ists, an equation which would not be appreciated at all by the rabidly anti-Zionist American Council for Judaism.

Whether Arab money helps finance black anti-Zionism is not known. Such is the belief in some Jewish circles. Featherstone, in August 1967, denied that SNCC, though sorely troubled by a depleted treasury, had received financial backing from Arab sources.

Arab students in the United States have done their best to cultivate black nationalist support.[74] Their tactic has been to tie their own struggle to the black liberation movement and to portray both American Negroes and Arabs as victims of colonialist repression. Illustrative of this is a statement by Arab students in the *Black Panther*, published in Oakland, California. Huey Newton—Panther Minister of Defence sentenced to prison after a shoot out in which he was badly wounded and an Oakland policeman killed—was described as a "freedom fighter" and a "political prisoner of the imperialists." From their own experience, the Arabs said, they knew Huey could not get a fair trial. "No Arab can claim that a Palestinian Guerrilla or One simply Accused of Being One, who is caught by the Racist Israelis can get a fair trial in Their Courts. And let us keep in mind the Great Similarity between the conditions under which the Black People live in the United States and those under which the Palestinian Arabs live in Israel."[75]

For its part the national Black Panther Party has openly identified with the Arab cause.[76] Identification with the Arabs by histor-

---

[74] In Detroit, one year after the June war, black students joined Arabs and an assortment of leftist groups to protest the appearance at an Israel Bond rally of Menachem Beigin, leader of the right-wing Gahal Party. Among other things Beigin was castigated because he stood for "Zionist Race Supremacy and Israeli Expansionism." Blacks were particularly angered by Israel's purported aid to reactionary and racist regimes in Africa. *South End,* which reported the Beigin incident, is the official student newspaper at Wayne State University. Since radicals gained control in 1967 the paper has been openly anti-Zionist and has praised the efforts of Al Fatah. See *South End,* 4 June 1968.

[75] *The Black Panther,* 7 September 1968. Those who consider Huey Newton a freedom fighter rather than a common criminal are not limited to the Panthers or Arab students in America. Without the publicity generated by the trial Newton may well have been imprisoned for life or sentenced to death.

[76] Eldridge Cleaver, the leading Panther luminary who is now in exile, recently asserted in Algiers: "The United States uses the Zionist regime that usurped the land of the Palestine people as a puppet and pawn." Stokely

ically aware black people is rather remarkable. Although Islamic cultural influences are of enormous significance in West Africa, Arabs were also the most important slave traders in East Africa. Countless Africans were forcibly transported to Arabia and other Muslim lands. Black slaves were a major commodity on which was based the economic well-being of Arab settlements dotted along the Indian Ocean.[77] It is not insignificant that within a few weeks after the Arab-dominated island of Zanzibar, once the leading slave market in the world, became independent in December 1963, an indigenous black revolution exiled the Sultan, massacred large numbers of Arabs, and sent many others packing to the Arab countries. These facts have not escaped the notice of all black men. As one reader of *Ebony* wrote to the editor of that Negro periodical

For any black man to think of himself as being a natural ally of the Arabs is comparable to the final thread of the screw being turned. . . . the Arabs, in league with the Portuguese, were the chief instigators and the main profiteers of the slave trade, the ones who set tribe against tribe in bloody massacre and then sat back and collected the human debris; the ones who raped and razed defenceless villages, enslaving men, women and children, after slaughtering the aged, infirm and those considered unsalable. . . . Indeed, it was the Arab who showed the white man what a fortune could be made in black flesh . . . I do not see how any black brother with even a passing acquaintance with our history, can proclaim himself in spiritual league with the Arab.[78]

Apparently, new vogues in racial nomenclature have facilitated the solidarity between some black nationalists and Arabs. More and more militant black Americans, especially the young, eschew the term "Negro." Sometimes "Negro" is used disdainfully to stigmatize one regarded as unduly moderate or compliant. Ordinarily, the preference is for "Afro-American" or "black." Until the mid-

Carmichael, a former prime minister of the Panthers, was in Algiers at the same time to attend the Pan-African Cultural Festival. He again expressed sympathy for the Arab cause. See the *New York Times,* 23 July 1969 and 25 July 1969. For additional pro-Arab expressions see *The Black Panther,* 12 October 1968; 21 December 1968; 4 January 1969; 2 February 1969; and 9 February 1969.

[77] Zöe Marsh and G. W. Kingsnorth, *An Introduction to the History of East Africa* (Cambridge: Cambridge University Press, 1965), p. 33.

[78] *Ebony,* November 1968, p. 16.

1960s "black" had a pejorative connotation for many Negroes. Now many light-skinned Negroes are proud to be so identified. For most nationalists the concept "black" has become synonymous with nonwhite. This semantic legerdemain makes it possible to characterize the ancient Egyptian and the Moorish civilizations, Christ and Hannibal as black.[79] It was in this vein that Malcolm, echoing Elijah Muhammed observed, "the red, the brown and the yellow are indeed all part of the black nation. Which means that black, brown, red, yellow, all are brothers, all are one family. The white one is a stranger. He's the odd fellow."[80]

Having redefined the meaning of black it is possible to include Arabs in the same racial family as Afro-Americans. Thus, a soapbox orator in Harlem haranguing his listeners about Zionist expropriation can talk glibly of his colored brothers or his black kinsmen, the Arabs. And *Muhammad Speaks* in treating the hostilities in June 1967, can talk of black men endemic to the population invaded by Israel.[81] Pragmatic diplomatic advantages aside, many color-conscious Arabs would not welcome news of this racial consanguinity.

If Arabs are perceived as black, then Israelis are seen as white. This is logical, if not quite accurate. For American Negroes the Jew is a Central or East European—a white man. Oriental Jews who now comprise slightly more than half of Israel's population have never been seen by American blacks. Those Jews from North Africa and the Middle East are often physically indistinguishable from Arabs in whose midst they lived for centuries. In other words, they, too, are "black" given the broadened connotation of that word.

It should not be inferred that anti-Zionism in some radical black groups flows from ignorance of the historical and ethnological complexities of the Middle East. At the core of their outlook are grievances against the white West in general and the United States in particular. Unable to make appreciable progress toward economic, political, and social equality in America, their strategy has been to forge ties with the Third World. They find inspiration in the revolu-

---

[79] *Playboy*, interview with Malcolm X, May 1963, p. 58.
[80] Ibid.
[81] *Muhammad Speaks,* 23 June 1967.

tionary words of Che Guevara and Frantz Fanon and strive to internationalize their struggle by linking arms with liberation movements across the seas.

Simply stated, their train of thought appears to be as follows: America oppresses black people. The same racist United States helped to create Israel in 1947–1948. Since then the Jewish state has been the West's foothold in the Middle East. Hence, America's ally is the black man's natural enemy.[82] Therefore, while Israel has added a new dimension to relations between blacks and Jews in America, the seemingly insoluble Middle East enigma cannot be disentangled from ghetto frictions or from black attitudes toward the United States and its white populace.

[82] This logic led *Muhammad Speaks* to look with suspicion at any solution to the Arab-Israeli problem proposed by the United States or Great Britain because "both . . . are racist Governments as attested to by the conditions of peoples of African descent." *Muhammad Speaks,* 16 June 1967.

} 6 {

SOME DILEMMAS
FOR THE
INTELLECTUALS

THE LATTER PART OF THE 1960s WAS MARKED BY SCHISMS IN THE ranks of some of the organizations in which Negroes and Jews had worked together earlier in the decade. Blacks are seeking to gain full control of their own movements, and the independence which ostensibly springs from such control. Jewish liberals and radicals, like their other white counterparts, in turn, have had to decide the extent to which they can support the various manifestations of black power as the struggle for black liberation moves into the urban North.

Over the years, contacts between blacks and Jews have constituted a goodly portion of the interaction between black and white intellectuals in the major urban areas. This has been particularly true in New York City, the leading cultural center in America and long the home of many radical political and artistic movements. As black consciousness emerges strongly, some black intellectuals feel that their relationship with Jews has to be altered if they are to develop full control of black political and cultural movements. Jewish critics and scholars have been among the chief interpreters of Negro social and cultural developments, and in years past, Jewish philanthropy, involvement in the civil rights movement, and general concern for the Negroes' welfare were welcomed enthusiastically. But now, given the critical need to control their own political and cultural institutions in America, an increasing number of Blacks deem it necessary to remove the vestiges of dependence on white outsiders.

The most extensive exposition of the argument that black intellectuals have been patronized and exploited by Jews is contained in Harold Cruse's *The Crisis of the Negro Intellectual.* A lengthy consideration of Cruse's interpretation of the nature of historic encounters between the Negro and Jewish intellectual is therefore merited.

For Cruse, the direction which Harlem takes is crucial to the future of black America. He states: "Harlem has, in this century, become the most strategically important community of black America. Harlem is still the pivot of the black world's quest for identity and salvation. The way Harlem goes (or does not go) so goes all black America. Harlem is the black world's key community for historical, political, economic, cultural and/or ethnic reasons."[1] The often-heard demand, "break up the Harlem ghetto," represents to Cruse "nothing but the romantic wail of politically insolvent integrationists, who fear ghetto riots only *more* than they fear the responsibilities of political and economic power that lie in the Harlem potential."

This emphasis on the importance of Harlem for black America sets in perspective Cruse's view of Jewish intellectuals to whom he assigns a large share of the responsibility for the demise of the Harlem renaissance of the 1920s. To summarize Cruse's argument: Jewish leftists, particularly those in the Communist party, put the Negro intellectual in a position "wherein representatives of another minority could dictate cultural standards to them." Overwhelmed at being "discovered and courted," Harlem intellectuals "allowed a bona fide cultural movement, which issued from the social system as naturally as a gushing spring, to degenerate into a pampered and paternalized vogue."[2]

During the 1930s—a period marked by Jewish dominance in the Communist party—assimilated Jewish Communists "assumed the mouth of spokesmanship on Negro affairs, thus burying the Negro

[1] Harold Cruse, *The Crisis of the Negro Intellectual* (New York: William Morrow, 1967), p. 12.
[2] Ibid., p. 52.

radical potential deeper and deeper in the slough of white intellectual paternalism."[3] Cruse was particularly angry that the party permitted Jews to maintain their cultural identity while it assumed that Negroes had no cultural identity to perpetuate. Cruse asserts that Negroes within the Party had the potential to Americanize Marxism:

It evidently never occurred to Negro revolutionaries that there was no one in America who possessed the remotest potential for Americanizing Marxism but themselves. Certainly the Jews could not with their nationalistic aggressiveness, emerging out of Eastside ghettos to demonstrate through Marxism their intellectual superiority over the Anglo-Saxon *goyim*. The Jews failed to make Marxism applicable to anything in America but their own national-group social ambitions or individual self elevation. As a result the great brainwashing of Negro radical intellectuals was not achieved by capitalism, or the capitalist bourgeoisie, but by Jewish intellectuals in the American Communist Party.[4]

Cruse resented what he conceived to be the subordinate role that the Negro intellectual has been forced to play to his Jewish counterpart over the years. He charged that the Jewish Communist intelligentsia established domination over the Negroes in the interpretation of the Negro question in the United States. "In the late 1940s and early 1950s the Communist Party, through the researches of Herbert Aptheker brazenly attempted to establish scholarly and theoretical dominance over Negro studies."[5] Allegedly, the Communists also had a pernicious influence on the Negro journals *Freedom* and *Freedomways* in the late 1950s and 1960s. The basic problem of the Negro intellectual of today, Cruse writes, is that:

The *interpretation* of the Negro is predominantly a white liberal affair, an alliance between white Christian and Jewish reformism. Within the scope of this alliance, the resulting ideology is preeminently of Jewish

---

[3] Ibid., p. 147, 148. Cruse continues: "These Jewish Communists were often more arrogant and paternalistic than the Anglo-Saxons, more self-righteous and intellectually supercilious about their Marxist line on America, than any other minority group. . . . One wonders how it was possible for Negroes to remain in the Party and accept such demeaning subordination."

[4] Ibid., p. 158.

[5] Ibid., p. 163.

intellectual origin. In fact, the main job of researching and interpreting the American Negro has been taken over by the Jewish intelligentsia to the extent where it is practically impossible for the Negro to deal with the Anglo-Saxon majority in this country unless he first comes to the Jews to get his instructions.[6]

Cruse, like a number of other black intellectuals, is understandably repelled by the notion put forward by a few rather naive Jews that the Negroes and Jews have faced similar problems in America. American Jews have never had any real political, economic, or cultural problems comparable to the Negroes'. There is no basis he feels, for the Jewish concern over anti-Semitism in America. Also "Jews have no honest cause for complaints inasmuch as they, as a group are by no means themselves immune to race prejudice."[7] He emphasizes that so far as Negroes are concerned Jews have not suffered at all in the United States. "The average Negro is not going to buy the propaganda that Negroes and Jews are 'brother sufferers' in the same boat."

The idea of Negro-Jewish unity has been largely a myth, Cruse contends. On the Communist Left, for example, "there has been an intense undercurrent of jealousy, enmity and competition over the prizes of group political power and intellectual prestige. In this struggle the Jewish intellectuals—because of superior organization, drive, intellectual discipline, money and the motive power of their cultural compulsions—have been able to win out." Cruse notes the call for Negro-Jewish unity was not a meaningful one and that "bonds of solidarity" only existed among a few leaders. This solidarity "was never a real fact down below among the black or Jewish masses, and it is misleading to claim that it was ever so. The relationships of Negroes to Jews, and vice-versa, have always been ambiguous . . . and are growing more so every day. The expansion in scope and quality of the Negro Civil Rights movement has

---

[6] Ibid., p. 270.

[7] Ibid., pp. 168–169. Cruse continues: "They are a group capable of becoming bankers financeers and merchant capitalists who hire Christians at high salaries, yet their absence on the executive boards of Christian capitalist firms is to Jews a sign of anti-Semitism. One might just as easily say that having become the most affluent group in America in per capita income and wealth, despite Anti-Semitism, is too much of a cross for American Jews to bear under 'democratic' capitalism."

brought to the surface the residual anti-Semitism that has always existed among Negroes, a group attitude which Jews themselves are at least partially responsible for fostering."

Cruse seeks to lay to rest the "Jew is the best friend of the Negro" myth and calls for a more realistic understanding of Jews by Negroes:

For many years, certain Negro intellectuals have been unable to face the Jews realistically. Among the many myths life and history have imposed on Negroes (such as that of Lincoln's "freeing" the slaves) is the myth that the Negro's best friend is the Jew. Far more accurately, certain Jews have been the best friends of certain Negroes—which in any case is nothing very unusual. There is little evidence that the Jewish group was much interested in the Negro's plight . . . prior to the age of Booker T. Washington and the N.A.A.C.P. era that followed.[8]

He notes that "certain Jews" were aware of the Negro's plight prior to this century. To "substantiate" this point, Cruse quotes a blatantly anti-Semitic passage by the great Russian writer, Feodor Doestoevsky. Doestoevsky wrote, in 1877 "The Negroes have now been liberated from the slaveowners, but they will not last because the Jews, of whom there are so many in the world, will jump at this new little victim."[9]

Cruse's portrayal of the problems and frustrations of black intellectuals in dealing with their white counterparts—Jew and Gentile alike—are insightful.[10] His argument for black writers, artists, and scholars to sever patronizing ties and his call for the black intellectuals to serve the pressing needs of the black community are also valid. But a major shortcoming, and a very serious one, of his analysis is his one-dimensional portrayal of the motives of Jews who down through the years have had dealings with Negroes. For example, his assessment of Jews and Negroes in the Communist party is not a balanced one. He alleges that Jews in the party intended as a group to subordinate and use blacks.[11] Somehow Jews

[8] Ibid., p. 476.

[9] Doestoevsky, *The Diary of a Writer* (New York: George Braziller, 1954), p. 642. Cited by Cruse, *Crisis of the Negro Intellectual,* p. 477.

[10] Cruse's own frustrations stemming from the infighting between his Harlem Writers Club and the Harlem Writers' Guild understandably added to his enmity toward the Communist Party.

[11] Negroes have been "used" in some instances by Communists, as they have

emerge as responsible for every major problem confronting the black intelligentsia, from the decline of the Harlem renaissance to the undermining of endeavors like *Freedomways*. Cruse presents a brand of anti-Communism combined with aspersions toward Jews which is readily marketable on the American scene.

Cruse's study contains some good reasons why, in retrospect, American Negro intellectuals may have been better off to have remained outside the Communist party altogether. But the simplistic impressions that Cruse creates of the motives of Jewish Communists and others on the Left do not wholly square with the historic realties of that period.[12]

Cruse also cannot tolerate the temporal successes of what he terms "Jewish nationalism," which culminated in the State of Israel. The frustrations which have accompanied attempts to engender a sense of black nationalism account for some of his antipathy toward Israel. He questions the loyalty of "a great proportion of American Jews" who function "as an organic part of a distant nation-state."[13] In order to discredit the "international machinations" that brought about the state of Israel, Cruse is not loath to trot out a number of anti-Zionist and right-wing writers who serve this purpose.

Robert Chrisman, editor of the new journal, *The Black Scholar,* has written that *The Crisis of the Negro Intellectual* is by far the most impressive history of black intellectual development to emerge in this decade. Indeed, it has the same quality of impact on black letters and the total American sensibility that James Baldwin's *Notes of a Native Son* and Ralph Ellison's *The Invisible Man* had before it. Like those works, Cruse isolates, defines, and crystallizes the major black concerns and climate of its time." Yet, there

---

been "used" by the major political parties in America down through the years.

[12] Nowhere in the book is there any mention of a comradeship shared by blacks and whites (often Jews) within the Party, that for all of its limitations was not matched within any other contemporary institution in the U.S.A. Where else in America except in certain predominantly Leftist or bohemian areas of New York could black men and white women walk arm in arm in relative safety? Which other group of whites were willing to go into the deep South in the 1930s and, at the risk of their very lives attempt to improve the condition of the Negro?

[13] Cruse, *Crisis of the Negro Intellectual,* p. 481.

are "confusions and contradictions" within the book. Among these is the nature of the historic relationship between Jews and Negroes: "There is a vicious anti-Semitism throughout the work. When faced with complexity, Cruse finds the nearest scapegoat and furiously lashes his way out of the jam. *The Crisis of the Negro Intellectual* is the crisis of Harold Cruse more than it is anything else. Where his vision of black experience should crystallize and develop a new intellectual framework, it lapses into a fog of personal confusion and spite, and imprecision on basic issues and concepts."[14]

One passage in Cruse's book points up a basic dilemma: whether the task of the intellectual should be to write white history, black history, or objective history. He relates that in 1965 playwright LeRoi Jones and Archie Shepp, a musician, began to express a cultural nationalism which was not only antiwhite, but was "specifically critical of Jewish whites." At the Village Vanguard in New York, Jones and Shepp had some exchanges with the audience during which Shepp mentioned the murder and martyrdom in Mississippi of Andrew Goodman and Michael Schwerner, both Jews. Shepp called the slain young men "artifacts" and said he was tired of talking about six million Jews in Europe. What about the five to eight million Africans killed in the Congo during King Leopold's day? In analyzing the situation Cruse declared that Jones and Shepp are confused on the Jews.

Shepp observed that the first victim, James E. Chaney, a Negro had been beaten into an unrecognizable state, while even in death the white lynchers had "embraced" their fellow whites by treating them "less harshly." There are profound moral and ethical problems involved here, but the question is—How far into the historical roots of these moral issues are Jones and Shepp willing to go? How far afield from New York City, where free speech is permitted all factions from Freedom Riders to Fascists, will Negro intellectuals go to search out the economic, cultural, political and imperialistic strands and bind them into a meaningful critique? If they reject Schwerner and Goodman today, they must reject John Brown(ism) of yesterday and expunge his name from Negro history, along with the Abolitionists as the precursors of paternalistic freedom assistance for blacks. But the Robesons,

[14] Robert Chrisman, "The Crisis of Harold Cruse," *The Black Scholar* 1, no. 1 (November 1969):78.

the Apthekers, the Shirley Graham DuBoises *et al.* would not like that.[15]

Cruse has stated the problem excellently, and one reads on expectantly for his own advice to the black intellectual. But instead the author evades the issue by adding rhetorically that his whipping boys, "the Robesons, the Apthekers and the Shirley G. DuBoises would not like that." Of course not. The question remains, "Would the Harold Cruses reject all the John Browns of yesterday and expunge their names from Negro history?"

In an article in *Liberator* entitled "White Liberals vs. Black Community," Lawrence Neal, like Cruse, regrets that "the dissemination and examination of the main features of Afro-American life and culture, are not in the hands of Black people themselves, but rather, in that of whites—specifically Jewish whites." This statement, writes Neal, "is not meant to vilify. It is simply a fact that cannot merely be whispered about any longer. Black intellectuals cannot expect any meaningful development until they (we) assume more power over all aspects of their (our) culture."[16]

Neal then points to the need for the Blacks to support their own organizations financially. CORE, for example, began to suffer "because Jewish money was withdrawn after a CORE official had uttered an anti-Semitic slur. (See Mount Vernon incident in chapter 7.) "It is a sad state of affairs when a so-called militant organization is dependent on support from outsiders whose interests lay elsewhere. No Jewish organization, on the other hand depends on Black money for support, and no Jewish organization would allow itself to fall into that kind of trap."

Neal goes on to observe that "the sociological study of Afro-Americans, aside from Du Bois, Clark, Frazier, and Drake, has rested primarily in the hands of people like Herskovits, Arnold Rose, Herbert Aptheker, Harold Isaacs and countless other Jewish scholars." It should be recalled in considering this point that for three decades prior to his death in 1963 Herskovits worked tirelessly in the field in which he had been a pioneer—Afro-American studies. He did yeoman work in dispelling pejorative myths about

[15] Cruse, *Crisis of the Negro Intellectual,* p. 486.
[16] Lawrence P. Neal, "White Liberals vs. Black Community." *Liberator* 6, no. 7 (July 1966):4.

the Negro's past. One of his main interests was the interaction of Europeans, Africans, and American Indian cultures in the New World, and he emphatically rejected the assumption that African cultures had disintegrated in the face of superior European civilizations in the Americas. It is ironic that Neal faults Isaacs for de-emphasizing the links Afro-Americans feel with Africa in view of the fact that Herskovits' critics have challenged what they regarded as his overemphasis of Africanisms among New World Negroes.[17]

Aptheker, the literary executor of W. E. B. Du Bois' papers, wrote about black history when it was given short shrift by most historians. His controversial but seminal research on slave insur-rections in general and Nat Turner specifically has provided black radicals with a good deal of historical ammunition. In recognition of his work, Aptheker was honored in 1969 in New York by the Association for the Study of Negro Life and History.

Prior to the 1900s there was little contact between Jews and blacks. Neal notes that a close relationship, albeit an uneasy one, began to emerge around 1917, when the NAACP, the Urban League, and various other Negro institutions were established.

It has continued up to the present. American Jewish intellectuals have taken a particular interest in studying all aspects of the "Negro Question." They have been communists fighting for the rights of Black workers. They have been critics and sociologists examining the phe-nomena of a displaced minority in the United States. . . . They have had an inordinate amount to say about the Black man's problem in America. They have attempted to wed our cause to theirs. And I sup-pose there is some underlying relationship between our problem and theirs, but the relationship has not been especially in our best interests. It is a precarious one which often assumes hypocritical dimensions."[18]

The authors, as outsiders, can only agree with the thrust of Neal's argument that blacks should assume more interest and par-ticipation in the uses and interpretations of their own culture. The need becomes imperative, considering the position of blacks in contemporary America. The need, however, is to produce addi-

[17] For a recent article stressing New World Negro-African links, see Robert Weisbord, "Africa, Africans and the Afro-American: Images and Identi-ties in Transition," *Race* 10, no. 3 (1969):305–321.

[18] Ibid., p. 5.

tional black sociologists, and to judge the nonblack sociologists, including those who happen to be Jews, solely on the quality of their work.

Pointing to a condition, which from the *Liberator's* point of view is deplorable, Neal observes that "the entire spectrum of Negro leadership is entangled in a weird relationship with the liberal Jewish establishment. Such entanglements create a false sense of unity between the two groups, and leaves the Negro leadership estranged from the black masses which they claim to represent." Neal asserts that the relationship of the black intellectual to the American intellectual establishment which, at least in his New York environs is primarily Jewish, is one of "master to slave, teacher to student."

He cites in the field of music Nat Hentoff as an authority on jazz "who has his hands in almost every area of Afro-American music and culture. . . . There are very few Afro-American critics and writers given as many opportunities to talk about things Black as Hentoff." It is questionable whether it is fair to use the master-slave analogy with Hentoff, long a serious student of jazz and a friend to many black causes. Hentoff, unfortunately, has no control over his pigmentation and ethnic origin.

A more legitimate complaint put forth by both Neal and Cruse is the lack of black access to and influence on America's communications and entertainment media. This "has been especially true of the Black musicians whose music is in great demand, but who profit very little from its exposure." Many Jews would reply instinctively and defensively that the entertainment arena was the first lucrative field to be opened up to Negroes, and that Jews were, by and large, among the first to recognize and provide some openings for Negro talent. Yet while Jews gave Negroes their "first break" most Jews in the entertainment world as elsewhere shared the broad societal attitudes of their contemporaries.

Although it is irrelevant and no consolation to a black today, it was perhaps no accident that a Jewish Jack Benny took on Rochester for his valet on their celebrated radio program. Benny made the big money and was the employer, of course, but one saving grace was that Rochester occasionally had the chance to good-humoredly put the white man in his place. For whatever it is worth, it is hard to think of many non-Jewish entertainers who would have gone even as far as Jack Benny a few decades ago. In general, though, Hollywood and Broadway have much to be ashamed of. Very little courage or initiative has been shown over the years to advance the course of racial justice in America. Jewish film magnates and producers have generally accepted and reinforced the prevailing mores of the day and the profit motive has ruled supreme. It is not a matter of oversight, as Harold Cruse accurately underscored, that no Hollywood studio has sought to do a movie of Ralph Ellison's *The Invisible Man*.

Neal concludes: "We do not need pathological love-hate relationships. We want to be free from cultural oppression and political and economic domination by outside forces. We refuse to pretend that we are not *suffering* at the hands of Jewish landlords. We refuse to sit idly by, and watch our culture being continually exploited by money hungry leeches playing hip." Until the last sentence the statement expresses a very legitimate concern. But why single out Jews? And are the bourgeoisie with beards who are making today's academic and cultural scenes peculiarly a Jewish phenomenon? The authors suggest that they as well as landlords are not confined to any particular group.

We might add, parenthetically, that the authors, both Jews, have been doing the very thing that distresses Cruse and Neal—subjecting blacks to a kind of scrutiny. Perhaps it is absurd for us to have concurred with some points and disagreed with others, in the sense that Cruse and Neal were not writing for the purpose of creating a dialogue with onlooking whites. Perhaps to a self-conscious proponent of a liberation movement anything is considered justifiable to advance the cause. Yet if one impugns the motives of specific groups or individuals one should expect to be challenged if his accuracy is questionable. There is today, fortunately, more of a quid pro quo as the trend is reversing—blacks are now providing some much needed analysis of Jews and other whites. Hopefully, in the painful process of talking past each other, some small exchange of ideas will take place.

The approach toward Jews and whites taken by Eldridge Cleaver, an activist-intellectual, differs from that of Cruse. A younger man, Cleaver did not have a background of frustrations emanating from encounters with the Old Left. Cleaver is not preoccupied with Jews but with the question of liberating the black man from an oppressive system controlled by whites of various ethnic and religious backgrounds. Cleaver welcomed the backing of empathetic whites in a *supportive* role for the Black Panther's struggle. Such a unity among whites and blacks was manifested in the electoral alliance between the exclusively Afro-American Panthers and the predominantly white Peace and Freedom Party during the 1968 elections. Cleaver ran for president on the Peace and Freedom ticket and Paul Jacobs, one of the many Jewish radicals in the movement, ran for U.S. Senator.[19]

What brings Cruse, Neal, and Cleaver close together is their common belief that the oppressive white heel on the black man's neck must be removed, forcibly if necessary. Also they believe that blacks should control their own communities and enhance their economic power, that they should enlarge their political power and rehabilitate their self-image.

Creative writers such as essayist-novelist James Baldwin and poet-playwright LeRoi Jones have also participated in the running debate on blacks and Jews. In recent years, a legion of black critics have chastised Baldwin for lacking black consciousness in his writing and thinking. Those who have chosen to follow a path leading to separatism do not like others to rekindle the fragmented hope that America is redeemable. It does not sit well with a number of these critics that Baldwin attempts to give a balanced picture of the Jews. Baldwin in recent years has been, as Leslie Fiedler put it, "caught between the exigencies of his poetic talent and his political commitment."[20]

Writing the piece, "The Harlem Ghetto: Winter 1948," for the American Jewish Committee-sponsored *Commentary* magazine made Baldwin susceptible to the criticism by various black radicals that he was soft on the Jews.[21] Cruse devotes several pages to "The Harlem Ghetto" which he denounces as "a chic piece of magazine journalism that rehashed all the time-worn superficialities of Har-

[19] For additional comments by Cleaver on Jews and Zionists, see Introduction, p. xxvi, and chap. 5, p. 107, of this book.

[20] Leslie Fiedler's essay in Shlomo Katz, ed., *Negro and Jew*, p. 30. Fiedler describes LeRoi Jones as "the victim of his own anguish and *mishigas*."

[21] James Baldwin, "The Harlem Ghetto: Winter 1948," *Commentary*, February 1948, pp. 165–170.

lem 'local color' and decrepitude. . . . Baldwin looks at the Jewish question with the eyes of a rather innocent and provincial intellectual," who bends "over backwards to avoid criticism of Jews while pretending to be angry with whites."[22] "It would not be correct," writes Cruse patronizingly, "to call Baldwin a Jew Lover, inasmuch as Baldwin simply loves everybody, even those he feels are against him. More exactly, he fits the category of apologist for the Jews."[23] A later essay in *The New York Times* on the phenomenon of anti-Semitism among Negroes did little to enhance Baldwin's stature among the black critics, although the essay presented a well-balanced critique of Afro-American views about Jews.[24]

A content analysis of LeRoi Jones' poems would merely belabor the point that the gifted poet does not regard Jews very highly. For example, the following lines are from his "Black Art:"

> We want poems like fists beating niggers out of Jocks or dagger poems in the slimy bellies of the owner-jews.

> Look at the Liberal spokesman for the Jews clutch his throat and puke himself into eternity.[25]

Jones' poetry of course is directed toward whites in general, although Jews receive more scornful allusions than any other ethnic group. The frequency of references to Italian-Americans has increased after Jones' scrapes with the Newark, New Jersey, power structure. In February, 1970 Jones spoke of Newark as a city that is "in control of an Italian nationalist army called the police department." The Jewish liberal and businessman are oft-selected targets for the social commentary which Jones is making. For Jones the terms liberal and Jew are almost synonymous.

In America's present polarized situation black and white radical intelligentsia alike tend to attack liberal "hypocrisy" more strenuously than the thinly veiled racism of a George Wallace. The latter has even been complimented for his honesty.

22 Cruse, *Crisis of the Negro Intellectual,* p. 489.
23 Ibid., p. 482.
24 James Baldwin, "Negroes Are Anti-Semitic Because They're Anti-White," *New York Times Magazine* (April 1967), p. 26ff.
25 LeRoi Jones, "Black Art," in LeRoi Jones and Larry Neal, eds., *Black Fire, An Anthology of Afro-American Writing* (New York: Morrow, 1966), p. 302.

Black intellectuals of various persuasions find some characteristics of a segment of the Jewish community distasteful. They find
repugnant the expectation that today every time an anti-Semitic
remark is made by a black, "responsible" Negro spokesmen are
supposed to publicly denounce it. They believe Jews are unneces-
sarily preoccupied with anti-Semitism. Another sensitive point is
the Jewish "we are your best friends" approach and the reminder
of what Jews have done for blacks over the years. Such reminders
are generally prompted by the belief that the Negroes do not appreciate what has been done for them. But, it should be noted, even
Israelis who have been largely dependent on financial support from
American Jewry do not like to be constantly reminded of what
American Jews have done for them.[26]

Many blacks are sensitive about being considered an appendage
of white (Jewish) liberalism and are anxious to assert their independence. The fact that liberal Jewish organizations in the past
have been in the forefront of supportive white groups of the civil
rights movement is not enough. In an age of "instant history"
blacks are interested in knowing what Jews and other white groups
are doing *now* to effectuate economic equality as well as equality
under the law.

Negroes also resent Jews' telling them that they understand the
Negroes' suffering because they have suffered. As chapter 1 made
clear, in America at least, Jews have not suffered anything comparable to Negroes. Harold Cruse, in a recent essay, is repulsed by
the twin ideas that "anti-Semitism and anti-Negroism were two
sides of the same coin," and "both Negroes and Jews were in the
same boat." Nothing provoked Cruse's enmity towards Jews more
during the 1940s and 1950s than being told by a Jew: "I know
how you feel because I, too, am discriminated against." For Cruse,
"the economic position of the Jews alone was enough to prove to
anyone that anti-Semitism had very little in common with anti-
Negroism."[27] Or as James Baldwin put it recently:

[26] There is a relation between this and the Jewish parents' syndrome (which
has been overworked ad nauseum in the recent spate of literature)—the
Jewish mother and her desire to evoke a constant flow of gratitude and
latent guilt from her children for all that she has done for them.
[27] Harold Cruse, "My Jewish Problem and Theirs," in Nat Hentoff, ed.,

It is true that many Jews use, shamefully, the slaughter of the 6,000,000 by the Third Reich as proof that they cannot be bigots—or in the hope of not being held responsible for their bigotry. It is galling to be told by a Jew whom you have known to be exploiting you that he cannot possibly be doing what you know he is doing because he is a Jew. . . .

One does not wish, in short, to be told by an American Jew that his suffering is as great as the American Negro's suffering. It isn't, and one knows that it isn't from the very tone in which he assures you that it is.[28]

We turn now to several of the problems confronting Jewish intellectuals in the quest for amicable Jewish-black relations. First, some Jewish intellectuals share, at least in part, the general societal prejudices against blacks. Such prejudice rarely appears overtly in their written work. But more pernicious are the biases and misinformation drawn from our collective past and educational processing. When the awareness of our biases does emerge, it may well be repressed because we do not wish to come to grips with it.

One Jewish writer who has honestly confronted his ambivalent feelings toward Negroes is Norman Podhoretz, editor of *Commentary* magazine. As a boy in Brooklyn he grew up "fearing and hating and envying Negroes." As an adult he admitted to still feeling these same emotions, "but not in the same proportions and certainly not in the same way."[29] Podhoretz acknowledges painfully that his negative feeling toward the Negro remains with him as an adult:

The hatred I still feel for Negroes is the hardest of all the old feelings to face or admit, and it is the most hidden and the most overlarded by

---

Black Anti-Semitism and Jewish Racism (New York: Richard W. Baron, 1969), pp. 172–173.

28 Baldwin, "Negroes Are Anti-Semitic Because They're Anti-White," pp. 135–136.

29 Norman Podhoretz, "My Negro Problem—And Ours." Reprinted from *Doings and Undoings: The Fifties and After in American Writing* (New York: Farrar, Straus & Giroux, 1963). The author continues: "I now live on the upper West Side of Manhattan, where there are many Negroes and many Puerto Ricans, and there are nights when I experience the old apprehensiveness again, and there are streets that I avoid when I am walking in the dark. . . . I find that I am not afraid of Puerto Ricans, but I cannot restrain my nervousness whenever I pass a group of Negroes

the conscious attitudes into which I have succeeded in willing myself. It no longer has, as for me it once did, any cause or justification. . . . How, then, do I know that this hatred has never entirely disappeared? I know it from the insane rage that can stir in me at the thought of Negro anti-Semitism, I know it from the disgusting prurience that can stir in me at the sight of a mixed couple.[30]

It takes a courageous forthrightness to make such an admission, inasmuch as intellectuals generally like to believe that they are immune from the emotional responses which move the mass of people.

Jewish intellectuals have sought dialogue with their Negro counterparts, but all too often in the past such dialogues have been primarily oriented toward Jewish interests. Such a dialogue was symbolized by a symposium sponsored by *Midstream* magazine in 1966.[31] The symposium brought together prominent Negro and Jewish commentators to discuss the alleged increase in the incidence of black anti-Semitism. The format essentially examined anti-Semitism in the black community. The participants in the symposium numbered twenty-five Jews and two Negroes. The symposium idea was commendable and a number of the essays were very informative and perceptive, but the significant fact remains that the focal point was black anti-Semitism and the participants themselves were overwhelmingly Jewish. The symposium scarcely provided any real encounter between Jewish and Negro intellectuals. (One may ask why there has never been a similar conference focusing upon the phenomenon of white-Jewish racism?)

The major cause for crisis in Jewish intellectual circles in recent years stems from the problem of how Jews should react to the black revolution. Some Jews have supported virtually all of the

---

standing in front of a bar or sauntering down the street. I know now, as I did not know when I was a child, that power is on my side, that the police are working for me and not for them. And knowing this I feel ashamed and guilty, like the good liberal I have grown up to be. Yet the twinges of fear and the resentment they bring and the self-contempt they arouse are not to be gainsaid."

[30] Ibid.

[31] The essays from the symposium appeared in the December 1966 issue of *Midstream* and were reprinted in paperback form, Shlomo Katz, ed., *Negro and Jew: An Encounter in America* (New York: Macmillan Co., 1967).

militant or extremist movements which have emanated from the black ghettos. In fact, a disproportionate amount of the white backing for black radical movements has been Jewish in origin. At the same time, a much larger group of Jewish intellectuals—mainly liberals—have either dropped out of primarily black organizations or, in some cases, have been pushed out. Jewish financial support for such previously racially mixed organizations as CORE and SNCC has dropped accordingly.

During the height of the civil rights movement headed by Dr. Martin Luther King, Jr., a great majority of Jewish intellectuals stood solidly in support of the Negro goals. A cleavage has since occurred in the ranks of Jewish intellectuals over whether militant blacks should be accorded support, ignored, or actively opposed. There has been considerable acrimony among those taking various positions. Representing a personal position on this question to the "right" of the cleavage point, the noted sociologist, Nathan Glazer, in one section of a *Commentary* article entitled, "Blacks, Jews, and the Intellectuals," contends that

the expansion of anti-Semitism among blacks, while fed by material already present at the grass roots, has largely been the work of the black intelligentsia—to use an unfortunately indispensable word— abetted and assisted and advised by a white, predominantly Jewish intelligentsia. When we attack black anti-Semitism, let us be perfectly clear that we are attacking the fruits of five years of growing rage and irrationality, centered among radical college students, but encouraged by a wide range of white intellectuals, many of them of Jewish origin.[32]

Glazer holds responsible "such gurus of the time" as Norman Mailer and Edgar Z. Friedenberg and their followers in the *New York Review of Books,* the underground press and elsewhere for promoting the notion that American middle-class society is racist and corrupt. "To be sure," he concedes, "there were materials for black anti-Semitism in the concrete contacts of blacks and Jews. But these materials had to be interpreted, the interpretations had to be spread among young whites," who in turn passed them on to the young blacks. The enraged nihilism that exists among many

[32] Nathan Glazer, "Blacks, Jews, and the Intellectuals," *Commentary* 47, no. 4 (April 1969):35.

white and Jewish intellectuals are major factors in the recrudescence of black anti-Semitism. It is ironic, according to Glazer's
analysis, that an advertisement by the International Committee to
Support Eldridge Cleaver in a recent issue of the *Black Panther*
included many distinguished Jewish intellectuals as sponsors.[33]
The same issue of the *Black Panther* contained an admiring story
on the Al Fatah, an Arab movement which seeks to destroy Israel.

"Let us recall," Glazer continues in the *Commentary* article:

> that Andrew Kopkind, writing in the *New York Review of Books*
> (edited by Robert Silvers and Barbara Epstein), glorified the violence
> and destruction of the Newark riots, and called for more. Let us recall
> that Paul Jacobs helped establish Eldridge Cleaver at *Ramparts,* that
> Robert Scheer edited his last book, that Jacobs and Paul Shapiro lost
> money when he jumped bail. Let us recall that Marvin Garson pub-
> lishes bloodthirsty prophesies in his *Express-Times* depicting an upris-
> ing in Berkeley in which hundreds of policemen are killed and the
> Chancellor of the University is murdered before a cheering revolution-
> ary tribunal, and that Max Scheer is the editor of the Berkeley Barb
> in which no act of violence by blacks against whites is criticized.[34]

Glazer does not want "to deprive blacks of all the credit for the
mood of violence which hangs over the country," but holds that
we must acknowledge that white intellectuals, meaning "in large
measure Jewish intellectuals, have taught violence, justified violence, rationalized violence."

In assessing what Glazer has written, it should be noted that he
chooses not to deal with whether the ideas which the Jewish intellectuals have "propagated so assiduously over the past five years
are understandable, excusable, or even right." Begging this question ignores an important consideration that must be looked at
when one appraises the volatile situation which has developed in
the country. In the *Commentary* article Glazer has singled out
Jewish radicals' alleged contribution to the climate of violence in

[33] Ibid. The sponsors included Allen Ginsberg, Herbert Gold, Norman
Mailer, Paul Jacobs, Edgar Friedenberg, Marcus Raskin, Jack Newfield,
Nat Hentoff, Susan Sontag, Arthur Waskow, Jules Feiffer, Robert Bru-
stein, Maurice Zeitlin, Noan Chomsky, Richard Lichtman, Robert Silvers,
Theodore Solotaroff, and others.

[34] Ibid., p. 36.

America, rather than concentrating on the underlying reasons why contemporary America is so fertile for such "violent" ideas.

Glazer understandably regrets that the question of black anti-Semitism has been immortalized by a *Time* cover story, and points out why it is better to confine the discussion of such problems to lower-keyed Jewish publications. One can only applaud the view that far too much has been made of black anti-Semitism in the mass media.

A concern expressed by Glazer, and shared by the majority of Jewish liberal intellectuals, is predicated on the belief that the United States has reached a fever point and must be cooled down, and that black militancy is potentially inimical both to American Jewry and to Israel. One can certainly understand much of the reasoning underlying this position. But the implicit assumption that there would scarcely be a militant black liberation movement afoot today were it not for Jewish radical intelligentsia is not tenable. This point of view may reflect a still prevailing viewpoint that Negroes cannot (or will not) do it on their own without Jewish patronage, a view that drives a new generation of proud young blacks up the proverbial wall.

Events of recent years at home and abroad have led to sharp divisions on the traditional American Left. Decent men like Nathan Glazer in 1968–1969 found themselves on one side of the dividing line peering across at equally decent radicals on the other side. They may share the same vision of a just society, but they differ in their approaches to the creation of such a society. There are thoughtful liberals who are afraid that the rhetoric and actions of the radical left will lead not to societal emancipation but to harsh repression by the Right—a repression in which mainstream America will acquiesce. There are also posturers on both sides of the dividing line, and this group includes a substantial number of nominal liberals, Jew and Gentile, who criticize radical approaches to change, but do next to nothing to ameliorate the societal problems that create the recourse to radicalism.

In *Beyond the Melting Pot,* published in 1963, Glazer and Daniel Moynihan argued that in New York City the larger American experience of the Negro, based on slavery and repression in the South, would be overcome as Negroes "joined society" as an ethnic group. Six years later, Glazer frankly acknowledged that this has not happened.[35] The optimism during the early years of the Kennedy Administration, during which time the data for *Beyond the Melting Pot* was collected, has not borne fruit. To justify their faith that the American system can be made operative to accommodate the needs of all of its peoples, liberal scholars are often tempted to see the changes they wish to see in statistical data. Illusions are sometimes created that conditions for America's minorities have been improving dramatically, when in reality little improvement has occurred.

Those to the right of the cleavage point—wherever it may be at any particular moment—hold the left primarily responsible for the present confrontation in American society. Those left of the cleavage point disdain the pollyannaish liberal scholarship that submitted that all was well with the American body politic, when indeed all was not well.

Jewish radicals support certain black radical groups for a number of reasons, ranging from the belief that this is the best way to bring about racial and social justice in America to the notion that any forces which might help to restrain unwarranted American interventionism abroad should be supported.

Seen from a radical viewpoint, the American system has always tolerated a certain amount of selective repression to contain or crush recalcitrant elements in society, while broader societal adjustments known as reforms are taking place. The present Establishment plans to finally bring the Negro into the mainstream of American economic life are opposed by some elements in the black community and their white radical allies who resist the terms under which such incorporation is taking place. Official support is being given to even rhetorically militant black groups if

[35] Glazer acknowledged that the statistics for the years 1950–1960 pointed to the stagnation of opportunities for Negroes; also that there had been a serious undercount in number of Negro males. Unfortunately, these dates were not taken into consideration in the prognosis for *Beyond the Melting Pot*. Nathan Glazer, "A New Look at the Melting Pot," *The Public Interest*, August 1969, pp. 180–187. Moynihan, currently an advisor to President Nixon on urban affairs, in his "benign neglect" memorandum of January 1970 still believes that substantial progress has been made by the Negro.

their programs are sufficiently reformist, while at the same time the more recalcitrant black groups are being crushed.[36]

Issues like the controversy surrounding the Black Panthers and their running dispute with "Authority" serve to draw a line between those who would push forward for radical change, even at the risk of societal upheaval, and those who would accept only controlled gradualist change. Many Jewish and Christian liberals are so taken aback by the occasional antiwhite rhetoric of Bobby Seale, that they are willing to look away when the civil rights of members of the Panther organization are violated. The rationale for this position is that the Panthers have gone beyond the bounds of permissible dissent; it is too bad that they must be repressed, but it is being done for the greatest good of the greatest number of Americans. In short, "let's not take any risks of upsetting the American applecart." Then there are those on the other side of the divide, among them Jewish intelligentsia who were identified with the advertisement supporting Eldridge Cleaver in the *Black Panther*. Those endorsing the advertisement believe that the United States should not force its dissidents to become political exiles. While one cannot generalize it can be said that they want to provide a buffer of support and protection for those dissident blacks who might be liquidated or otherwise removed from the scene. Many of the attorneys, like William M. Kunstler, who provide legal defense for blacks, are Jewish.[37] Although some of the advocates of the *Black*

---

[36] Developing this point an article in *Leviathan:* "Closely linked to these plans to incorporate blacks into the political economy is a systematic program of repression of those elements in the black community—and within the white radical movements as well—who are attempting to create bases from which to resist this incorporation. Repression is nearly always, as we have suggested, doubleedged: aid and encourage those groups that have mastered an effective—in this context, militant—rhetoric, but which also have a reformist program; at the same time, smash the more 'recalcitrant' groups. Thus, the Ford Foundation shows extensive noblesse oblige to CORE and its attempts to promote black capitalism in Cleveland while the Justice Department prepares, according to recent reports, Smith Act indictments against the Black Panthers." David Wellman and Ian Dizard, "i love ralph bunche, but i can't eat him for lunch," *Leviathan* 1, no. 4 (July–August, 1969):49.

[37] A coalition of experienced lawyers and young staff, many of whom are Jewish, formed a Law Center for Constitutional Rights to provide counsel and represent people and organizations in the anti-Establishment "Movement." One of the group's prominent lawyers is William Kunstler, who

Panther and supporters of Cleaver assuredly would not agree with their views on Al Fatah, the cruel nature of the confrontations of our times forces conscientious individuals to act in a manner that is not always 100 percent consistent.

---

since the early 1960s has been involved in much of the major civil rights litigation, and who has more recently served as attorney for H. Rap Brown and some members of the Black Panther Party. (A number of the New York Civil Liberties Union officials who have provided legal assistance for the Panthers are also Jewish.)

The Law Center lawyers often find themselves defending clients who have expressed anti-Jewish and/or anti-Israeli sentiments. Mr. Kunstler, when asked about this, remarked that "the visible enemy in the ghetto is often the Jewish landlord and shopkeeper. . . . Maybe by their association with us, the anti-Semitism, much of which is rhetoric, is being dissipated." *New York Times,* 17 August 1969.

} 7 {

FROM DIXIE TO
MOUNT VERNON TO
WASHINGTON SQUARE

PRIOR TO WORLD WAR II, JEWISH ORGANIZATIONS DEVOTED ALMOST
all of their energies to the fight against anti-Semitism, although
some individual Jews were leading benefactors of Negro education
and others supported the causes of the NAACP. Feeling more
secure in postwar America, Jewish agencies began to include within
the scope of their activities concern over the widespread discrimination against the Negro. The focal point for this emphasis was
the civil rights movement, through which valuable legal assistance
was provided for Negroes. Another way in which Jewish organizations indirectly assisted the gradual growth of Negro rights was
by combatting Jewish exclusion from hotels, clubs, and the like.
In working against the "exclusionist principle" through court action, Jews helped other minority groups who were treading the
same path. American Jewry had felt the inner hurt of injustice and
had fought within a harsh but open society to obtain their rights.
Geared to combatting prejudice against themselves, Jewish organizations subsequently compiled a notable record, especially as compared with most other sectarian groups, in fighting against deeply
ingrained religious and racial prejudice. While some members and
backers of Jewish organizations were afflicted by the same bigoted
racial attitudes which permeated other segments of America, the
fact remained that a substantial part of the organized Jewish com-

133

munity continually stood on or near the forefront of supportive white groups seeking to gain equality under the law for the Negro.

The Anti-Defamation League of the B'nai B'rith beginning in the late 1940s actively worked to get civil rights legislation into the federal statute books.[1] Spokesmen for the group gave testimony before and strongly favored the report submitted by President Truman's Committee on Civil Rights. The report concluded that great numbers of Negroes were denied protection from lawless violence, arbitrary arrest, and punishment and that their rights to equal opportunity in employment, education, housing, health, recreation, and transportation were systematically violated throughout the nation. The response of the 80th Congress, however, was to bury the report.

The Negro struggle for legal desegregation of the public schools received strong Jewish support. In the landmark 1954 *Brown v. Topeka Board of Education* case, the ADL was a "friend to the court," drawing upon its experienced personnel and extensive research facilities. After the desegregation ruling was reached the local ADL and B'nai B'rith in several southern states like Alabama disavowed the work of the national organization. As the movement to end de facto segregation headed North, the ADL filed a number of amicus curiae briefs and sought to promote community acceptance of desegregated schools.

Along with the ADL, the American Jewish Committee and the American Jewish Congress filed legal briefs in major civil rights cases dealing with housing, employment, education, and public accommodations.

The American Jewish Congress was the most active Jewish group in terms of taking the initiative to promote desegregation in the North. In 1954, the New York City chapter of the Congress filed the first brief in the North (in Englewood, New Jersey) against de facto segregation. Taking a more advanced position at the time than the national civil rights organizations, the Congress

---

[1] Accounts of the ADL's role in the civil rights movement are drawn from John P. Roche, *The Quest for the Dream* (New York: Macmillan Co., 1963), pp. 234–251, and the ADL pamphlet, *Not the Work of a Day* (New York, 1965), pp. 47ff, and from conversations with ADL officials.

attempted to persuade the NAACP to take a more activist stand in the New York City school situation.[2]

Jewish national organizations helped in the movement which led in 1957 to President Eisenhower's signing the nation's first civil rights bill in eighty-two years. During the Kennedy administration they worked for a broad civil rights bill. After Kennedy's untimely death, several hundred Jewish lay leaders joined with their liberal counterparts of other backgrounds in calling for the immediate passage of the far-reaching 1964 Civil Rights Act.

Jewish religious leaders, such as Rabbi Abraham Heschel, along with like-minded Christian counterparts, were among the distinguished advocates of the civil rights bill. Several days before the Senate voted on the 1964 bill, a group of sixteen reform rabbis headed by the Director of the Commission on Social Action of Reform Judaism, Albert Vorspan, expressed their feelings by flying to St. Augustine, Florida, to participate in a desegregation demonstration.[3]

During the summer of 1964 a significant percentage of the twelve hundred youths recruited by CORE, SNCC, SCLC, and the NAACP to work in the deep South were of Jewish background. The volunteers worked to encourage voter registration and to provide educational opportunities for children.

Other Jews, for example Jack Greenberg who succeeded Thurgood Marshall as director counsel of the NAACP Legal Defense and Educational Fund, have been part of the ongoing day-to-day struggle to promote integration. More obscure, but also significant, are the contributions of realtor, Morris Milgram, a trailblazer in integrated housing.

At the time of the historic 1954 Supreme Court ruling on school desegregation, Jewish national organizations lauded the decision. The implementation of the ruling was something else again, however, especially in the deep South. The reaction of rabbis and Jewish congregations in the South was one of caution for the most

2 David Rogers, *110 Livingston Street* (New York: Random House, 1968), p. 144.
3 Henry Cohen, *Justice, Justice,* rev. ed. (New York: Union of American Hebrew Congregations, 1969), p. 18.

part. It was not, as Robert St. John superficially describes it, a situation in which "throughout the region rabbis mounted their pulpits and spoke out fearlessly."[4] Indeed it would have been most surprising if this had been the case.

Within the region of the old confederacy are approximately two hundred thousand Jews, who represent only about seven-tenths of one percent of the region's population. Many southern Jews view themselves as a potentially vulnerable minority, and fear civil rights activism for this reason among others. Most are middle and upper-middle class socioeconomically and most are business-men, white-collar workers and a few planters. In an excellent article dealing with southern Jews and the civil rights movement, P. Allen Krause raises the question: "Where, then, does Southern Jewry stand on the issue of segregation?"[5] Are they fighting friends, frightened friends, or foes of the Negro activists? They are, in the writer's opinion, something of all three—with emphasis on the middle epithet.

Without a doubt, Southern Jews do include vocal and active desegre-gationists—but their number is small. They would usually be . . . first generation southerners—people like Harry Golden. In addition, they are to be found almost invariably in other than Deep-South commu-nities. There are also vocal, card-carrying Jewish segregationists—who are not so out of fear but out of conviction. More often than not they will be [long residents of the South for two or more generations]—but they too are a distinct minority—amounting most likely to a percentage about equal to their liberal coreligionists. The vast majority of southern Jews—some 75 per cent of them—are in the middle, somewhat am-bivalent about the whole issue, but tending toward thoughts sympa-thetic to the Negro.[6]

---

[4] Robert St. John, *Jews, Justice and Judaism* (New York: Doubleday, 1969), p. 297.

[5] P. Allen Krause, "Rabbis and Negro Rights in the South, 1954–1967," *American Jewish Archives* 21, no. 1 (April 1969): 20, 47.

[6] Ibid., p. 23. Krause cites some opinions of others on southern Jewry and civil rights. In his analysis of "Iron City," sociologist Theodore Lowi characterized almost all southern Jews as "publicly conservative," and noted that the majority are probably "privately conservative" as well, for their values "are homogenized under the pressure of southern consensus on the most important political and social issue of all." Lowi, "Southern Jews: The Two Communities," *Jewish Journal of Sociology* 6 (July 1964): 111. The Reverend Fred Shuttlesworth, close colleague of Dr.

There are few conservative and even fewer orthodox rabbis in the South, and these have for the greatest part been conspicuously absent from the civil rights movement. Most congregations have reform rabbis, many of whom have taken a stance within their own congregation against segregation—but generally in "carefully worded, non-inflammatory rhetoric." There are few rabbis who have stepped beyond the general position of their congregations and become actively involved in the civil rights struggle.

Among those who "joined word to deed" in the deep South were Rabbis Ira Sanders, Perry Nussbaum, Alfred Goodman, Charles Martinband, and Jacob Rothchild. Rabbi Rothchild had a somewhat less arduous task than the other aforementioned in that his congregation was in Atlanta, which by southern standards was perhaps the city most open to racial liberalism. In 1957 he joined with seventy-nine other clergy to issue the "Atlanta Manifesto"—one of the earliest and most significant clerical statements on desegregation. Also, Rothchild organized seminars to help prepare his congregants for desegregation. On 12 October 1958 he was "rewarded" for his effort by having his synagogue dynamited by white extremists. Within an eight-month period five Jewish community centers in Miami, Nashville, Jacksonville, Birmingham, and Atlanta were desecrated by similar explosions. Rabbi Rothchild, in appraising the situation, said that the anti-Semitic group who bombed the synagogue "misread the attitudes of the community." The bombing created a reaction of outrage and as a result made it more possible to speak out on desegregation to middle-of-the-road Atlantans who were shamed by the bombing of the synagogue.[7]

In a number of southern communities, Reform rabbis have "played valuable secondary or supportive roles" in the civil rights struggle. But Rabbi Charles Martinband is distinguished in having been on the front line for eleven years (1951–1962) in battling segregation in the very conservative town of Hattiesburg, Missis-

Martin Luther King opined that "the response of southern Jews to the [civil rights] movement certainly compares favorably with that of numerous other white groups." But Aaron Henry from Mississippi in a letter to Allan Krause in 1966 remarked, "You asked about the Jews in the South and rabbis particularly. Sorry, they are not with it." Krause, "Rabbis and Negro Rights in the South," pp. 22–23.

[7] Krause, "Rabbis and Negro Rights in the South," pp. 38–39.

sippi. Hattiesburg is a town of less than 50,000 inhabitants with a Jewish population of about 175. Rabbi Martinband was criticized by his congregants and the community at large for his "open association with Negroes on an at-home social basis, his refusal to keep to himself his ideas about the evil of segregation, his very active participation in the Southern Regional Council, and the numerous speeches he made at nearby Negro colleges." He also had to contend with the local White Citizen's Council in pursuing an active relationship with Negroes. Yet, in standing up for his principles in a forthright, but nonhistrionic way, Martinband amazingly won the grudging respect of enough of his fellow townsmen to be given the "key to the city" when he left Hattiesburg in 1962.[8] (It was the same Hattiesburg in which Rabbi Arthur Lelyveld of Cleveland, a counselor of the Council of Federated Organizations (COFO), was badly beaten in 1964.) All in all, the southern rabbis have played, according to Krause, a fairly respectable role, but one that certainly could be much improved upon. It is perhaps unrealistic to have expected Southern Jews to be among the foremost activists.

The southern rabbi has been open to sharp criticism by his northern counterparts for not being in the vanguard of the civil rights activists. Some from the North made weekend trips to join the civil rights campaigns in Selma, Montgomery, and St. Augustine, Florida, and felt free to criticize the tepidness of their colleagues in the South. But as the problems of race relations moved north, many Rabbis along with their congregants and others in the liberal community, found themselves in positions where they have backed away from ethical challenges. We in the North have learned that it is not so easy to be courageous on our own home grounds.

It is indeed ironic that in the 1960s "law and order" rapidly gained acceptance as our national credo, and yet the constitutional rights of black Americans are still flagrantly violated on a continuing basis. The decision of the United States Supreme Court in *Brown v. Topeka Board of Education* notwithstanding, segregation in the public schools is commonplace. Integration in the South has been circumvented by a variety of "legal" maneuvers. In the North de facto segregation is perpetuated in the name of the sacrosanct

[8] Ibid., pp. 40–41.

neighborhood school concept. Resistance to change in the field of public education—at first opposition to busing and other plans devised to promote racial mixing in the schools, and, more recently, opposition to "community control" in the black ghettos—has contributed to the growth of Jewish-Negro tensions.

In February 1966 an emotion-charged incident dramatized the problem. It happened in Westchester County's Mount Vernon, a suburb of New York City. It occurred at the time when the attention of civil rights advocates was focusing more and more on racially based housing and educational patterns in the North. A new theater of operations had been opened in the war over integration. Mount Vernon was but one battlefield in that war.

By 1966 the dispute over racial imbalance in Mount Vernon's schools had generated much bitterness. James E. Allen, Jr., then New York State Commissioner of Education, had ordered the town to develop an acceptable integration plan by March 15. At a meeting of the local board of education held to discuss the school crisis, Clifford A. Brown, a thirty-two-year-old CORE official and a probation officer, heatedly remarked to the audience which included a number of Jews: "Hitler made a mistake when he didn't kill enough of you."[9] The Jewish president of the Mount Vernon Parents and Taxpayers, a foe of Brown's on the volatile school issue, was one of those toward whom the comment was directed. A substantial number of the estimated twelve to fifteen thousand members of the Jewish community were reported to have been opposed to or indifferent to Negro aspirations for integration.

Brown's outburst elicited a series of protests from both groups and individuals, black and white. One hundred and ninety-five well-known blacks in Mount Vernon went on record as condemning "any inflammatory, irresponsible or reckless statement which tends to divide this community along racial or religious lines." Although Brown was not mentioned by name, racism and bigotry were strongly denounced. The group promised to strive for an improved Mount Vernon "in cooperation with all racial and reli-

---

[9] *Daily Argus* (Mount Vernon), 4 February 1966. The population of Mount Vernon is approximately 45 percent Italian, 30 percent Negro, and 15 percent Jewish. The Jewish population has been declining since the end of World War II.

gious groups in the spirit of brotherhood."[10] Not unexpectedly, spokesmen for Jewish organizations in Westchester—the Anti-Defamation League of B'nai B'rith, the American Jewish Committee, and the American Jewish Congress—criticized what they called the "descent to gutter anti-Semitism."[11]

CORE also found the Brown obscenity "intolerable." James Farmer, long an eloquent champion of human rights and then National Director of CORE, unequivocally disavowed the slur and ordered an investigation which would concern itself with the context of Brown's statement.

Will Maslow, Executive Director of the American Jewish Congress, was not satisfied with CORE's reaction. He found it "tepid and ambiguous" and evidence of a flabby moral fiber.[12] Maslow promptly resigned from the national board of CORE. In a letter of resignation addressed to Farmer, he expressed his inability to understand why Brown had not been suspended immediately. Moreover, he asked directly: "Can you conceive of any context that would make Mr. Brown's outrageous statement permissible? Can you conceive of any situation that would justify the kind of tirade that calls for more acts of genocide?"[13]

Shortly thereafter, Farmer issued an even stronger denunciation. Noting that the objectionable comment had been uttered in a heated atmosphere against a background of the "intolerable delaying tactics" of the school board, he stated nevertheless, "there is no room in CORE for racism or bigotry."[14] In his opinion, there was no possible justification for such a comment. At the urging of David Livingston, a Jewish labor leader who was one of thirty-eight members of CORE's national advisory committee, a meeting of that body was quickly called. Livingston's stated purpose was

[10] Ibid., 9 February 1966.
[11] Ibid., 8 February 1966.
[12] *New York Times,* 9 February 1966.
[13] The letter has been reproduced in the *Congress Bi-Weekly,* 21 February 1966. The wisdom of Maslow's resignation at a time when Jewish-Negro unity was critically needed has been doubted by some in the Jewish social action agencies. Their feeling was that Maslow's action while understandable, may have psychologically widened the gap between the two communities at precisely the wrong time.
[14] *New York Times,* 10 February 1966.

to eliminate "all taint of anti-Semitism within CORE." He said bluntly: "There can be no compromise with ovens for Jews."[15]

Clearly, the situation was a fluid one. On February 8, Brown resigned. An attempt a few months later to elect him an officer precipitated the expulsion of the entire Mount Vernon chapter. In the wake of the February incident, CORE had been inundated with protest mail and had found it necessary to devote countless hours to repudiating bigotry.[16] Financial contributions had declined sharply despite the repudiation. Lincoln Lynch, then Associate National Director, was quoted in the *New York Times* as saying that whites were responsible for about three-fourths of CORE's financial support "and you could say that Jewish contributions have been predominant."[17] While CORE's assault on the government's Vietnam policy may have alienated some contributors, the publicity given to Brown's horrifying utterance and what some felt was CORE's mishandling of the matter were probably the critical factors. It can also be assumed that some liberal sensitivities were also bruised by civil rights agitation in their own northern bailiwick.[18]

In July 1966 the Mount Vernon episode was referred to in an article published by the *Liberator*. The author, Louise R. Moore, argued that American blacks ought to follow the pattern set by the Mau Mau in dealing ruthlessly with blacks who conceived of themselves as white. Negro traitors had to be liquidated. She charged that more than six black leaders had been bought off by white money in the preceding six years and "there are plenty more for sale." In that connection she cited a "blatant example" in Westchester. "The Jewish leaders of National CORE forced the resignation of Mr. Brown and the dissolution of the Mount Vernon chapter."[19]

Actually Brown had apologized for his remark which was made, he said, "at an emotional moment." In fact, he had done so during the same February 1966 meeting at which the outburst oc-

[15] Ibid.
[16] Ibid., 28 May 1966.
[17] Ibid., 25 July 1966.
[18] Ibid.
[19] Louise R. Moore, "When A Black Man Stood Up," *Liberator*, July 1966, p. 7.

curred.[20] Some weeks afterward at a two-day conference held at
Vassar to examine the community tensions which had been brought
to a head by the remark, Brown's justification was that he desper-
ately wanted to dramatize the black case and to "shake up" the
white man. However, in a letter to the editor of the *Liberator* in
February 1967, Brown admitted that a year earlier, "I had not
yet reconciled in my own mind whether I meant that remark or
whether it was an impulsive reaction to the degrading things we
were being called by the whites in attendance."[21] He subsequently
decided that he was wholeheartedly opposed to genocide. In the
interim he also reached other conclusions about the Jew. He rejected the idea that the Jew had been the Negro's best friend. He
accepted the idea that the Jew's "financial generosity has had dia-
bolical strings attached." In addition, he became convinced that
the "Jew's notorious reputation for exploitation of minorities is
now well established."

Allegedly, Brown's comment had provided some paternalistic
Jews with the pretext for ending their support of CORE. In the
same *Liberator* letter, he characterized the Jew as "a peculiar
breed" who "will contribute money to a civil rights group with
one hand, and with the other . . . will sign his name to a petition
to keep Black people out of his neighborhood." Jewish social action
agencies, e.g., B'nai B'rith and the American Jewish Congress,
were called "hypocrites." "What steps have they taken to expose
and crack down on their own brothers who make fortunes out of
our misery and off our backs? I accuse them of doing nothing.
Nothing at all!"

Brown's experience had also revealed who the "Uncle Toms"

---

[20] *Daily Argus,* 4 February 1966.

[21] In February 1966 James Farmer observed that Brown's reference to
Hitler was "voiced out of emotional disturbances." After a Negro woman
had begun to speak at the meeting, whites in the crowd, Farmer alleged,
cried out "tell the black son of a bitch to sit down." According to the
Times, reporters present had not heard any such remark. See *New York
Times,* 10 February 1966. However, David Rogers speaks of a Jewish
leader present at the meeting who recalled afterwards that a number of
anti-Negro slurs preceded Brown's outburst. According to this unidentified
individual Negroes were characterized as persons who did not value education, who were incapable of learning and were uncivilized. David
Rogers, *110 Livingston Street,* pp. 161–162. According to the *Daily Argus*
of 4 February 1966, someone in the audience yelled to Brown, "you're a

were. They were readily identifiable by their defense of "whitey." Supposedly that defense was motivated by a fear that the "master" would be angered and would discontinue his financial support.[22]

Martin Luther King's name was *not* specifically mentioned, but undoubtedly he would have qualified for Brown's wrath. Shortly after the incident in Mount Vernon Dr. King wrote a column entitled "The Black Man and His Jewish Brother" in which he recorded his sadness upon reading about an anti-Semitic remark by "one of the leaders of a fine and militant civil rights group." Significantly, he interpreted the outburst as anti-man and anti-God rather than anti-Jewish. Coming from a black man's lips, he found the statement "singularly despicable" because "black people, who have torturously burned in the crucible of hatred for centuries, should have become so purified of hate in those scorching flames as to be instinctively intolerant of intolerance."[23]

In terms of race relations what transpired in Mount Vernon in 1966 was both an echo of the past and a harbinger of future crises. An appreciable number of Jews—exactly how many or precisely what percentage of the total Jewish population is not known—had functioned as white Americans in dealing with black Americans. Either because they felt sincerely but probably without any justification that their children's education would suffer from integrating Mount Vernon's schools or simply because of race prejudice, many Jews behaved in a way considered detrimental to the best educational interests of the black community. Charles Silberman, author of *Crisis in Black and White* who resides in Mount Vernon, is reported to have said of the fracas that it "stripped the veneer of liberalism from the Jewish community."[24] As has usually been the case historically, the reaction of most Jews to the black man's drive for equality and integration was not meaningfully different from that of other ethnic minorities. There is no evidence that the Italian-American community in Mount Vernon was any more sym-

---

racist," but this was reported to have happened after the Hitler remark. Brown's rejoinder was allegedly: "I'm a racist and proud of it. I hate all whites."

22 *Liberator,* February 1967, p. 22.
23 *Afro-American,* 3 March 1966.
24 Quoted in James Yaffe, *The American Jews: Portrait of a Split Personality* (New York: Random House, 1968), p. 26.

pathetic to integration. Indeed, Jews were numbered among the leading proponents of integration in that community.

Black attitudes toward their Jewish neighbors were divided. Clearly, Brown's anti-Semitic sentiments were not typical.[25] They were disavowed repeatedly. But once again it is difficult to calculate the extent to which black rage generated by the opposition to school integration was translated into generalized distaste for Jews.

Unhappily, subsequent conflicts over public education have also aggravated ethnic tensions. On 30 November 1967 Cecil B. Moore exploded during a court hearing in Philadelphia. Under discussion was a suit instituted by the school board seeking an injunction to restrain black power demonstrations at Philadelphia's public schools. Moore, who was representing leaders of Philadelphia CORE and the Black People's Unity Movement, loudly told the special counsel for the Board of Education: "You're playing footsie with racist bigots! You and the rest of the Jews get out of my business." As the special counsel tried in vain to reply Moore shouted: "I said, Jew, get out of my business."[26]

1966 and 1967, years in which the civil rights movement with its legalist emphasis was competing with the power-oriented black revolution, were marked by other disturbing examples of Negro-Jewish disharmony. Less dramatic than the school confrontations was a three-part series, entitled "Semitism in the Black Ghetto," written by Eddie Ellis. The series appeared in the *Liberator* whose editor-in-chief is Dan Watts, an intelligent and articulate black nationalist who was formerly an architect.

The first installment appeared in January 1966, and attempted to explain the manifold sources of the "intense anti-semitism [*sic*]

---

[25] Brown was quoted almost verbatim in January 1968 at a meeting of the Port Chester, New York, Anti-Poverty Association by a black power advocate who said: "Hitler was stopped too soon, he was only allowed to kill six and a half million Jews." See *Westmore News,* 8 February 1968. And in September 1967 members of Brooklyn CORE entered PS 9 and confronted the school's administrators. Among the remarks made on that occasion were, "the Germans did not do a good enough job with you Jews." This statement was quoted in a preliminary report of the Anti-Defamation League, *Anti-Semitism in the New York City School Controversy* (New York: 1969).

[26] *New York Times,* 10 December 1967.

feeling" in the black ghetto. Ellis inveighed against the ghetto butcher, the corner grocer, the absentee landlord, and the agent of the collection or credit agency. "In most cases these 'cats' are Jewish." He went on to say that the segment of the Jewish population which is responsible for the inferior meat, the contaminated food, and the dilapidated buildings had become affluent through their exploitation of Negroes over many decades.

Moreover, Ellis was galled by the killing of an "unarmed" Negro by a policeman of the Jewish faith. Worse still in his view, the Shomrin Society, a fraternal order of Jewish policemen in New York City, honored both a civilian who aided the policeman and the judge who presided when the grand jury cleared the officer of any wrongdoing. Ellis wrote: "It's not difficult to determine who is a friend and who is a foe when events like this take place."[27] The facts of this individual case, like so many of its kind, are unclear, but there are obviously cases in ghetto areas where police have killed unarmed Negroes with impunity.

In subsequent articles Ellis went far beyond the distressing ghetto frictions. He assailed what he described as Jewish domination of Negro educational institutions and civil rights organizations. Just two years after emancipation he alleged, white liberal money, often Jewish money, was channeled southward to support Negro schools. "Freak factories," Ellis called them, "because they produced freak Black men with white minds." Negro students were taught to be humble and dependent upon the white man, and to meekly accept their own inferiority.[28]

Preeminent among the philanthropic foundations which supposedly subjected black institutions to "Zionism" was the Julius Rosenwald Fund. Ellis deplored the early support given the NAACP and the Urban League by Rosenwald. The foundation's substantial contributions to Howard University Ellis branded "white chauvinism" because the university "was run by a series of white presidents up until 1926." Although it subsidized promising black scientists, writers and artists, Ellis said the fund "was hostile to any Negro who showed independence in his thinking with regard

[27] Eddie Ellis, "Semitism in the Black Ghetto," *Liberator,* January 1966, p. 6.
[28] Ibid., April 1966, p. 14.

to racial or economic problems."[29] No evidence for the charge was adduced by Ellis. Furthermore, he accused the foundation of discouraging other philanthropies from supporting Atlanta University where W. E. B. Du Bois was then conducting sociological research on the Negro. No evidence for the charge was cited by Ellis. The truth is that the Rosenwald Fund in 1931 gave Du Bois a grant to commence work on his classic *Black Reconstruction*.[30]

Rosenwald's benefactions have not been ignored by other chroniclers of the Negro experience. John Hope Franklin, the distinguished Negro historian, has pointed out that "between 1913 and 1932 the Fund aided in the construction of more than 5,000 school buildings in 15 Southern states. . . . When the program was completed more than 30 per cent of all the Negroes in school in the South were housed in buildings that had been constructed under the Rosenwald aid program."[31] At a time when there was a conspicuous paucity of facilities for recreation and guidance for urban blacks the Rosenwald philanthropy fostered the development of Negro YMCA's on a matching fund basis.[32] In addition, as Chandler Owen indicated in 1941, it was the first of the major foundations to appoint black men to sit on its board of directors.[33]

Rosenwald himself served on the Board of Trustees of Booker T. Washington's Tuskegee Institute. Washington's advocacy of industrial education is now viewed with contempt by militants and perhaps rightly so. But to pillory Rosenwald and by clear implication Jewish supporters of Negro education is unfair. When, in 1948, the Rosenwald Fund discontinued its operations, eulogies appeared in a variety of black publications. A letter to the editor of the *Pittsburgh Courier* even asserted: "One Jew did more for

[29] Ibid., p. 15. Eric Williams received a Rosenwald fellowship in 1940 to study social and economic conditions in the West Indies. Williams, of course, was anything but an "establishment" historian.
[30] Herbert Aptheker, "Du Bois As Historian," *Negro History Bulletin*, April 1969, p. 16. Aptheker is Du Bois' literary executor.
[31] John Hope Franklin, *From Slavery to Freedom: A History of Negro Americans* (New York: Alfred A. Knopf, 1967), pp. 547–548.
[32] August Meier, *Negro Thought In America, 1880–1915: Racial Ideologies in the Age of Booker T. Washington* (Ann Arbor: University of Michigan Press, 1966), p. 133.
[33] *Chicago Defender,* 8 November 1941.

colored people than all the rest of white America put together. His name is Julius Rosenwald."[34]

Other reckless statements of Ellis' should be mentioned. Jewish wealth was so omnipotent, he contended, that it could "destroy any Black man who voiced dissent towards the practices of the established order."[35] Thus, the Rosenwald-funded NAACP coopted Du Bois and gave him a "powerless" position as editor of its organ, *The Crisis*. Far from being "powerless," Du Bois exercised a good deal of independence in that capacity. Indeed, *The Crisis* was seen as "Du Bois Domain" and, according to one biographer, Du Bois conceded that the editorship of *The Crisis* was "the only work" in the NAACP that was of real interest to him.[36]

Having "absorbed" Du Bois "the Jewish money behind the N.A.A.C.P" used him "to silence any other critics of their policies." In this way Ellis explained Du Bois' opposition to Garvey's particular version of black nationalism. "The old divide and conquer game; play one 'nigger' off against another, and we didn't even 'dig it' . . . then." Needless to say, no substantiating evidence was produced by Ellis. That the brilliant and perceptive Dr. Du Bois could have been so manipulated is highly unlikely.

Jewish funding also supposedly explained Jewish "control" of most civil rights organizations in the sixties. Of these the NAACP and the Urban League received the brunt of Ellis' criticism. On the other hand, SNCC, a grass roots organization, has tried to "cleanse itself of this diseased Zionist influence."[37] Knowingly or unknowingly, Ellis used the terms "Jew" and "Zionist" as synonyms. As previously noted, that habit is not uncommon in certain black nationalist quarters.

Ellis' articles evoked the predictable condemnation from Jewish agencies. More importantly, their publication prompted James Baldwin and Ossie Davis to dissociate themselves from the *Liberator*. Both men later explained their rationale in *Freedomways*, a New York black quarterly. Baldwin writing from Istanbul thought

---

[34] *Pittsburgh Courier*, 27 March 1948.
[35] *Liberator*, April 1966, p. 15.
[36] Elliot Rudwick, *W. E. B. Du Bois: Propagandist of the Negro Protest* (New York: Atheneum, 1968), p. 151.
[37] *Liberator*, April 1966, p. 16.

it distinctly immoral and unhelpful to blame Harlem on the Jew. "For a man of Editor Dan Watts' experience, it is incredibly naive." Obviously with anti-Semitism in mind, Baldwin said he believed it was a disservice to Negroes to "take refuge in the most ancient and barbaric of the European myths."[38]

Ossie Davis' letter in *Freedomways* exploding the myth that black nationalism and anti-Semitism are inseparable was especially incisive. Davis is an accomplished actor and playwright. His credentials as an activist in the struggle for racial justice are equally impressive. A self-styled black nationalist, Davis delivered a poignant eulogy at the funeral of Malcolm X.

In Davis' estimation Ellis had exceeded the bounds of black nationalism. He believed the *Liberator* article to be racist in nature. "I still respect Dan Watts. But 'Semitism in the Black Ghetto' blows it for me, but good and but definitely. This is where I get off!" Davis was upset about Ellis' "wild and unsupported contentions." He was especially caustic in dealing with Ellis' claim that Jewish philanthropic and civil rights activities were part of a Zionist scheme to cast Negroes rather than themselves in the familiar role of scapegoat. "Mr. Ellis doesn't even offer us a 'Protocols of Zion,' . . . who in his right mind can argue that what was done and is being done by Jews in particular, whether good or bad, is part of a gigantic plot to dupe and take advantage of Negroes, a deliberate agreed-upon 'Zionist' 'Jewish Community,' 'Semitic' plot against Negroes?"[39]

Davis then addressed himself to those blacks who have emulated white racists in the practice of stereotyping. Exploitation in Harlem is a fact. "But," Davis asked rhetorically, "are Jews the only ones who profit from this exploitation?" "No" was his categorical answer. He doubted seriously that Jews profited more than other ethnic groups. Continuing his analysis of the ghetto scene he wrote: "Whatever Jews are guilty of exploiting Harlem, are not guilty because they are Jews, but because—along with many Catholics, Protestants, and Negro and white—they are exploiters. In a

[38] *Freedomways* 7, no. 1 (Winter 1967): 77. Kenneth Clark, according to a *Time* story on the *Liberator* stated that the magazine's only importance was that it demonstrated that "Negroes are no more immune to racial hatred and anti-Semitism than are whites." See *Time,* 17 March 1967.
[39] *Freedomways* 7, no. 1 (Winter 1967):77–78.

war against all exploiters whomsoever, I am an ally. But Mr. Ellis seems to be calling for a war against Jews. If that is the case, I am an enemy."[40] Black nationalism, Davis saw as legitimate and honorable, analogous to Irish nationalism or Zionism. But black racism he found abhorrent. The difference was fundamental. Regrettably, Davis' letter did not enjoy the currency it deserved.

Because anti-Semitism is sometimes found in the ranks of black nationalists, some Jews no less given to generalization than anti-Semites themselves, reject black nationalism in toto. Just as unfortunate is the fact that some Jews have imputed Ellis' thinking not merely to all militants but to practically the entire black community.

Not so, Harry Fleischman, race-relations coordinator for the American Jewish Committee, remarked. He hailed the Davis and Baldwin letters as "welcome evidence of militant Negro intellectuals who are fighting valiantly against anti-Semitism not only of the Klan, but also of some Negroes."[41] Dan Watts' response was completely different. He attributed the resignations of Davis and Baldwin as contributing editors to "economic pressure by Jews." Watts reiterated the charge that the principal exploiters in the black-inhabited inner city were Jewish landlords and storekeepers. He declared that he had hoped the Ellis articles would promote dialogue between black and Jewish community leaders. As reported in the *New York Times,* Watts accused B'nai B'rith and the American Jewish Committee of practicing "McCarthyism" by trying to depress the *Liberator'*s circulation which he estimated to be some twenty thousand as of 1965.[42]

Readers of the *Liberator* were clearly split in their reaction to the Ellis series. One letter to the editor began "Shame on you! Shame on your thinking!" Another found it curious in view of the "way Christians have (and still do) treated negroes [*sic*]" that

40 Ibid., p. 78.
41 *New York Times,* 28 February 1967.
42 Ibid. Three years after the Ellis articles were first published, Watts in an editorial, "Censorship Liberal Style," reviled the "house niggers" Davis and Baldwin. Career advancement had been their reward for performing a "hatchet job." Watts contended that reprisals had been taken against militants who refused to knuckle under. Newsstands and distributors were pressured into returning the *Liberator,* February 1969, p. 3.

Negroes are not anti-Christian instead of anti-Jewish. The writer "T.G." (his race is not indicated) asked: "Do you really believe Harlem would be any different if Christians owned more stores and apartment buildings?" On the other hand, a letter from Philadelphia implied that Davis and Baldwin were not free to express their true feelings because of their reliance upon Jews for food, clothing, and shelter. The ubiquitous Clifford Brown was also concerned about black leaders being "siphoned off by the dollar." He reviled Davis and Baldwin as the "re-incarnation of Booker T. Washington's attitudes of compromise and accomodation [sic]."[43]

Brown's caustic views had not been conceived in a vacuum, however, and in some ways were both symptomatic and reflective of the societal cleavages of our time. The frustrations engendered by the sluggish response of white America to the civil rights movement came to the surface in the mid-1960s. As Lew Smith, an organizer for Operation Bootstrap in Los Angeles, succinctly put it: "How would you like to have Congress debate for the last ten years how much of a man I'm going to be?" The compilers of the Kerner Report documented what blacks had already known, that racism permeated the entire fabric of American society. The nation's schools, including many of the finest universities in the land, were no exception. Institutionalized racism reflective of society as a whole was evident in the admissions policies, curricula, faculty and administrative hiring practices, and in the general relationship to the outside community of most centers of higher education. The escalation of the war in Vietnam and the general dissatisfaction of many youths with the values symbolized by the faceless, bureaucratized multiversity added to the growth of the new campus radical movement. Racism in America became linked in the minds of some of America's most gifted young people, white and black alike, with the policies of imperialism on the international sphere. The murder of Martin Luther King, Jr., long the foremost advocate for nonviolent socio-political change, was the final straw so far as some Afro-Americans were concerned. With the rising tide of black impatience, with the growth of Afro-American consciousness and identity, with spontaneous ghetto rioting threatening to develop into

[43] All of the letters can be found in the *Liberator*, April 1967, pp. 21–22.

insurrection, and with demands being put forth centering on recruitment and admission policies and black studies programs, America's educational establishments belatedly began to respond to the grievances of the black community.

The movement for change came to New York University, as well as to the other universities in the New York metropolitan area. NYU's past traditions were relatively conservative, due in part ironically to the fact that its percentage of Jewish students and faculty was not as great as those in some of the city colleges. Through the years, NYU had not attracted large numbers of Jewish students of proletarian and socialist backgrounds as had a tuition-free school like the City College of New York. Its percentage of students from nonwhite minority groups was also relatively low. But particularly after King's death, NYU, like many other universities, pledged to recruit and educate a substantially increased number of black students.

This led to the series of events at NYU in 1968 that came to be known as the "Hatchett affair." These events placed in bold relief the tensions in contemporary urban America between blacks and whites in general and blacks and Jews in particular. The Martin Luther King, Jr., Afro-American Student Center was established at NYU at the request of black students. The purpose of the Center was to provide a place where they could receive counseling on nonacademic matters, meet informally, and hold cultural and social events. While the facilities were primarily for the black students, the Center's activities would also relate to and enrich general student life and learning at the University. To serve as director of the Center, NYU appointed Mr. John F. Hatchett who had been recommended for the position by a black student group. A resident of the Washington Square area, the thirty-seven year-old appointee had been educational assistant at the Washington Square Methodist Church. A graduate of Wayne State University with a theological degree from Boston University, he had later taught at several southern Negro colleges and was at the time of his appointment a Ph.D. candidate at Columbia University. From 1966 to early 1968 Hatchett had served as a substitute teacher in the New York public school system. In February 1968 he was dismissed by the New York City Board of Education for taking his pupils, without the permission of the school principal (but reportedly with the parents' permission) to a memorial service for Malcolm X. According to University officials, Hatchett was selected on "the strength of his personal recommendations, the quality of his writing on Afro-American culture and on religion, and his evident personal integrity and seriousness of character."[44]

Ostensibly, NYU officials who hired Hatchett were not aware of a controversial article published that past winter which had been criticized in a statement issued jointly by the American Jewish Congress, the Protestant Council of the City of New York, and the Catholic Interracial Council. The article which had appeared in the Afro-American Teachers Association Forum dealt with the New York School desegregation controversy.[45] Part of the piece was a critique of two teachers—one Jewish and one black, who taught along with Hatchett in Public School 68 of the Intermediate School 201 complex, one of the city's three experimental districts in the school decentralization project. Entitled "The Phenomenon of the Anti-Black Jews and the Black Anglo-Saxon: A Study in Educational Perfidy," the article attacked the aforementioned two teachers for their criticisms of the Intermediate School 201 project at a United Federation of Teachers meeting. The piece began:

We are witnessing today in New York City a phenomenon that spells death for the minds and souls of our Black children. It is the systematic coming of age of the Jews who dominate and control the educational bureaucracy of the New York Public School system and their power-starved imitators, the Black Anglo-Saxon. It is the avowed thesis of this paper that this coalition or collusion or whatever one chooses to call it, is one of the fundamental reasons why our black children are being educationally castrated. . . . In short our children are being mentally poisoned by a group of educators who are actively and persistently bringing a certain self-fulfilling prophesy to its logical conclusion.[46]

Anticipating the charge of anti-Semitism which might be levied against him, Hatchett continued: "The reader may ask why I have

---

[44] Internal, About NYU: For Faculty and Administration 3:35 (13 August 1968): 2.

[45] Afro-American Teachers Forum 2 (November–December 1967):2.

[46] Ibid., p. 1. Hatchett's percentage of New York public school teachers who are Jewish was somewhat inflated, as was his figure that 90–95 percent of assistant principals and principals of the schools were Jews.

singled out Jews? It is not a matter of singling out; it is a statistical fact (even though the Board of Education refuses to release the data), that Jewish teachers comprise between 80–85% of the teaching staff of this system. . . . In educational or political language this degree of representation inevitably means control."

Not surprisingly the Hatchett article drew a sharp response from Jewish organizations in New York.[47] Upon learning of Hatchett's selection, the American Jewish Congress wrote to Chancellor Cartter of NYU criticizing the appointment and requesting that it be rescinded. On behalf of the Congress, David Haber, pointed out that Hatchett's article embraced a "racist interpretation" of the New York school problem. "It is one thing," he wrote, "to criticize the faults of our public school system. It is quite another to attribute these faults to a Jewish conspiracy. There is no room for racists in the struggle against racism. Those who would participate in the struggle for equality must recognize that they will accomplish nothing toward their goal if they tolerate anti-Semitism, publicly proclaimed or privately whispered."[48]

In response to criticisms of its judgment, NYU officials declared that they had no knowledge of the controversial article prior to Hatchett's appointment. Concerned with adverse Jewish reaction,

[47] Well mobilized to combat the phenomenon of anti-Semitism in America such organizations as the Anti-Defamation League, the American Jewish Committee and the American Jewish Congress have substantial financial resources at their disposal, experienced staff members and close contact with political and labor organizations and the information media. These organizations are in a position, particularly in the New York metropolitan area, to mobilize a good deal of pressure on matters which interest them —comparable Negro organizations are quite frankly not as successful in similar endeavors. And it is only natural, when the threat is against Jewish interests, that the Jewish organizations react strongly. Interestingly enough, for several years the Jewish groups by and large did not play up incidents involving derogatory remarks by Negroes about Jews, and actually ignored some anti-Semitic public remarks in the interest of not provoking greater intergroup hostility. By 1968, however, the officials of Jewish organizations were feeling considerable pressures from their members. In an atmosphere heated by the recriminations of school controversy, several Jewish agencies for several months changed their tactics and drew attention to many utterances by blacks about Jews.

[48] Quoted by Lois Waldman in "What Price Peace at NYU?" *Congress Bi-Weekly* 35, no. 10 (16 September 1968):3. The American Jewish Committee Institute of Human Relations in the 13 August 1968 newsletter to its New York members noted that Jewish contributors had responded

NYU officials met with the groups, including the Protestant and Catholic organizations which had originally condemned the article. The Jewish agencies pointed out that as director of the Afro-American Center, Hatchett would have "substantial opportunities for communicating his distorted racial and religious attitudes to impressionable black students." For NYU to appoint a man with racist anti-Semitic views to an important post gave legitimacy, respectability, and acceptability to those views.[49]

The University representatives countered by saying that, had they known about the article in question, Hatchett would not have been appointed. However, Hatchett had been selected by black students and had been approved by a group of black faculty members. To remove him would pose a threat of campus disruption and possible violence both to NYU and to the Jewish community in New York. It was suggested that the involved Jewish organizations had the responsibility to help assuage the public criticism which they had initiated and thus help NYU out of a delicate situation. Representatives of the non-Jewish religious councils present then suggested that Hatchett be contacted for a clarifying statement of his position.[50]

Hatchett had written in his by now celebrated article that it was impossible by definition for a black man in America to be a racist, since "racism connotes power and Black people in white America are clearly powerless."[51] The gist of his rebuttal to charges against him was simply: "I am not an anti-Semite. The thrust of the article was not aimed at Jews just because they were Jews. The tone of the article was anti-Establishment. That is, it was against those in a position to change the system."[52]

heavily to the fund-raising drive for the NYU Center, and said "sullied is the memory of Martin Luther King, Jr., whose name the center bears." Edward Moldover, then urban affairs chairman of the American Jewish Committee's New York chapter, in a telegram to the NYU chancellor wrote: "Whatever his credentials, a man who in his public statements appeals to racial and religious hatreds sullies these credentials and, in turn, the institution with which he is formally associated." *New York Times*, 26 July 1968.

49 *Congress Bi-Weekly*, 16 September 1968, p. 4.

50 Ibid.

51 "The Phenomenon of the Anti-Black Jews and the Black Anglo-Saxon," *Afro-American Teachers Forum* 2 (November–December 1967):3.

52 *New York Times*, 25 August 1968.

The American Jewish Congress was not satisfied, however, and maintained that Hatchett had not backed down on the views expressed in the article. Referring to a recent interview of Hatchett in the *Village Voice,* a Congress spokesman declared that Hatchett had reaffirmed the substance of his anti-Jewish characterizations while denying that he was anti-Semitic.

At that juncture NYU sought the good offices of Arthur Goldberg, former Supreme Court justice and erstwhile United Nations ambassador. Shortly thereafter NYU announced that it was retaining John Hatchett on the basis of a plan put forward by Goldberg and Federal Judge Constance B. Motley. In a letter to President Hester of NYU, Goldberg stated: "The references in Hatchett's article to Jewish teachers and administrators are completely unfounded and cannot be condoned. As a result of my frank and candid talk with Mr. Hatchett, I believe he now understands the injustices and dangers inherent in the kind of criticism he voiced in the article."[53]

Using Goldberg's statement to support his position, President Hester announced on August 9 that NYU would retain Hatchett. Hester submitted that if Hatchett was an anti-Semite "in the classic sense, we could not keep him in the position." But, he continued, "I do not believe he is prejudiced against Jews as an ethnic group. . . . His article is meant to be critical of the Establishment, what he considers to be the Establishment in the public schools, and I think it is true that there is a preponderance of Jewish teachers and administrators. . . . I can understand how someone might make references [to the Jewish Teachers Organization] and at the same time not be anti-Semitic." Hester reproached those groups which had labeled the Hatchett article "black Nazism!" They could not see, said Hester, that Hatchett had not attacked Jews as Jews. He went on to describe Hatchett as a moral man who would like to work for racial justice and harmony. The Martin Luther King Center itself would "establish a place in the university for dialogue about the black experience, which includes the very serious criticisms of many black intellectuals of conditions in our society.[54]

[53] *Congress Bi-Weekly,* 16 September 1968. Mr. Goldberg later was elected president of the American Jewish Committee.
[54] *New York Times,* 25 August 1968.

The position taken by the NYU administration was in accord with that recommended by fifteen of the sixteen representatives of NYU's major student organizations. The student leaders, some of whom were Jewish, urged that Hatchett be retained in the post "to forestall a destructive breakdown" in relations between Jewish and black students on campus. NYU's black students were also virtually unanimous in their support of Hatchett's retention, and criticized the way in which the public media had treated the NYU situation.[55]

The New York Civil Liberties Union also voiced its support for the retention of Hatchett on the grounds that "a man's right to employment must be based on his professional performance and not on his private thoughts, words, beliefs, or associations.[56] This reasoning was contested by NYU philosophy professor, Sidney Hook, among others, who argued that the NYCLU position "overlooks the key fact that a man's beliefs may be highly relevant to his professional tasks." The nature of Hatchett's position at NYU required a person "whose qualifications include absence of racial bias and prejudice."[57] Obviously, the civil liberties aspect of the case were complex and arguments could be mustered on both sides.

The defense of the Hatchett appointment by President Hester

[55] In a letter to the *New York Times* (7 August 1968) Leonard H. Burg, vice-president of the Black Allied Student Association bitterly wrote: "When news of the appointment was released to the press they did a good job of ignoring the vast potential of such a unique experiment on a large urban campus and sensationally overemphasized Hatchett's article. . . . Any normally intelligent person, devoid of paranoia and oversensitivity who has objectively read the article would know, as Hatchett has stated, that he is not in the least bit anti-Semitic."

[56] The NYCLU statement which was not overly enthusiastic in its support of Hatchett read in part: "Without getting into the merits of the particular article by Mr. Hatchett, let us make it clear that we yield to no one in our abhorrence of anti-Semitism. Nevertheless, we call upon NYU to keep paramount the well-established principle of academic freedom that university employees should be appointed solely on the basis of ability and competence in their professional fields. . . . We have defended the rights of a policeman to belong to the John Birch Society and of a welfare worker to belong to the Ku Klux Klan. In each instance, we have done so because we believe that a man's right to employment must be based on his professional performance and not on his private thoughts, words, beliefs or associations." Press release, 26 July 1968.

[57] Hook argued that the NYCLU had confused two things: a citizen's legal right to express racialist ideas which flow from his civil right to hold

brought a renewed rush of criticism by Jewish organizations. For example, the Union of American Hebrew Congregations denounced the remarks as a "tortured and outraged effort to deodorize the noxious anti-Semitism of Hatchett's article." Hester stood accused by the Synagogue Council of America, and other groups, for having made an "unpardonably imprudent and insensitive" defense of a "scurrilous anti-Semitic article."[58] (The criticisms, it might be noted, were not extended, at least publicly against the highly-respected Arthur Goldberg who in a mediatory role had recommended that Hatchett be retained in his post.) Jewish opinion resented the fact that a man who had made anti-Semitic remarks was being protected from public censure.[59] A few days later Hester stated: "I regret that my comments on the language used by Mr. Hatchett have been misinterpreted as a defense of his article." He now recognized "the oversimplification in my references to the complex phenomenon of anti-Semitism."

The affair had by this time taken on the aura of a comic opera, and would have had its humorous side had the consequences for race relations not been so serious. Just as the furor over the appointment had about died down, another incident occurred which quickly led to Hatchett's dismissal. On October 8, speaking before seven hundred students at NYU's Bronx campus, Hatchett put UFT president, Albert Shanker, as well as Hubert Humphrey and Richard Nixon, in the same bag by saying that "all have something in common—they are racist bastards." This was too much for the

---

foolish and dangerous beliefs, and the right to hold a specific job whose qualifications include absence of racial bias and prejudice. Letter to editor of the *New York Times,* 27 July 1968.

[58] *New York Times,* 4 September 1968.

[59] This point of view was later articulated in an article by Marie Syrkin who wrote that President Hester should be able to recognize the phenomenon of anti-Semitism in Hatchett's opus. "In Poland, Czeckoslovakia or Soviet Russia anti-Semitic functionaries attack their scapegoats as 'Zionists'—it used to be 'rootless cosmopolitans.' Everyone knows what is meant. . . . Mr. Hatchett did not bother with such subterfuges."

The Syrkin article concluded with a warning that anti-Semitism "is latent and endemic, and can become epidemic whenever social tensions seek an easy focus for their discharge. . . . to allow Negro extremists, without meaningful opposition, to utilize this familiar technique because Negroes, in a paradoxical sense, have become untouchables, is a dangerous development, boding good neither to Jews or Negroes, nor to the country as a whole." *Mainstream,* November 1968, pp. 3–9.

NYU administration, even though the remark was made in the context of an impassioned talk during the New York school strike. Not only Jewish teachers, but the whole of Establishment America, in the persons of the two presidential candidates (and by extension the NYU administration itself) were being denounced.

Condemnation of Hatchett's outburst came immediately.[60] With the full backing of the NYU University Senate, President Hester announced Hatchett's dismissal. The principle reason for the action, he said, was that Hatchett "has proved to be increasingly ineffective in performing his duties because of the incompatibility of many of his actions and public statements with the requirements of his position in the university. . . . A major objective of the center is to work towards improving relations among all religious and ethnic groups." Hatchett's performance was "impossible to reconcile with that objective."[61]

In a statement following his dismissal Hatchett declared that he was being punished because he had spoken freely and openly of some of the ills of society. Student protests broke out immediately at the two NYU campuses, led by the Black Allied Students Association, the Students for a Democratic Society, and the Peace and Freedom Party. A boycott of classes was urged and peaceful picketing took place. Meanwhile leaders of the black students group met with university officials and expressed their dissatisfaction with the procedure taken in dismissing Hatchett without consulting them first.[62] Finally, a black ad hoc committee and the university agreed upon a compromise settlement according to which Hatchett would remain as an adviser to black students on the campus. The students had to pay for his office space and Hatchett could use his year's severance pay for salary. Two buildings on the Bronx campus

---

[60] For example, Dore Schary, president of the ADL, said that Hatchett's remarks "once again demonstrate the kind of irresponsible, intemperate, indeed inflammatory remarks Mr. Hatchett showed in earlier anti-Semitic statements and writings." New York Times, 10 October 1968. A New York Times editorial of 10 October, "Insult to Dr. King's Memory," called for Hatchett's dismissal. Similar sentiments were expressed in the other New York daily newspapers.

[61] New York Times, 11 October 1968.

[62] New York Times, 15 October 1968.

which had been briefly occupied were then vacated. The student strike continued for a few more days and then ended.

Estimates of the participation in the strike varied widely; on October 16, a spokesman for the Ad Hoc Committee of Black Student Organizations, representing the university's 2,500 black students said that 18,000–22,000 students supported the boycott while the university chancellor said that 90–95 percent of the University's 42,000 students were attending classes.

Most people appeared to be placated by the settlement reached. Some, however, remained dissatisfied with Hatchett's dismissal.[63] Afterwards the University renewed its pledge to support the Martin Luther King, Jr., Center and announced that in September 1969 the Center would be operated by an independent board of black students and faculty. The university president also acknowledged that the black student groups should have been consulted on the matter of Hatchett's dismissal.[64] One could project from the terms of the NYU settlement that program directors such as Hatchett would have to act within a certain code of civility. The established order in New York had said that there were some breaches of conduct on interracial matters which could not be tolerated.

There is a great deal of truth in the contention that nonwhites are oppressed within the prevailing educational structure, but Hatchett's loose inferences that one group, the Jew, was somehow responsible for the situation was unwarranted. Hatchett never seemed to understand the basic point his critics were making. He maintained that he was not singling out Jews *as Jews.* For instance, when asked at a talk to NYU freshmen why he spoke as if it were just Jews who were doing the persecuting, Hatchett retorted: "What just about every detractor has failed miserably to comprehend is that nowhere and at no time have I ever discussed all of anybody."[65]

---

[63] As one individual put it: Hatchett was suspended because he exposed the tactics used both in the community and at NYU to perpetuate the oppressive status quo." Ronald Banks in a letter to the Editor in *Liberator* 8, no. 10 (October 1968):22.

[64] *New York Times,* 2 November 1968.

[65] Joe Pilati, "Orienting the Frosh to the Ivory Tower," *The Village Voice,* 26 September 1968.

Hatchett's grievances as a black man in America are most understandable. As he said during a marathon "sensitivity" session between a group of blacks and Jews held in Washington, D.C.: "My ancestors were brought as animals, beasts of burden, and spawned in a country founded in violence."[66] He called for Jews, if they meant what they said, to put themselves on the line and challenge white American institutions. Later in the session he remarked that Jewish teachers were castrating Negro children. He declared that he was a black man trying to find his own identity and was "not preoccupied with white men and Jews."

During the session, Paul Jacobs, a Jewish radical, pointed to Richard Cohn of the American Jewish Congress and asked why he had not invested a dime to call Hatchett on the phone to try to learn what he meant to say in his controversial article.[67] Jacobs went on to note that those involved in the New York school dispute were very anxious to talk with the press and other media, but avoided communicating with their antagonists. The sad reality was that neither side in the Hatchett dispute was able to communicate with or understand the other.[68]

In sum, in suburb and city, in public schools and private universities, some black Americans and some Jewish Americans found themselves in tragic conflict. The Mount Vernon and Washington Square controversies and the *Liberator* series were but prologues. The worst was yet to come—the New York City teachers' strike and its legacy of fear and mistrust.

[66] The encounter sessions held over an eleven hour period were sponsored by the National Educational Association. Segments of the sessions were telecast under the appropriate heading, "Some of My Best Friends" by National Educational TV in 1969.

[67] Ibid.

[68] A spokesman for a major Jewish organization told the authors that unsuccessful efforts were made by NYU and by the church groups which tried to serve as mediators to get Mr. Hatchett to consider a modification or an explanation of the statement. Additional attempts to find an opening to cool the tensions purportedly were without avail. "This plus the repeated emphasis of the issue by the *Jewish Press* made it impossible to lower the level of hostility."

} 8 {

THE NEW YORK
SCHOOL CRISIS AND
ITS AFTERMATH

INTERRACIAL TENSIONS IN NEW YORK CITY HAVE BEEN EXACER-
bated in recent years, particularly by the issues of quality and
control of public school education. As the percentage of Negroes
and Puerto Ricans has increased in the public schools the achievement level of school children has declined. In his book, *110 Livingston Street,* David Rogers points to the growing disparity between national standards and the average New York City student's
achievement in arithmetic and reading. In recent years "reading
scores have gone down, dropout rates have gone up, community
protest has increased, and the middle class has been steadily with-
drawing its children from the public schools."[1] The longer black
students remain in school the further they fall behind their white
counterparts; those blacks who manage to graduate from high
school in New York City are, on the average, three and one-half
years behind the white graduates.

In the years following the 1954 Supreme Court decision on
school desegregation the New York City Board of Education made
plans to rezone districts, "pair" schools, and establish educational
complexes and parks. While the plans appeared progressive, they
were scarcely implemented.

[1] David Rogers, *110 Livingston Street* (New York: Random House, 1968),
pp. 5–6.

The demographic patterns in New York City have been similar to those of many other urban centers in the North. Ironically, New York schools were even more segregated in 1965 than they were a decade earlier. This was due in part to the continuing influx of Negroes and Puerto Ricans into the city and the simultaneous move of large numbers of whites to suburban areas. The withdrawal of additional middle-class children from public schools and their enrollment in private or parochial schools has added to the problem. While there is a strong racial component to this pattern, there is also the important consideration that the overall quality of many public schools has been declining. This decline has been particularly true in the nonwhite neighborhoods, as the educational gap between predominantly black and predominantly white schools increases yearly.

In 1967, whites (including in this instance Puerto Ricans) made up 60 percent of Manhattan's total population but accounted for only 28.72 percent of that borough's public school enrollment.[2] Rogers notes that on Manhattan's Upper West Side (from 66th–122d Streets) many reform Democrats who have been strong proponents of civil rights and school desegregation have given up the public schools and are sending their children to private schools. According to Rogers: "These people may not be running away from the Negro and Puerto Ricans. They are simply convinced of the inferior education in public schools."[3]

Despite its acceptance in principle by city and school officials, desegregation has not become a reality. Increases in young, low-income Negro and Puerto Rican families whose birth rates are

[2] According to Board of Education figures, the total number of schools with 90 percent or more Negroes and Puerto Ricans at the elementary school level and 85 percent at the junior high and high school level, increased from 118 in 1960 to 201 in 1966. These schools accounted for 23 percent of all public schools by 1966. Generally speaking the trend has been toward more segregation for nonwhite students. The Central Zoning Unit of the Board of Education, *Ethnic Distribution of Pupils in the Public Schools of New York City,* 24 March 1965 and 15 June 1966. Quoted in Rogers, *110 Livingston Street,* pp. 15–16.

[3] Ibid., p. 56. According to a recent study by two sociologists, "among community facilities which attract and keep residents, schools are considered the most important." See Seymour Sudman and Norman Bradburn, *Social Psychological Factors in Inter-Group Housing: Results of a Pilot Test* (National Opinion Research Center, May 1966), p. 10.

higher than those of whites, and the spreading out of the ghettos make it hard to improve the racial balance. There are also "chronic scarcities of trained and committed staff, building space and funds." Rogers observed further that the actual school construction and site selection decisions were at wide variance with the Board of Education's stated desegregation policies. Recommendations that new schools be located in the fringe areas between Negro and white areas have for the most part been neglected. The teachers' union, the United Federation of Teachers, by and large, has not been responsive to recommendations that more qualified teachers be transferred to ghetto schools.[4] The union's stance has been determined largely by the fact that the great majority of better qualified teachers prefer to teach in white schools which have more facilities, better prepared students, and fewer disciplinary problems. Only the most highly motivated, if given an option, would volunteer for a ghetto area.[5]

By 1963, Negro leaders in New York were openly expressing their frustration with the lack of any appreciable progress in desegregation. Prodded by the NAACP and other civil rights groups, the Board of Education sought a new approach to the problem. In accord with recommendations by a committee headed by State Education Commissioner James E. Allen, Jr., plans were made to bus some Negro children into white districts to help correct racial imbalance in the schools. At this point, a number of liberal groups in New York City—the Anti-Defamation League, the American

[4] For a broader discussion of "The Failure of Desegregation," see Rogers, *110 Livingston Street*, pp. 15–35.

[5] In the black ghettos it is not difficult for the average teacher to form negative views of the students; views which the students reciprocate in kind. Whites today who think ghetto youths are unteachable should read Michael Gold's views, and those of his Jewish friend, "Nigger," of their first-grade teacher. "O irritable, starched old maid teacher. O stupid, proper unimaginative despot, O cow with no milk . . . it was torture to you, Ku Kluxer before your time, to teach in a Jewish neighborhood.

"I knew no English when handed to you. I was a little savage and lover of the street. I used no toothbrush. I slept in my underwear, I was lousy, maybe. To sit on a bench made me restless, my body hated coffins. But Teacher! O teacher for little slaves, O ruptured American virgin of fifty-five, you should not have called me 'Little Kike.'

"Nigger banged you on the nose for that. I should have been as brave. It was justice." Michael Gold, *Jews Without Money* (New York: Avon, 1965), pp. 22–23.

Jewish Committee, the Liberal Party and the New York Civil
Liberties Union—expressed opposition to the bussing of white
children for desegregation purposes. Only the American Jewish
Congress backed "the demand of civil rights groups for citywide
pairings and other nonvoluntary plans."[6]

With scant results from desegregation programs, concerned
Negro parents began in the mid-1960s to change tactics. The inability of the schools—for whatever reasons—to educate their children, led to an emphasis on the need for community control of
schools. Hopefully, this would increase the effectiveness of the
school administration and teachers, by bringing closer cooperation
between parents and teachers and by staffing schools with more
teachers who are responsible to the needs and problems of black
students. The turn toward community control coincided with the
nascent black power movement, thus setting the stage for conflict
between elements of the black community on the one hand, and the
teachers' and supervisors' unions and the central school board on
the other.

During the winter of 1966–1967 School Superintendent Bernard
Donovan, black community leaders, teachers' union representatives, and Ford Foundation personnel drew up plans for three
experimental school districts. Shortly thereafter, Mayor John
Lindsay's Advisory Panel on Decentralization issued a report—
called the Bundy Plan after Ford Foundation President McGeorge
Bundy—under which thirty to sixty local school boards would be
elected primarily by the school children's parents. These local
boards would have final authority over key areas of school policy,
most importantly budget, curriculum, and personnel.[7] The Bundy
Plan immediately came under attack by the United Federation of
Teachers, the Council of Supervisory Associations, and the Board
of Education which successfully led the lobbying against its passage
at the spring session of the state legislature in Albany.[8]

Nevertheless, three experimental districts were set up at Ocean
Hill-Brownsville, the Intermediate School 201 Complex in Harlem,

[6] Rogers, *110 Livingston Street*, pp. 26–27.
[7] Maurice R. Berube and Marilyn Gittell, eds., *Confrontation at Ocean Hill-
Brownsville: The New York School Strikes of 1968* (New York: Praeger,
1969), p. 14.
[8] Ibid., p. 15.

and the Two Bridges Model District in the Lower East Side of Manhattan. Over the next two years these experimental districts, particularly Ocean Hill-Brownsville, became the center of a controversy which threatened to divide an already beleaguered city.

This is not the place to recount in full detail the step-by-step buildup of the Ocean Hill crisis or to attempt an in-depth analysis of the extent to which each of the parties involved was responsible for what ensued. Much has already been written on the subject, and it should be noted that interpretations of the same events by different observers vary considerably.[9] (This is not surprising, as the entire city became increasingly polarized by the controversy, particularly during the school strike in the fall of 1968.) Our basic intent here is to consider the effects of the decentralization controversy on race relations, particularly between the black and Jewish communities focusing on the reaction within both communities to the school crisis and to other tension-provoking incidents.

Ocean Hill, the focal point of the school controversy, is sandwiched between the slum districts of Brownsville and Bedford-Stuyvesant in the East New York section of Brooklyn. According to Martin Mayer's account, "less than a fifth of its adult population was born in New York City; less than a third completed high school; only two-fifths have lived in the area as long as five years; more than half the households subsist on less than $5,000 a year; about 70% are Negro, about 25% are Puerto Rican. . . . Most people live in deteriorating rooming houses and tenements."[10]

---

[9] Among the studies generally sympathetic to the UFT's position in the Ocean Hill controversy are Martin Mayer, *The Teachers Strike: New York, 1968* (New York: Perennial Library Edition, 1969); Naomi Levine and Richard Cohen, *Schools in Crisis* (New York: Popular Library, 1969); Maurice J. Goldbloom, "The New York School Crisis," *Commentary* 47, no. 1 (January 1969):43–58; and the publications of the various Jewish agencies in New York. Maurice Berube and Marilyn Gittell, ed., *Confrontation at Ocean Hill-Brownsville* personally favored the Ocean Hill Governing Board's position, although the essays in their book represent the various sides of the dispute. Those writing in the *New York Review of Books* and the *Village Voice* (Nat Hentoff, for example) generally opposed the Union stance and its supporters. For critical review of Martin Mayer's book (which had first appeared as an article in the *New York Times Sunday Magazine*, 2 February 1969), see Jason Epstein, "The Real McCoy," in the *New York Review of Books*, 13 March 1969, pp. 31ff.

[10] Mayer, *The Teachers' Strike*, p. 18.

Friction existed between the Ocean Hill Governing Board and the UFT almost from the inception of the decentralization experiment. The UFT's grievances were sharpened by the hiring of Rhody McCoy as unit administrator. The union expressed concern that its teachers were often made to feel uncomfortable at teachers' meetings in McCoy's district.[11] The Ocean Hill Governing Board countered accusations made against it by stating that the New York City Board of Education had denied meaningful assistance to Ocean Hill and was bent on pushing the locally administered district into chaos.[12]

After a year of tension, an incident occurred which brought the conflict between the UFT and the Governing Board to a head. In May 1968 McCoy transferred thirteen union teachers, five assistant principals, and one principal to central headquarters for reassignment to other schools outside the district. All were considered unsympathetic to the decentralization experiment. Superintendent of Schools Bernard Donovan ordered the nineteen to return to their schools and to ignore the transfer. Parents from Ocean Hill-Brownsville then blockaded the school entrances and avowed the ousted teachers would not be permitted to return. On May 5, police admitted the teachers to the school. From that time forth the situation was volatile. Black parents charged the city with racism and police brutality and were in turn accused by the UFT of vigilantism and black racism. The UFT successfully lobbied in Albany against further plans to decentralize the city school system and flooded local newspapers with antidecentralization advertise-

---

[11] For a discussion of the "harassment" of a number of union teachers at teachers' meetings in Ocean Hill schools, see Eugenia Kemble's article in the UFT publication, *United Teacher, Local 2*, AFL-CIO, 20 December 1967.

[12] Richard Karp, writing in *Interplay Magazine* (August–September 1968) charged: "The Board of Education was not alone in its determination to disrupt and discredit community control. It had powerful allies of the kind that shows how politics makes strange bedfellows. Among them was the giant UFT, the board's traditional foe, with its loyal legions of white, middle-class teachers. The UFT had seen, in the events of the previous year that the Board of Education was beginning to lose its grip on the school system. It could no longer be depended upon to preserve the status quo. The union itself would have to fill the gap and become the first line of defense against reform." Reprinted in Berube and Gittell, eds., *Confrontation at Ocean Hill-Brownsville*, p. 69.

ments stating that local school districts would operate "on the basis of local prejudices based on color, race, or religion."[13]

After negotiations in September 1968, the Ocean Hill-Brownsville board agreed to take back ten transferred teachers, but refused to give them classroom assignments. The UFT would not accept this and called for a strike. In violation of the Taylor Law forbidding strikes by public employees, 54,000 out of 57,000 UFT teachers stayed out of work on opening day.[14] In Ocean Hill-Brownsville only a small number of union teachers appeared for work, but these were complemented by a large number of hastily recruited, nonunion teachers. An estimated 70 percent of the 350 newly recruited teachers were white; somewhat over half were Jewish. An agreement was reached on September 11, but the union teachers returning to Ocean Hill-Brownsville reported that they were being jeered by students and harassed by "outsiders."[15] The Ocean Hill-Brownsville Governing Board explained that the community "had risen spontaneously" to keep the nonsympathetic union teachers out. A second citywide teachers strike ensued.[16]

Schools reopened after a compromise under which union

13 Ibid., p. 75.
14 Mayer, *The Teachers' Strike*, p. 67. It can be said that the Taylor Law in itself may well be outmoded. Leaving aside the question of whether or not the teachers' grievances justified a strike, it appears inequitable that public employees in general are not afforded the same right to strike as those unionized workers employed in the private sphere.
15 Ibid., pp. 74–75. To resolve the problem Mayor Lindsay sought the intervention of Commissioner Allen and labor mediator Theodore Kheel, who suggested as a "compromise" the suspension of the Ocean Hill-Brownsville Governing Board and the transfer of the by-now celebrated ten teachers. The Governing Board was furious at the proposal, and "moderate" blacks like the respected educator, Kenneth Clark, were angered at Commissioner Allen for equating the supposed rights of ten teachers with the educational hopes of the Negro community.
16 Ibid., pp. 70–71. The returning union teachers were told to report to the I-55 auditorium for an orientation session with McCoy. "When the teachers arrived at the auditorium, they found about fifty Negro men, some wearing helmets, carrying sticks or with bandoliers of bullets, who shouted curses at them. The eighty-three teachers clustered in the center of the auditorium, terrified, and McCoy entered. As he started to speak, choruses of jeers drowned him out, and after a few minutes he left. . . . The teachers were told from the crowd that if they came back to the district, they would be carried out of it in pine boxes. Finally McCoy returned. If the teachers still insisted on returning to the district, he said, they should report to their schools at one o'clock."

teachers were reinstated along with principals from PS 271 whom the union had opposed.[17] By this time, however, the UFT realized that it was in a position powerful enough to get all of its demands accepted. A third strike was called. While the first two strikes had a great deal of popular support, the third strike (which lasted five weeks) exasperated many people in the city. There was criticism of the union in the city's major newspapers, but this did not increase popular support for the Ocean Hill-Brownsville cause. Mayor Lindsay made a number of public statements against the union leadership, but ultimately he and his supporters within the city establishment accepted the union demands. With all the forces of the white power structure acquiescing to the UFT, Rhody McCoy gave in to what he called "the degrading and humiliating terms" of the deal which ended the strike. Perhaps McCoy had no viable alternative, even though the settlement was worse than any he had refused to accept in earlier months. Frustrations were rapidly mounting in the black community in Brooklyn and open conflict between blacks and the forces of authority might have resulted. Needless to say, there would have been little doubt as to the outcome of such a conflict. And the black children—whose welfare had been the prime motivation for the experimental districts in the first place—could scarcely have been helped by such a course of events.

[17] It should be noted the transferral of teachers from one school to another in the New York public school system has been an arbitrary practice. Principals often transfer teachers without the prior consent of the teacher, and the teacher himself rarely protests. At the same time it is acknowledged that once a teacher becomes licensed in New York City it is virtually impossible to remove him from the system. According to Berube and Gittell only a dozen teachers had been dismissed from the school system in the five-year period to 1968, and these were for very serious reasons. Berube and Gittell, eds., *Confrontation at Ocean Hill-Brownsville*, p. 82.

Had the Ocean Hill-Brownsville Governing Board sent the thirteen teachers, one or two at a time, to the Board of Education they may have carried it off. (Some observers have suggested that the governing board welcomed a confrontation situation at the time.) But the transfer of a sizeable number of teachers and principals in one group at a time when tensions were high led the Union to believe that its authority was being challenged. The UFT position gradually hardened to the point where the teachers had to be taken back and the Ocean-Hill Brownsville Governing Board suspended.

The UFT's argument on behalf of the ousted teachers and principals was first based on the rights of its members to receive due process of law. As a standard practice in the New York school system, teachers could be transferred from one district to another at the discretion of the superintendent alone. Hundreds of such transfers took place yearly without UFT objection. One grievance which had been put forth by some teachers in the past was that the UFT had been indifferent to complaints that they had been unfairly transferred. (In and of itself the practice of transfer or dismissal of teachers without the implementation of due process is objectionable. In that sense the UFT was justified in protesting the transfer of teachers from Ocean Hill. While the UFT's action in this case apparently was not primarily motivated by a passion for justice, the issue which it raised was still a legitimate one.)

In September, however, the UFT shifted its emphasis from the "due process" issue to the spectre of black "militants" taking over the school systems in the ghetto areas. The implicit argument was that such a tendency had to be nipped in the bud, lest the "militant" elements, heartened by their successes, become more difficult to deal with later.

But what about the effects of the school decentralization dispute on Negro-Jewish relations? The latent racial overtones of the dispute surfaced quickly. The fact was that Rhody McCoy and a large majority of the Ocean Hill-Brownsville governing board were black, while the ten teachers seeking reinstatement in Ocean Hill-Brownsville were Jews. Albert Shanker, the outspoken UFT president, and most of the union leadership and membership, were Jewish. A substantial majority of the school supervisors and administrators in black ghetto areas were also Jewish, as were a number of the members of the Board of Education.

During the heated atmosphere of the strike period several different pieces of extremist literature came to light. A viciously anti-Semitic tract was placed in some union teachers' mailboxes in JHS 271 and PS 144 in Brooklyn. It read in part:

If African American History and Culture is to be taught to our Black Children it Must be Done By African Americans who Identify With And Who Understand The Problem. It Is Impossible For The Middle East Murderers of Colored People to Possibly Bring To This Important

Task The Insight, The Concern, The Exposing Of The Truth That is a *Must* If the Years Of Brainwashing And Self-Hatred That Has Been Taught To Our Black Children By Those Bloodsucking Exploiters and Murderers Is To Be OverCome. The Idea Behind This Program Is Beautiful, But When The Money Changers Heard About It, They Took Over, As Is Their Custom in the Black Community. If African American History And Culture Is Important To Our Children To Raise Their Esteem Of Themselves, They Are The Only Persons Who Can Do The Job Are African-American Brothers and Sisters, And Not the So-Called Liberal Jewish Friend. We Know From His Tricky, Deceitful Maneuvers That He is Really Our Enemy and He is Responsible For The Serious Educational Retardation of Our Black Children. We Call On All Concerned Black Teachers, Parents, And Friends to Write to The Board of Education, To the Mayor, To The State Commissioner of Education To Protest The Take Over Of This Crucial Program By People Who Are Unfit By Tradition And By Inclination To Do Even An Adequate Job.

The UFT irresponsibly reprinted as a one-page leaflet hundreds of thousands of copies of the above message along with a letter attributed to one Ralph Poynter, and circulated it to its members and others in New York's Jewish community. (Poynter's piece was a militant demand for absolute black control over the schools in black areas, but did not contain anti-Semitic references.) At the bottom of the leaflet was the caption in bold letters—"IS THIS WHAT YOU WANT FOR YOUR CHILDREN? THE UFT SAYS NO!"

Various groups in the city began to take positions either supporting or opposing the UFT's tactics in dealing with the Ocean Hill situation. One organization which strongly opposed the UFT's actions on the "Poynter Leaflet" and the anti-Semitic issue generally was the New York Civil Liberties Union.[18] Previously, in a statement issued early in October on the teachers' strike, the NYCLU had chastised the Board of Education and the UFT for creating

---

[18] The NYCLU in a rebuke to UFT declared that holding the Ocean Hill-Brownsville Local Governing Board responsible for Ralph Poynter's statements "makes about as much sense as holding the American Jewish Congress responsible for Albert Shanker's statements, which is to say it makes no sense at all." *Memorandum from New York Civil Liberties Union to Special Committee on Religious and Racial Prejudice,* 26 November 1968, pp. 3–4.

the due process issue "out of thin air." The statement noted that "disenchanted black parents decided that since they were again struck with a de facto segregated school, they might at least run it themselves."[19]

A second report drawn up by Ira Glasser for the NYCLU and released on November 26 came out even more strongly against the UFT for exacerbating racial tensions in the city.[20] Having been identified with one side in the dispute, the NYCLU office and its personnel received numerous hate calls and a considerable number of hate letters from those who supported the teachers' position. Many of these letters to Glasser, himself a Jew, could have been written only by fellow Jews. This hate mail was virtually indistinguishable from the few pieces of hate literature written by blacks which had been given citywide publicity by the UFT. The NYCLU report denied that the proponents of community control were the only ones using intimidation and other such tactics.[21]

The report said, in part: "It is always difficult to assess blame for individual incidents or to prevent individuals from expressing racial hostility. . . . But we do have the right to expect responsible organizations and responsible leaders to refrain from official and systematic expressions which have the effect of arousing such incidents." According to the NYCLU "the UFT leadership, and in particular Albert Shanker, systematically accused the Ocean Hill-Brownsville Board and Rhody McCoy of anti-Semitism and ex-

---

[19] Ira Glasser, "The Burden of the Blame—New York Civil Liberties Union Report on the Ocean Hill-Brownsville School Controversy," quoted in full in Berube and Gittell, eds., *Confrontation at Ocean Hill-Brownsville*, pp. 104–119.

[20] *Memorandum from NYCLU to Special Committee on Religious and Racial Prejudice.*

[21] Ibid., p. 1. "Any allegation that threats, intimidation, racial slurs or religious epithets came only or primarily from proponents of community control is contradicted by the evidence we received. In fact, because after October 10th we were identified with one side of the dispute, we received numerous hate calls and a substantial amount of hate mail primarily from those who sided with the striking teachers. Similarly, most reports of intimidation we received tended to come from those against the strike alleging incidents of harassment by striking teachers and their supporters. Thus, the overwhelming proportion of incidents of which we were made aware were allegedly perpetrated by striking teachers and their supporters."

tremism, and then 'proved' those accusations only with half-truths, innuendoes, and outright lies."[22]

The NYCLU report concluded that the UFT and its President, Albert Shanker, had compounded their errors by using such un-subtle "code words" in their campaign as Nazi, mob rule, vigilantes, extremists, criminals, black militants, and black racists. "By in-cessant use of such words; by the fraudulent leaflets, and by the whole tone and tenor of the campaign, the UFT did what no one else has ever before been able to do in this city. It legitimized liberal racism."[23]

The central figure in the NYCLU report was, of course, Albert Shanker. It is typical of the irony of our times that Shanker should have become the principal character in the confrontation with the Ocean Hill-Brownsville Governing Board. Shanker had been, in Martin Mayer's words, "the leading integrationist in the New York labor movement."

The teachers and supervisors unions, with predominantly Jewish leadership, came to be supported by almost all of the organized Jewish groups and agencies in the city. On the other hand, most Negro groups, regardless of how they had felt earlier about the school decentralization issue, came to support the Ocean Hill-Brownsville governing board during the confrontation.[24]

Those who have defended the UFT's position contend that the

---

[22] Ibid., p. 2. "Official UFT leaflets have made it appear as if the Ocean Hill-Brownsville Board was directly responsible for anti-Semitic literature that the UFT knew had no connection with the governing board. . . . These smears are vicious and inexcusable. They have whipped up religious terror, released race hatred and opened sores in the community that will not be easily or quickly healed."

[23] Ibid., p. 10.

[24] Speaking of the polarization which took place, Maurice Berube in *Confrontation at Ocean Hill-Brownsville*, pp. 146–147, wrote: "Who are the militants for community control that so worry the UFT? An old integra-tionist activist core (Rev. Milton Galamison, Annie Stein, Rev. Herbert Oliver, Ellen Lurie, Preston Wilcox, to name a few) is joined with younger black and white activists. True, some black anti-Semites have latched onto community control, but they are not representative and have been disowned.

"Who supports the UFT? A few prominent social democrats and lib-erals like Michael Harrington, Jewish groups who are rightly anxious over black anti-Semitism, others who are plainly anxious about blacks, and that anti-Semitic, anti-black white constituency (Many Catholics) who sup-

union was far from racist in its policies, that the strikes were actually in the long-term interests of the black and Puerto Rican communities. The suggestion has been made that Rhody McCoy and the governing board had wanted a confrontation and got it, but without the results which they desired.[25] In defending the "merit system," which had been attacked as an obstacle to Negro advancement and a device for protecting the ethnic status quo, Maurice Goldbloom has argued with historic justification: "The merit system has served one minority after another in its struggles to circumvent the barriers of discrimination. Negroes, too, are finding the civil service a relatively smooth road to advancement." By this reasoning it was presumed that more Negro teachers and administrators would eventually work their way into the school system.[26]

Jewish complaints that the Ocean Hill Governing board had permitted anti-Semitism to flourish among the teaching staff were for the most part overstated. The governing board could not have afforded to permit overt anti-Semitism to exist in the Ocean Hill schools because, among other reasons, the schools were dependent upon Jewish teachers. Over half of the 350 new teachers who were hastily recruited to fill vacancies in the schools in the summer of 1968 were Jewish.[27] Most of these teachers would not have coun-

---

ported PAT [Parents and Taxpayers]. Quite a coalition. Certainly the larger segment would most probably support local control in the white South, but not the urban black North."

[25] Rhody McCoy was quoted in the *New York Times* of 16 May 1968 as declaring, "Not one of these ['transferred'] teachers will be allowed to teach anywhere in this city. The black community will see to that." Quoted in Maurice Goldbloom, "The New York School Crisis," *Commentary* 47, no. 1 (January 1969): 54.

[26] Ibid., p. 58. Goldbloom noted that Negroes are "proportionately more numerous in the post office and many other federal departments than in the population as a whole." While that observation is in itself correct, it is highly doubtful that a substantially increased number of Negro teachers and administrators will be produced unless a massive effort is made to improve the quality of the public schools in the ghetto area.

[27] A full-page advertisement in *The New York Times* entitled "Anti-Semitism? A Statement by the Teachers of Ocean Hill-Brownsville to the People of New York" sought "to scotch the rumors and hysteria about anti-Semitism, racism and revolution being the underlying causes of the problems of Ocean Hill-Brownsville." The statement signed by almost four hundred teachers, many of them Jewish, observed that "black people

tenanced a school system in which anti-Jewish feeling was rampant.

The Ocean Hill Board, resenting the implication that it had approved the placing of the anonymous hate literature in Jewish teachers' mailboxes, subsequently deplored the anti-Semitic literature.[28] While the Governing Board did repudiate several anti-Semitic remarks which had been made around the schools, however, it did not feel obliged to be any more responsible for intemperate remarks or behavior on the part of a few blacks than Jewish organizations were responsible for racist remarks made by individual Jews.[29] (It might be added that Jewish religious leaders resented any intimation that they could or should exert control over Jewish secular leaders such as the president of the UFT.) One may ask, however, whether McCoy, Reverend Oliver, and others should have gone further in repudiating anti-Semitic statements by a handful of blacks during the school strike, if only to help allay Jewish fears and to set the anti-Semitic charges to rest. On this latter point, it must be considered that Jews, because of their historic experience as a people, are highly sensitive to any threat of anti-Semitism. It might have been useful, once the anti-Semitic ploy had been injected into the Ocean Hill controversy, for McCoy and the Governing Board to have issued additional unequivocal statements against anti-Semitism and racism. Had such

will be turned away from anti-Semitism and white will be turned away from anti-Negro feelings only through the establishment of trust and confidence between both groups in day to day relationships." These teachers were attempting to establish such relationships. *New York Times,* 11 November 1968.

[28] The Board said: "The Ocean Hill-Brownsville Governing Board, as well as the entire Ocean Hill-Brownsville Demonstration School District, has never tolerated anti-Semitism in any form. Anti-Semitism has no place in our hearts or minds and indeed never in our schools. While certain anti-Semitic literature may have been distributed outside our school buildings, there is absolutely no connection between these acts and the thoughts and intents of the Ocean Hill-Brownsville Governing Board. We disclaim any responsibility for this literature and have in every way sought to find its source and take appropriate action to stop it." Quoted in Fred Ferretti, "New York's Black Anti-Semitism Scare," *Columbia Journalism Review,* Fall 1969, p. 23.

[29] Answers cannot be readily provided to such questions as: Were Rhody McCoy and the Ocean Hill Governing Board seeking a confrontation when they transferred the union teachers? Could a compromise have been worked out so that the union would not have felt the need to lock horns with the Governing Board?

statements been made and had they been given as much attention by the media as ethnic slurs, then the real issues of Ocean Hill would not have been so blurred in the eyes of Jews.[30]

The Ocean Hill-Brownsville situation brought out the antagonisms that had long been building up in the city. More than any other white group in New York City, Jews had supported reformist causes in the past, but their traditional ardor for reform seemingly had diminished. For example, it is estimated that only half of New York's Jews had supported Mayor Lindsay's proposed civilian review board which, among other functions, would have provided a check on police abuses in the ghetto areas. An increasing number of Jews also opposed proposals for low-income housing for blacks in predominantly Jewish neighborhoods.

Several other conflicts after the school strike further increased Jewish-Negro tensions in New York City. One incident was the dispute which developed over the reading of an anti-Semitic poem on WBAI-FM on 26 December 1968. The poem, written by a fifteen-year-old schoolgirl, was read on the "Julius Lester Program" by Leslie Campbell, a controversial teacher at PS 271 in Ocean Hill-Brownsville. Campbell had been suspended from his position for harassing union teachers, but had been reinstated by a state panel which found the evidence insufficient to warrant disciplinary proceedings.

A few verses of the poem read as follows: "Hey, Jew Boy, with that yarmulka on your head / You pale-faced Jew boy—I wish you were dead."[31] The poem, "dedicated" to Albert Shanker, was char-

---

30 An article by New York newsman Fred Ferretti, who covered the school strike for WNBC-TV, strongly criticizes the media coverage of the period. The *New York Times* coverage, with the exception of several analytical articles and editorials, left much to be desired. "Columnist Murray Kempton in the New York *Post* was an oasis of reason amid the general shrillness of that paper's daily coverage (the reporting of Kenneth Gross excepted.) The *Daily News* saw little need to discuss issues when there was so much juicy confrontation to report on. . . . TV's concept of objective coverage was to read the *Times,* discover the day's issue, get a UFT spokesman, then a spokesman for the beleaguered schools, and have them speak to the issue. . . . There was, with the predictable exception of Harlem's *Amsterdam News,* no real effort made to present the black man's side of the conflict." Ferretti, *New York's Black Anti-Semitism Scare,* pp. 27–28.

31 The "poem" author was "sick of hearing about the [Jewish] suffering in

acterized by Campbell as having a "tremendous sense of truth."[32]

The UFT wrote to the Federal Communications Commission vigorously protesting that "WBAI-FM was being used to spread anti-Semitic propaganda in general and attacks against New York teachers in particular." Shanker said that the reading of the poem by Campbell ought to provide new grounds to reverse his reinstatement. "This city was going to have to decide," he declared, "whether its teachers were to teach anti-Semitism or understanding and brotherhood."[33]

The UFT protest prompted a flood of protest. Among those who joined the mounting "siege" of WBAI were the President of the New York City Council, Francis X. Smith, who called for a suspension of WBAI's license,[34] the Anti-Defamation League, the Workmen's Circle, the New York Board of Rabbis, and Congressman Emanuel Celler of Brooklyn. On January 26 the Jewish Defense League, a militant group organized several months earlier, presented a list of demands which included the cancellation of the Julius Lester show and an apology from WBAI for its "insensitivity and complicity" in broadcasting the program.

WBAI, a station licensed to the Pacifica Foundation of Berkeley, California, and supported by listener contributions, rejected demands that it forbid expressions of an anti-Semitic nature in any of its programs. It also resisted the pressures to eliminate the Julius Lester Program. The station's manager, Frank Millspaugh, re-

---

Germany and spoke of the Jews' hatred for black Arabs." It concluded:

Then you came to America, land of the free,
And took over the school system to perpetuate white supremacy.
Guess you know, Jew boy, there's only one reason you made it—
You had a clean white face, colorless and faded.
I hated you Jew-boy, because your hang-up was the Torah,
And my only hang-up was my color.

Reprinted in the B'nai B'rith publication, *Metropolitan Star* 24, no. 8 (January 1969):1.

[32] *New York Times,* 16 January 1969.

[33] Ibid.

[34] The Council President's decision to ask the FCC to suspend WBAI's license was prompted by the comment of a black guest, Tyrone Woods, on another of Julius Lester's programs. According to *The New York Times,* 24 January 1969, Woods had remarked that Hitler didn't make enough lampshades out of Jews.

marked that he knew Mr. Lester's intent was "to demonstrate what a lot of people don't want to take seriously—the strong and growing hostility and resentment of Jewish whites among ghetto blacks." The chairman of the WBAI board, Dr. Harold Taylor, formerly president of Sarah Lawrence College, said censorship demands could not be accepted because they were contrary to the spirit of the First Amendment's protection of the right to freedom of expression. He asserted WBAI's responsibility to present views which might well be odious to everyone connected with the station as well as to various sectors of the public. In the case at hand "the anti-Semitic views were deeply repugnant" to everyone at the station, but steps taken to censor such views would "fall into the trap of those who would refine the rawness of truth in order to make it socially convenient. To be informed of the existence and extent of dangerous social forces is the first step toward coping with them."[35] The station also has the responsibility, Taylor continued, to provide a forum to counter the dangers of bigotry by "informed and enlightened analysis." He thus invited WBAI's critics to help solve the problems of community unrest and racism.[36] It was announced that the station was reviving its "Jewish Commentary" series "to insure that matters affecting the Jewish community will have immediate response from recognized leadership within that community."

In expressing support for WBAI, Nat Hentoff observed that "there is no station in the city on which a wider spectrum of opinion has been and can be expressed." This included the Ku Klux Klan and the young black man who said on Lester's program: "As far as I am concerned, more power to Hitler. He didn't make enough lampshades out of them."[37]

[35] "WBAI-FM Rejects Jewish Groups' Demand on Anti-Semitism," *New York Times,* 28 January 1969.

[36] *New York Times,* 7 February 1969. Taylor's position was supported by a letter to the *Times,* 1 February, written by Eric Salzman and signed by twenty-four members of the staff and volunteers at WBAI. The letter asked rhetorically: "would the critics of WBAI prefer that we made a compact (or a law) to pretend that anti-Semitism does not exist and let the virus spread in darkness and silence?"

[37] Nat Hentoff, "The Siege of WBAI," *Village Voice,* 6 February 1969, p. 9. Hentoff also notes a "Letter from a Listener" published in the February 1969 WBAI folio. The "listener," a black, young woman twenty-three years of age, wrote: "contrary to fanning the flames of anti-Semitism, WBAI is in fact helping what small minority of black listenership that it

Julius Lester said that he had been aware of the poem's contents prior to the program and encouraged Campbell to read it when the latter seemed reluctant. He remarked that the critics of Campbell and WBAI failed to mention that he had expressed the hope that the poem would raise issues for rational discussion.[38]

In late March the Federal Communications Commission ruled that it did not have the authority to judge or act on the controversial WBAI case. Remarks made on the Julius Lester show were held to be protected by the free speech guarantee of the First Amendment. The FCC went on to say that WBAI had fulfilled its responsibility under the "fairness doctrine" to present contrasting viewpoints on controversial matters, and that the station had made its facilities available to a wide range of spokesmen "to counteract the effect of bias and prejudice by a fair and judicious treatment of the entire subject."[39]

A dispute also developed over several reportedly anti-Semitic references in an introductory essay to a Metropolitan Museum of Art catalog for the "Harlem on My Mind" exhibition. Like the WBAI altercation, the controversy stemmed from the words of a teenage black girl. The essay by sixteen-year-old Candice Van Ellison included the following controversial passages: "Behind every hurdle that the Afro-American has yet to jump stands the Jew who has already cleared it," and the already exploited black "was allowed to be further exploited by the Jews."[40] Also: "One

has to realize that the Jew is not his real enemy, although he is his most immediate scapegoat."

[38] Nat Hentoff, "Blacks and Jews: An Interview with Julius Lester," *Evergreen Review* no. 65 (April 1969): 22. When asked in an interview why he did not comment on the content of the poem, which was admittedly anti-Semitic, Lester replied: "I think you have to consider the genesis of the poem. To my mind, the poem is an act of self-defense, because of the racism which was involved in the teachers' strike. The black community was attacked head-on, and specifically in Ocean Hill-Brownsville where this girl is a student. And so, as far as I'm concerned, she is defending herself with the only weapon at her command. She is hurt and therefore she is going to hurt back as much as she can. I think one of the difficulties is that people are equating the poem with the traditional anti-Semitism, which is rooted in God knows what—Christ-killers and what have you. That has no relationship to the black community."

[39] *New York Times,* 29 March 1969.

[40] The essay itself was actually a school term paper which had come to the attention of Mr. Allen Schoener when Miss Van Ellison was working

other important factor worth noting is that, psychologically blacks may find anti-Jewish sentiments place them, for once, within a majority. Thus, our contempt for the Jew makes us feel more completely American in sharing a national prejudice."[41]

Ironically, the last remark was a paraphrase from the book, *Beyond the Melting Pot,* by sociologists Nathan Glazer and Daniel Moynihan. What Glazer and Moynihan had actually written was:

Now admittedly everything we have to say to explain Negro-Jewish relations is also true (to some extent) of Italian-Negro and Irish-Negro relations. And yet there is less feeling expressed against the Irish and Italians. Perhaps, for many Negroes, subconsciously, a bit of anti-Jewish feeling helps make them feel more completely American, a part of the majority group. There are probably other irrational bases for this anti-Jewish feeling—anti-Semitism is a complicated thing—and yet the special tie-up of Jews with liberation is certainly important.[42]

There is clearly a difference in connotation between the passage as paraphrased and the passage in *Beyond the Melting Pot.* On this Professor Glazer commented: "Here is this thing being attacked for anti-Semitism that's quoted from a book which is clearly not." The controversy showed the change in the atmosphere in that American Jews were, for the first time in many years, worried about anti-Semitism.[43]

The protest against the "Harlem on My Mind" catalog was directed particularly against Thomas Hoving, director of the Museum, who according to the *New York Post* saw "nothing

---

under him in the Urban Art Corps program. Schoener, who is Jewish, as a member of the New York State Council of the Arts, directed the compilation of the "Harlem on My Mind" catalogue. In Miss Van Ellison's original essay there had been direct quotes from *Beyond the Melting Pot,* but Schoener had directed her to drop the quotes and paraphrase without making specific reference to the Glazer-Moynihan study. When Thomas Hoving, Director of the Museum, raised the question of the public reaction to the introductory essay before the catalogue was published, Schoener reportedly replied that the introduction would be considered anti-Semitic. "I would not edit an anti-Semitic work," he remarked, adding that Jewish liberal intellectuals had already encountered many of the sentiments in the essay. *New York Times,* 1 February 1969.

[41] *New York Times,* 1 February 1969.
[42] Nathan Glazer and Daniel Patrick Moynihan, *Beyond the Melting Pot,* (Cambridge: Massachusetts Institute of Technology Press, 1964), p. 77.
[43] *New York Times,* 29 January 1969.

inflammatory" about the essay and reportedly added, "if the truth hurts, so be it." Francis Plimpton, a long-time public servant and a trustee of the Museum, also drew flak after reportedly saying, "It's just one of those things. A young lady wrote a piece about Harlem as she saw it."[44] In a statement prior to the opening of the Museum exhibit, Dore Schary of the Anti-Defamation League termed the girl's essay "ridden with frustration and anger" and said "we cannot ignore a great institution as respectable as the Metropolitan Museum of Art's giving such a statement credence or significance."[45] Justice Botein of Mayor Lindsay's Special Commission on Racial and Religious Prejudice criticized Mr. Hoving and Random House, the catalog's publisher, for being "grossly negligent and irresponsible" in refusing to delete remarks that had anti-Semitic overtones. In a full-page advertisement in *The New York Times* on January 31, the American Jewish Congress published a statement, "The Enemy is Silence" which began: "It is important that every American understand the anger and dismay that swept the Jewish community when the Metropolitan Museum of Art published the racist catalogue for its exhibit, "Harlem on My Mind." We have had a long experience with the big lie—in this case, the lie that the Negro plight is the result of some kind of conspiracy by the Jews."[46]

Political officeholders and aspirants began to voice their displeasure. For example, James Scheuer, a candidate in the Demo-

[44] *Metropolitan Star,* January 1969, p. 11.

[45] *New York Times,* 18 January 1969. Addressing himself to Mr. Hoving's remark that "if the truth hurts so be it," Schary commented: "There can be no temporizing with Mr. Hoving's cavalier assessment of what is obviously an insult and attack on Jews who, despite the hasty appraisal of a few blacks, have been a central core in the fight for black freedom, equality and opportunity."

[46] *New York Times,* 31 January 1969. The AJC statement continued: "What troubled us profoundly was the silence of those (black and white) who, by failing to speak out, gave their consent to a group libel and the scapegoating of a people. But there is more to it than that. Anti-Semitism threatens not only the Jewish community but the survival of democracy. It imperils the Negro community because it is part of racism. . . . It is a sickness from which too many Americans still suffer—those born into security and ease who have never known the whiplash of prejudice and those who have experienced too much of it and seek in despair and desperation to turn it against others. . . .

"The time has come to renew the alliance for freedom our common past

cratic mayoralty primary, denounced the catalog introduction as "crude and obvious, virulently anti-Semitic and anti-ethnic." Mayor Lindsay termed the essay "racist" and called for its removal from the catalog. Hoving's feeling was that everyone was overreacting to the situation, but by January 30 he responded to the growing pressure and withdrew the catalog saying, "the continuing controversy over the distribution of the catalog is aggravating an already tense situation in New York."[47]

A few Afro-Americans expressed concern, as Charles Kenyatta of the Harlem Mau Mau Society put it, that Jewish leaders were blowing the Museum incident far out of proportion and that this was in itself an indication of Jewish anti-Negro feeling.[48] The exhibit as a whole was criticized by some because it offered a white man's view of Harlem and did not include works by contemporary black artists. Others did not believe that the positive side of Harlem life had been presented. In accord with this view, the Reverend Henry D. Rucker called the exhibit an insult to black people because it revived aspects of Harlem's history that were "better off dead."[49] From another vantage point, some Afro-Americans viewed the Museum venture as a step in the right direction. One thing on which virtually all blacks could agree was that the hysteria over the essay of a teenage girl was uncalled for.[50]

Needless to say the controversy over the exhibit and demonstra-

---

and common aspirations once forged. Together we must speak out against those who exploit differences and incite hatred. Together we must condemn anti-Semitism and anti-Negroism out of the respect we owe ourselves and each other."

[47] The publisher, Random House, had already sold 16,000 out of the 40,000 soft-cover copies of the catalog. Saying that it was "an error in judgment" to have published the book in its present form, the president of Random House said the 4,600 hard cover copies selling in bookstores would not be withdrawn as it would serve no useful purpose and "might set a dangerous precedent with respect to freedom of the press."

[48] Ibid.

[49] *New York Times,* 20 January 1969.

[50] *Amsterdam News,* 1 February 1969, commented in an editorial: "And now, if the overblown black-Jewish confrontation was not enough, they're trying to bring other racial groups into the "Harlem on My Mind" exhibit rhubarb at the Metropolitan Museum of Art as being victim of insult. Harlem, itself, is divided on this exhibit, but the present hysteria over an exploited introduction by a teenage girl causes the whole community to be branded, by some, as anti-everything but black."

tions outside the museum by a black group and by the Jewish Defense League greatly increased the exhibit's attendance. On opening day a steady stream of patrons viewed the exhibit, while thousands more milled around outside and traffic was almost brought to a standstill. When the catalog was withdrawn, *The New York Times* of January 31 remarked editorially that this was a "half-baked solution to a second-rate show and a third-rate catalog."[51]

A casualty of the rise in black-Jewish passions was William H. Booth, New York Commissioner for Human Rights. Booth stood accused by a number of Jewish groups of having maintained "sustained silence" on the subject of anti-Semitism during the New York school decentralization controversy.

On 17 December 1968, Mayor Lindsay told a group of concerned rabbis and synagogue officials that Booth could have done a better job of looking into the anti-Semitic incidents during the school strike. He said that Booth's failure had resulted from human error and that at times Booth had indeed "helped greatly to alleviate tensions." However, he felt that Booth should have acted "sooner and faster" in the matter of anti-Semitic literature.[52]

Charges against Booth were also made by the New York Board of Rabbis which asserted that Booth had shown a "singular insensitivity to anti-Semitic incidents. In asking Mayor Lindsay not to reappoint Booth as Human Rights Commissioner, Rabbi Gilbert Klaperman, president of the Board, said that Booth had not discerned anti-Semitic incidents in a memorial service held for Malcolm X in East Harlem a year earlier and had "whitewashed everybody."[53]

Booth's term as Human Rights Commissioner officially expired on 26 December 1968. Under mounting pressure, Mayor Lindsay on 5 February 1969 named Negro lawyer Simeon Golar to replace Booth, who had continued on a holdover basis as commissioner.

Blame for the deteriorating racial condition had to be placed somewhere. *The New York Times* editorialized that the shift in Human Rights Commissioners "serves the best interests of the

[51] *New York Times,* 31 January 1969.
[52] Ibid., 5 February 1969.
[53] Ibid.

city," and that "Mr. Booth has shown himself singularly insensitive to vicious anti-Semitism and black racism recently generated by hate-mongers in the city." The Human Rights Commission had also "not been functioning properly—not maintaining communications among various New York groups, not investigating vigorously enough the circulation of hate literature and the sharp upsweep in incidents of racial vandalism."[54]

Booth's dismissal was angrily challenged by many Afro-American organizations, ranging from nationalists to the moderate NAACP, of whose National Executive Board Booth was a member. Among those who charged that Booth had been removed under the pressure of "white blacklash" was state NAACP chairman, Donald Lee. Generally speaking, white city officials of both major parties conceded that complaints from leaders of the Jewish community had influenced Mayor Lindsay's decision, but that, in the words of City Council President Francis X. Smith, Mr. Booth had been dropped because he had evinced "a lack of sensitivity to anti-Semitism."[55]

In a rejoinder, the Commission of Human Rights staff which had served with Mr. Booth, prepared a lengthy report summing up the Commission's work on behalf of Jewish individuals and groups during Booth's period as chairman. The report answered the various charges that had been levied against the Commission. For example, during the Ocean Hill-Brownsville school crisis in 1968 "the Commission succeeded, through its good offices, in convincing the author of an anti-Semitic leaflet, describing Jewish people as 'Mid-East murderers,' to withdraw it from circulation. For the record, this same leaflet, with another piece of literature, was circulated in 500,000 copies by the UFT throughout all school districts falsely as representing the opinion of the Ocean Hill-Brownsville community."[56] Booth's criticism of the UFT during the school strike was directed at the UFT's actions as a labor union and "certainly had nothing to do with the ethnic composition of its membership." After citing numerous instances of actions

54 Ibid., editorial "Replacing Mr. Booth."
55 Ibid., 5 February 1969.
56 "Involvement of the City Commission of Human Rights with the Jewish Community of New York During the Chairmanship of William H. Booth," News Release, 4 February 1969, pp. 1–2.

on behalf of complainants of Jewish origin, the report noted opinion within the Jewish community which supported Booth.

The *Long Island Press,* a paper with a Democratic political orientation whose editor was Jewish, ran a strong editorial which stated that Booth "has performed great service as a vital bridge between black and white communities and as a zealous protector of human rights."[57] Albert Vorspan, Director of the Commission on Social Action of the Union of American Hebrew Congregations, said on February 2 that "to try William Booth in the press and to call for the revocation of [WBAI's] license without due process is to foster a contempt for the democratic process among Jews."

Speaking for himself, Booth stated that the problems of fighting anti-Semitism are the same as those in fighting racism of all kinds. Given the size of the staff and allocated funds it was hard to see how the Commission could have been more effective.[58] He wrote later that whenever there were allegations of discrimination against Jewish people the cases were thoroughly investigated. "Yet, seldom was any substantial evidence presented to show such discrimination. Whenever, in a few instances such evidence was provided, the commission proceeded vigorously, and most often to a successful conclusion."[59]

One sign of Mayor Lindsay's response to mounting Jewish complaints was the creation of a new agency to deal with the incidents of anti-Semitism and black and white racism generated by the

[57] *Long Island Press,* 2 January 1969.
[58] Commission on Human Rights, news release, p. 6.
[59] Nat Hentoff, ed., *Black Anti-Semitism and Jewish Racism* (New York: Richard W. Baron, 1969), p. 124.

Reviewing the origins of the criticism levied against him as Human Rights Commissioner, Booth wrote in 1969: "First public exposure of allegations of my 'softness' on anti-Semitism came in February, 1967. One of our fifteen commission members, Rabbi Julius Neumann, held a press conference at the City Hall press room to announce his resignation because of my alleged failure to 'see' discrimination practiced against non-black people. A series of six or seven charges against me were answered by my office in detail, and without rebuttal. But Rabbi Neumann was given the full 'profile' treatment by *The New York Times* and my answers to his charges were given short shrift. The charges never were forgotten and were built upon when anti-Semitism became the *cause célèbre* in our city in 1968." Ibid., p. 120.

school strike.[60] A task force appointed in November 1968 under the chairmanship of Bernard Botein, a former presiding appellate division judge, was charged with the responsibility of reporting back within five weeks "on the current conditions of racial and religious prejudice, focusing primarily on the school dispute." Their report made in January concluded that

an appalling amount of racial prejudice—black and white—in New York City surfaced in about the school controversy. . . . The anti-white prejudice has a dangerous component of anti-Semitism. Black leaders sincerely tend to regard this anti-Semitism as relatively unimportant in the school controversy, since in their struggle for emergence their preoccupation is with discrimination, notably in education, employment and housing and not with defamation, oral or written. Jews, in turn, are outraged by anti-Semitic defamation itself, fearful that such apparent indifference may spark violence and other forms of anti-Semitism well beyond defamatory expressions.[61]

The report pointed to a difference in the styles of white and black bigotry. Bigotry emanating from black extremists was "open, undisguised, nearly physical in its intensity—and far more obvious and identifiable than that emanating from whites. On the other hand, antiblack bigotry tended to be expressed in more sophisticated and subtle fashion, often communicated privately and seldom reported, but nonetheless equally evil, corrosive, damaging and deplorable."[62] The most objectionable aspect of the report to many blacks was the equation of the prevalence of white and black bigotry.

The Botein Committee chose not to name "blameworthy individuals or organizations," saying more investigation and further analysis was necessary. It lamented that the conflict between Jews and blacks should have grown so massively, in that these two

---

[60] Ibid., p. 2. To avoid duplication of effort, the Human Rights Commission then concentrated on holding hearings on school decentralization and teacher training and curriculum, leaving out the subject of anti-Semitism and black and white racism to avoid interference with the Botein Committee.

[61] Statement of the Special Committee on Racial and Religious Prejudice, 17 January 1969, pp. 5–6.

[62] Ibid.

groups "for many years have so successfully cooperated with each other in attempting to promote a higher level of human dignity, racial and religious understanding and equality of opportunity for men of all colors and creeds."[63]

"There is room for dissent, protest and militancy," the report continued, "but anti-Semitism, racism and violence are out of bounds in any community discussion of complex problems." Lack of communications was pointed to as a "major failure" between black and white communities. Among the specific recommendations made by the Committee was a call for "the voluntary creation of a continuing citywide conference composed of representatives of the recognized non-official human relations, religious and civil rights agencies resident in New York City." The report closed with a recommendation that an ongoing group be established by the Mayor for the purpose of investigating the whole range of racial, religious and ethnic conflicts.

In effect the Botein Committee confirmed that which should already have been known—that strong prejudices exist in many whites and nonwhites alike in New York City. In observing that the limited communications which had existed between ethnic groups were breaking down, the report pointed to the need for new and more meaningful forms of communication. The overriding concern of the Committee was that people speak out against racism and bigotry in an orderly manner. Otherwise "the tensions between the races will intensify and tear the city apart."

Feeling increased pressures from many elements within the Jewish community, several prominent Jewish agencies then decided to bring the anti-Semitism issue to the fore. The apparent strategy was to prod city officials and moderate Negro organizations and spokesmen to act more decisively on the matter. On 22 January 1969 the Anti-Defamation League of the B'nai B'rith released a twenty-five page "preliminary report" for the public's edification. The news release for the city's newspapers began as follows: "Raw undisguised anti-Semitism is at a crisis level in New York City schools, where unchecked by public authorities it has been building for more than two years."[64] The document drew the following

63 Ibid., p. 8.
64 New York Times, 24 January 1969.

conclusions about anti-Semitism in and around the public schools:

1. It has been perpetrated largely by black extremists.

2. Its growth has been aided by the failure of city and state public officials to condemn it swiftly and strongly enough, and to remove from positions of authority those who have utilized anti-Semitism, including representatives of the Council Against Poverty, the city's official anti-poverty agency.

3. There is a clear and present danger that school children in the city have been infected by the anti-Semitic preachings of black extremists who, in some cases, are teachers and to whom these youngsters increasingly look for leadership.[65]

Specifically with reference to the third point, the ADL report accused officials of the Afro-American Teachers Association and other "militants" involved in the school dispute of creating hostility in school children directed against Jewish teachers.[66]

The ADL, which had served as the staff group in putting together the Botein Committee report, went well beyond the stance taken a week earlier in the Botein report. The ADL chronicled incidents ranging from the Board of Education hearings of 1966 to the "Harlem on My Mind" exhibit catalog and the WBAI controversy.[67]

The day following the announcement of the ADL report Mayor Lindsay told a press conference that the Board of Education

---

[65] Anti-Defamation League, press release, 23 January 1969, p. 1.

[66] *New York Times,* 23 January 1969. To support these charges the report included statements and writings of those accused of anti-Semitism, e.g., Albert Vann, head of the Afro-American Teachers Association and acting assistant principal of PS 271 in Ocean Hill-Brownsville, Luis Fuentes, principal of PS 155 and Leslie Campbell, a teacher at PS 271.

[67] Ibid. The ADL asserted that "black separatists and other militants" have deliberately created "a pattern of anti-Semitism" to further their objectives of greater control within the public schools. A first manifestation of such a pattern occurred in a speech by Mr. Melvin Pritchard during the Board of Education hearings of 17 August, 1966, on a proposal to use federal funds to aid private and parochial schools. Mr. Pritchard was quoted as saying: "One particular ethnic group of non-Christians are willfully, deliberately and intentionally depriving American citizens of their right to first class education in the community public schools of this city, state and nation."

should publish a code of ethics for teachers to make clear what is "intolerable" with regard to anti-Semitic and racial slurs. Neither antiwhite nor antiblack sentiments, behavior, or attitudes were to be permitted. Lindsay denied the ADL assertion that anti-Semitism was at a crisis level in part because of the failure of his administration to take a stand against it. However, he did thereafter respond more quickly to the requests by Jewish groups that he use his office to help eradicate any anti-Semitism. With the mayoralty elections coming up in the fall of 1969, having already alienated many of the groups which had backed him in 1965, Lindsay could ill afford to cut himself off from a substantial portion of the New York Jewish community. In an effort to relieve growing tensions in the city, Lindsay sought to pursue a course which would placate Jewish moderates.[68]

Concurrent with the ADL document there occurred an outpouring of Jewish indignation over the alleged upsurge in Negro anti-Semitism. Charges were made by a number of Jewish spokesmen that Negro leaders had ignored black anti-Semitism.

For example, Will Maslow, executive director of the American Jewish Congress, chastised American Negro leaders for turning blind eyes to anti-Semitism in the black community. While acknowledging that manifestations of anti-Jewish feelings came predominantly from a handful of extremists, he held that "Negro leadership is to blame for failing to repudiate and denounce even those isolated and sporadic utterances." Nonetheless, he continued, American Jewish organizations would not abandon their efforts to help Negroes find more jobs and to improve their living conditions and educational opportunities. Maslow opined that Negro anti-Semitism hurt the antiracist cause in America more than it harmed the Jews.[69]

---

[68] *New York Times,* 1 February 1969. A week after the ADL report on anti-Semitism was released Mayor Lindsay was the guest of honor at a dinner for national leaders of the ADL. He asked the ADL leaders to help him find "a middle ground of moderation and reason" to ease racial and religious tensions. The Mayor was lauded by ADL president Dore Schary and received several standing ovations.

[69] Maslow stated that "organized Jewry has entered in the war against poverty, not to win gratitude, but to help bring about that equal society in which Jews can be secure." Quoted in the *New York Times,* 7 January 1969.

Interviewed after publication of the ADL report, Maslow reflected: "What appalled most of the leaders of the Jewish community was the utter silence of the Christian community and Negro leadership in the face of flagrantly anti-Semitic utterances and articles. For example, it would have been tactically wise and expedient for the Ocean Hill school board to have denounced the black anti-Semites; instead they kept quiet."[70]

According to an analysis in *The New York Times* by Henry Raymont, the general themes of Jewish discontent were:

1. That anti-Semitic utterances and literature employed by a handful of black power extremists in the school dispute is tolerated by too many Negroes as a convenient weapon in their competition for jobs held by Jews in the teaching, school administration and social welfare fields.

2. That public officials and non-Jewish civic leaders did not speak out soon and vigorously enough at the first signs of anti-Semitic propaganda during last fall's series of school strikes.

3. That by using anti-Semitism as a political strategy, black power extremists may be finding unwitting allies among politicians eager to maintain racial peace in the cities.[71]

Rabbi Richard Rubinstein, a University of Pittsburgh chaplain, attempted to propound the point that Establishment-black coalitions were being set up at the expense of other groups. Jewish interests, were of course, the easiest and most convenient to sacrifice. An example of the new alliance was the decision by the Ford Foundation to aid the movement for local control of schools in New York City. Rubinstein's thesis was rejected by a spokesman for the Ford Foundation, Francis Keppel, who had participated in the drafting of the school decentralization project. The project had been conceived in the interest of the city as a whole, and he had not counted on the fallout which later developed.[72]

The flow of Jewish attacks on black extremism continued into February and then gradually subsided. One of the final broadsides

[70] Ibid., 26 January 1969.
[71] Ibid., 25 January 1969.
[72] Ibid.

came at a meeting of the B'nai B'rith's governing board in Washington. There Rabbi Jay Kaufman, the organization's executive vice-president, told his colleagues that Negro extremists were using anti-Semitism as "a conscious and cynical deceit" and declared that effective counteraction must come from within the Negro community itself. Anti-Semitism was a device to subvert the Negro community which was used by black leaders to "serve their own power needs and ambitions." The anti-Jewish manifestations in the Negro community were termed "rare to the American continent though classical in Europe."[73]

Sociologist Earl Raab took issue with those who say that anti-Semitism is just an expression of hostility toward whites or a rhetorical weapon. He observed that "the ideology of political anti-Semitism has precisely always been poetic excess, which has not prevented it from becoming murderous."[74]

In an article in the January issue of *Commentary,* Mr. Raab maintained that anti-Semitism as a cultural form in America is not obsolescent.[75] One does not even have to be an anti-Semite in order to engage in or support anti-Semitic behavior. To support this point Raab wrote that while the majority of Negroes might be opposed to anti-Semitic rhetoric, few were willing to do anything about it. Many middle-class blacks "are horrified by all this, . . . but on the community level where the pressure is they are likely to say that it would not do for them to attack such manifestations, because it would seem to be an attack on the militant movement itself."[76] Thus the black power movement could be anti-Semitic without a corps of anti-Semites. Raab also put forth a suggestion that the black power movement in some large cities is seeking to gain concessions from the WASP establishment at the expense of Jewish interests.[77]

There was a variety of responses by Afro-Americans to the

[73] Ibid., 3 February 1969. Rabbi Kaufman continued: "Unable to offer any constructive program to mitigate the suffering of deprived Negroes in the ghetto, they offer them the jobs Jews have attained through training, labor, proficiency and seniority. It is a cheap and larcenous scheme."
[74] Ibid., 29 December 1968.
[75] Earl Raab, "The Black Revolution and the Jewish Question," *Commentary* 47, no. 1 (January 1969):23–33.
[76] Ibid.
[77] Ibid.

much-publicized treatment of black anti-Semitism. Those who had been involved in cooperative ventures with liberal Jewish organizations over a long period feared a division in the Jewish-Negro coalition in New York City. Talk of Jewish retrenchment was viewed with great concern by such "moderates" as Whitney Young and Bayard Rustin. Young, executive director of the Urban League, warned Negroes and Puerto Ricans that anti-Semitic expressions "damage the cause of community control" of the school. He noted that the National Urban League had frequently attacked anti-Semitism and felt that the "delicate and critical" nature of the present crisis required reaffirmation of the League's long-standing position.[78]

Bayard Rustin (who had been cut off from the majority of black intellectuals by his support of the UFT during the school strikes) asserted: "Negro leaders have a moral obligation to fight against anti-Semitism. Jews have been in the forefront of the civil rights fight and probably made more of a contribution than any single group. We cannot be timid and we cannot be silent. Negro children who themselves have been brutalized by racism ought not to be further brutalized by teaching them anti-Semitism and religious prejudice."[79]

The Southern Christian Leadership Conference, under the direction of Martin Luther King's successor, Ralph Abernathy, commented in a February letter to its supporters: "In some urban centers anti-Semitism has been employed to pit Negroes against Jews. Anti-Semitism is intolerable and immoral. We will fight it, as we always have, as contemptible opportunism—as harmful to black people as to Jews—because it fosters the poison of racism generally."[80]

Some prominent Negro "moderates," however, were put off by

[78] *New York Times,* 9 January 1969. One of two incidents which reportedly prompted Young's remark was the publication of an editorial critical of Jews in a recent issue of the bimonthly Afro-American Teachers Forum which read in part: "How long shall the black and Puerto Rican communities of New York City sit back and allow the Jewish-dominated Federation of Teachers to destroy our every effort to rescue our children from those incompetent teachers whose only goal—aside from receiving fat paychecks—is stifling our children's intellectual growth?"

[79] Ibid., 26 January 1969.

[80] SCLC letter dated February 1969.

the nature of the campaign against anti-Semitism. Dr. John Morrill of the NAACP reacted negatively to what he termed Jewish "demands" that "responsible" Negro leaders respond with reassurance on behalf of the Negro community every time an instance of Negro anti-Semitism is publicized by the news media. This reflected an inability on the part of Jews to distinguish friend from foe.[81]

Floyd McKissick, in his column in the *Amsterdam News,* wrote that the conflict between Jews and blacks in New York is not the result of anti-Semitism on the part of blacks. He observed:

It is the result of legitimate conflict of interests. It is the result of an outraged community to exploitation, an outrage which would be directed against any exploiter, regardless of ethnic background. Blacks speak in terms of Jews when they speak in terms of exploitation, [but] the real exploiter is the big corporation and the millionaires, mainly Anglo-Saxon, who control the corporations. Both Jews and Blacks are victims of the same oppressive system. But within that system, Jews have advantages over Blacks—advantages gained by the fact of their whiteness, and advantages gratefully accepted. It is difficult for any group to relinquish an advantage just as it is difficult for any individual to do so. But if this city is ever to reach bearable sanity level, some groups must give up some advantages.[82]

A Negro churchman, Reverend Canon Walter D. Dennis, termed a series of demands made by the New York Board of Rabbis to curb anti-Semitism as "intemperate and rash." The demands had included the withdrawal of WBAI's license by the FCC and the replacement of William Booth as Human Rights Commissioner. Dennis said that "only time will tell whether or not [the demand for Booth's removal] will have the effect of moving many moderate black leaders into the camp of the militants and extremists." He advised that "what is now needed is a moratorium on intemperate demands by the Jewish community" and a "cessation of injudicious remarks by the black community." Reverend Dennis exhorted that "anti-Semitism must be condemned wherever it is found and responsible people must do all in their power to eradi-

---

[81] *New York Times,* 13 April 1969.
[82] Floyd McKissick, "Anti-Black and Anti-Jew," in the *Amsterdam-News,* 8 February 1969.

cate this menace from among us, but scapegoating, book burning and unconstitutional prohibition of free speech is certainly not the way to go at it."[83]

From the standpoint of a black activist deeply involved in the decentralization dispute, the chairman of the IS 201 complex, David Spencer, rapped the Jews for denouncing as "militants" those blacks who stood up for their rights.[84]

One unidentified Afro-American upbraided Jews for finding anti-Semitism where none existed. Speaking at one of the series of private meetings of religious and community leaders called by Mayor Lindsay in February he remarked that "the first thing that happens when a synagogue is set on fire, you look for a black." He then noted that most of the captured arsonists in the spate of synagogue fires thus far were whites, and some were Jews.[85]

Opinion among the non-Jewish intellectual community was split, but sympathy for the blacks appeared to increase as Negro-Jewish tensions mounted. One nonpartisan observer, John Leo, writing in the liberal Catholic journal *Commonweal* remarked that Negro anti-Semitism had quickly become the number one political issue in New York City. Mayor Lindsay found himself going from synagogue to synagogue in an effort to soothe a Jewish community which found itself "in high anxiety, if not frenzy about Negro hatred for Jews."[86]

How did the emotions rise to such a fever pitch? Leo cites as a key step the decision by Albert Shanker of the UFT to repro-

[83] *New York Times,* 10 February 1969.

[84] Ibid., 1 February 1969.

[85] Ibid. 22 February 1969.

[86] John Leo, "Black Anti-Semitism," *Commonweal* 89, no. 19 (14 February 1969):618. Frenzy was not too strong a word for it according to Leo. He spoke of one Jewish friend telling him how the Gentile was determined to raise the black men at the Jew's expense, so that Gentiles and blacks could turn on the Jew together. Another Jewish friend counted on Leo as "one of the people who will help get my children out when the pogrom comes to New York." Leo wrote that "the same adrenalin flows among leaders of the Jewish service organizations. One told me Murray Kempton [columnist of the *New York Post*] was 'a son of a bitch' for finding an Anti-Defamation League report on black anti-Semitism incoherent and inconclusive. Another reportedly called Thomas Hoving, Director of the Metropolitan Museum, a 'racist bastard' to his face, after an anti-Semitic remark was somehow allowed to stand in a teenage Negro girl's introductory essay to a museum catalogue."

duce and circulate in large quantities anti-Semitic handbills which had come out during the "long complicated dispute which pitted a largely Jewish union against a pugnacious group of community leaders in Ocean Hill-Brownsville." Until that time the issue "had not entered the public consciousness as a stark Negro-Jewish battle." Prior to that time

anti-Semitic sallies by LeRoi Jones and the SNCC leadership had alerted the Jewish community nationally to the possibility of black frustration pouring into the ancient mold of anti-Semitism, even though there was scant evidence that the possibility was becoming a reality. And Jews were well aware that by the accident of the city's social history, the vast bureaucracies which irritate the Negro most—schools and welfare, primarily—are disproportionately Jewish. By another accident, Negroes in the ghetto come into disproportionate contact with Jewish landlords and entrepreneurs.

But be this as it may, "it was Shanker's handbills which provided the spark." To call one's opponents (the Ocean Hill-Brownsville Governing Board) anti-Semitic "is equivalent to labeling someone a pinko while Joe McCarthy was riding high."[87]

Jewish anxiety was further increased by the mayor's Special Committee on Racial and Religious Prejudice report (the Botein Committee) and the Anti-Defamation League report which declared respectively that there was an "appalling amount of bigotry" and that anti-Semitism had reached a "crisis level" in New York.[88]

Leo suggested that Murray Friedman's article in the January 1969 issue of *Commentary* should be read as a gentle reminder that "what appears as classic anti-Semitism among New York blacks should not be interpreted in the light of six million dead in Hitler's Europe, but in the light of the normal roughhouse of good old American ethnic politics tied to the consciousness of Black Power." Leo concluded that "we do not know if anti-Semitism [had become] a significant factor in the Negro community,

[87] Ibid., pp. 618–619.
[88] Ibid. For the ADL to have found a "crisis level" of anti-Semitism based on a few scurrilities "is the kind of racial smear" that invites the creation of a Negro Anti-Defamation League. Such a NADL might find a crisis in Jewish business ethics because two color TV's have been repossessed without cause."

though we are entitled to suspect that Shanker and the ADL may easily make it so."[89]

A small segment of Jewish opinion also strongly opposed the overreaction to incidents of black anti-Semitism. A group calling itself the Jewish Citizens Committee for Community Control took a full-page advertisement in the *New York Times* on March 16 to reprint an article which had appeared earlier in the biweekly journal, *The Public Life*. The article was entitled "How New York Jews Were Turned Against Black Men: Exploding the Myth of Black Anti-Semitism."[90] The piece accused several of the Jewish service agencies, particularly the Anti-Defamation League, of blowing out of proportion a number of incidents surrounding the New York School strike and making it appear that black anti-Semitism was endemic in the city.

The *Public Life* article, written by Walter Karp and H. L. Shapiro, asserted that the UFT and other opponents of school decentralization created the black anti-Semitism issue "to break the alliance between the liberal Jewish middle class and the black people of the city," thus destroying the decentralization experiment. The Jewish organizations, one by one, were then pressured to follow suit. The Jewish agencies themselves had "neither the power, nor being for the most part liberal minded, the desire to exaggerate charges of anti-Semitism—especially against black people." The article went on to contend that "from 1966 to the fall of 1968, it was the consistent policy of almost every major Jewish organization to *minimize* the significance of occasional reports of black anti-Semitism."[91] The ADL as late as October 1968 denied there was any organized effort behind the anti-Jewish leaflets distributed during the school strikes."[92] Yet the same ADL in its January 1969 report spoke of "proof" of a dangerous effort to

[89] Ibid. As one of Leo's "friends" put it: "I never never thought I'd live to see New York Jews running around in circles like a bunch of *Brooklyn Tablet* Catholics."

[90] Walter Karp and H. L. Shapiro, "Exploding the Myth of Black Anti-Semitism," *The Public Life* 1, no. 8 (21 February 1969), reprinted in the *New York Times,* 16 March 1969, p. 7E.

[91] Ibid. For example, on 28 April 1966, an American Jewish Congress spokesman coined the term "Jewish backlash" and denounced stories of black anti-Jewish sentiment as "overblown."

[92] Ibid. *The Public Life* article recalled the five-year study conducted by Gary

drive Jewish personnel out of the schools.[93] According to the *Public Life* article even the most prominent of the Jewish organizations succumbed to pressures and accepted the myth of snowballing black anti-Semitism. This in turn confirmed its existence for the thousands of Jews who had resisted the UFT's "propaganda."

By mid-March 1969, the Anti-Defamation League began to reappraise the rigid position adopted several months earlier on the question of black anti-Semitism. Two unpublished critiques of the ADL report which were circulated privately among New York Jewish organizations undoubtedly helped prompt the reappraisal. On February 6 Leonard J. Fein, director of research for the Harvard-MIT Joint Center for Urban Studies and also chairman of the Commission on Community Interrelations of the American Jewish Congress, wrote that blacks were very sensitive about the anti-Semitism issue, and that the matter should be dealt with carefully and precisely. "A continuation of the vague but panicked rhetoric which has marked so much of the debate" was not needed. He cited the ADL report as having exacerbated an already volatile issue:

It fails to distinguish between gutter anti-Semitism . . . and the statements of public men; it equates vulgar imprecation and sophisticated if specious reasoning; it neglects entirely the counter provocations, which though they can never justify anti-Semitism, at least help to explain it. As a result, it does not contribute to either understanding or constructive action; it merely inflames.[94]

A second critique was written by Henry Schwarzchild, currently a fellow at the Metropolitan Applied Research Center and a mem-

---

Marx for the ADL, published in May 1967, which found that blacks were the least anti-Semitic group in the country, that they were less likely than any other white group to vote for a candidate who ran on an anti-Semitic platform, and that the more "militant" a black was the less likely he was to be anti-white and anti-Jewish.

[93] Ibid. Four of the seven incidents cited as proof in the ADL dossier involved "Sonny Carson and two of his sidekicks in a rump organization known as Brooklyn Independent CORE. The expulsion of the Jews —surely a pivotal point in demonstrating the danger of black anti-Semitism—turns out to be the theme song of a one-man band."

[94] Quoted in Ferretti, "New York's Black Anti-Semitism Scare," p. 26.

ber of the Commission on Religion and Race of the Synagogue Council of America. The critique began with a remark made a year earlier by the national director of the ADL, Ben Epstein, which read: "the Jewish Community would be well advised . . . to drop preoccupation with Negro anti-Semitism, which only serves to divert energies from the civil rights struggle." Schwarzchild then criticized the ADL for doing just the opposite in its controversial report.[95]

This reappraisal also was partially due to the work of Kenyon Burke, the ADL's recently appointed Director of Urban Affairs. Burke, incidentally, was the first Negro selected for an important position dealing with community relations by any of the major Jewish service agencies. In a memorandum dated 19 March 1969 circulated among ADL regional directors, Burke in effect stated that Jewish organizations were overplaying the theme that Negro leaders were not speaking out against anti-Semitism. His covering notes for the memorandum read in part:

We have heard from our constituency with discouraging frequency in the past few weeks whenever a black extremist has received publicity as the result of an anti-Semitic Statement. The burden of the complaint has been, "Why doesn't the Negro leadership speak out against anti-Semitism and Racism?" I have therefore gathered together excerpts of editorials that appeared in the black press and a significant number of statements made by responsible black citizens that were published in the white press throughout the nation. . . . The common thread running through all their statements is the denouncing of anti-Semitism and Racism. This compilation makes an impressive document that effectively deals with the pervasive feeling that "Negroes have not spoken out."[96]

[95] Schwartzchild asked, rhetorically, why black organizations had not compiled a report on anti-black sentiment in the Jewish community, and then replied: "Negroes are not interested in a nosecounting contest with the ADL over which minority group has suffered more verbal assault, even though they could win this sad competition hands down. Negroes are now struggling to end the oppressive force over them of fundamentally racist liberal institutions of the society. It is liberal racism which is the enemy. And this produces puzzlement, discomfiture and resentment among liberals, intellectuals, and in the Jewish community." Ibid., p. 27.
[96] Memorandum to ADL Regional Directors by Kenyon C. Burke, 19 March 1969.

To make its point the memorandum listed among others statements by Whitney Young, Roy Wilkins, Bayard Rustin, Ralph Abernathy, Carl Rowan, Judge William Booth, M. Brent Oldham, Congresswoman Shirley Chisholm, Judge Raymond Pace Alexander, Reverend Canon Walter Dennis, John Sengestacke (editor of the *Chicago Defender*), several Harlem residents, Councilman Thomas Bradley (of Los Angeles), Robert Magnum, Floyd McKissick, and editorials from the *Minneapolis Spokesman,* the *Louisville Defender,* the *Call and Post* (Cleveland), the *Amsterdam News,* and *Crisis* (the NAACP monthly).

Some of the individual and editorial criticisms of anti-Semitism had been made in recent months and may well have been elicited by appeals of Jewish groups. The statements were most welcome. Nonetheless, it was becoming increasingly understood that leaders of the moderate Negro organizations have little or no influence on the kinds of individuals who would make blatant anti-Semitic remarks. The ADL came to realize that Negro moderates who identified too closely with the Jewish or white establishment tended to lose what little rapport existed between themselves and the black ghetto dwellers.

Some Jewish religious leaders had not been drawn into the fray with the black community over the anti-Semitism issue. In late January a biracial Committee to Stop Hate was formed. The Committee asked rhetorically in its newspaper advertisements: "Shall we split into warring tribes or unite in solving the problem? Will *you* pledge brotherhood with us?" Seeking to curb aroused passions, other Jewish and Negro clergymen began to meet in a search for racial peace.

At a Harlem meeting of fifty rabbis, white ministers and priests, and Negro clergy, Albert Vorspan of the Union of American Hebrew Congregations deplored the recriminations between Negroes and Jews. Despite the shouting and anger, he said, there remains the identity of interests of two minorities seeking meaningful and peaceful coexistence in a pluralistic society.

Vorspan spoke of the factors which have led to the deep psychological insecurity afflicting Jews, culminated by the Nazi holocaust and Arab hostility toward Israel. He referred to the recent pictures of Jews hanged in Iraq after conviction for "espionage."

He said: "I see an anxiety [in New York's Jewish community] which borders on hysteria . . . a profound visceral reaction." Speaking next, the Reverend Wyatt Tee Walker, a Negro, said: "It was heartening for me to hear of your paranoia, because it allows for me to admit for the Black community our schizophrenia."[97]

In February 1969 the Ford Foundation gave a grant of $54,500 to help support a continuing program of bringing rabbis and Negro clergy together for dialogue. Other clergy urged a cooperative council to tackle neighborhood problems arising from racial tensions. Such a venture was organized by an interracial group of clergy on New York's West Side.[98]

Jewish community leaders began to realize that the fear of anti-Semitism might severely hamper continued Jewish support for the civil rights movement. An appeal was made by the Central Committee of American Rabbis that the voice of Reform Judaism "must not be silenced by the summer soldiers and the fair weather patriots who were for racial justice when the going was easier, but now counsel abject silence or even outright opposition to the just demands of black Americans." A statement issued by the conference held that Jews particularly should be understanding of the Negroes' "painful withdrawal into separation and nationalism" after many years of little real progress. It continued: "We Jews, who for so long feared and hated the truncheon of the oppressor, should understand the feelings of the black community in a country whose law enforcement officials are rarely black, and, more often than not, appear the instrument of the white man's oppression."[99]

The setting up of a "hot line" linking various human relation agencies in New York to assure prompt communication and joint action on community problems, particularly between the Jewish and Negro communities, symbolized a growing awareness that the old contact between communities was inadequate. Another meaningful act, in this case primarily designed to reawaken the consciousness of Jews, was the interracial, interfaith Passover seder

[97] "Fifty Rabbis and Negro Clergymen Searching for Racial Peace," *New York Times,* 31 January 1969.
[98] Ibid., 6 February 1969.
[99] Ibid., 8 February 1969.

held in Washington, D.C. on April 4, the first anniversary of Martin Luther King's death. A gathering of rabbis, black community organizers, and white radicals broke matzos together and read from a Freedom *Haggadah* put together by Arthur Waskow, fellow at the Institute for Policy Studies. Included in the *Haggadah* were quotes from such latter-day prophets and judges as Eldridge Cleaver, Martin Buber, Hannah Arendt, and A. J. Muste. The retelling of the Passover stressed the struggles of Negro and Jew alike to seek liberation from modern-day pharoahs.[100]

In May the American Jewish Congress announced that it was seeking to avoid the "dialogue syndrome" and to concentrate on working with Negroes on specific problems of mutual concern. A specific need was to halt the panic and physical decline in Jewish neighborhoods once Negroes began to move in. The Congress felt that by bringing members of the Jewish community into direct and productive contact with Negroes living and working in the same communities, panic might be prevented and with it "the deterioration and blight that comes from fear."[101] In some cities the Congress was trying to prevent the "panic flights" of such Jewish institutions as community centers and synagogues from the central city.

The American Jewish Committee has also stepped up its efforts to promote racial equality. It is helping blacks to establish businesses in the ghettos in New York, Miami, St. Louis, Cincinnati, and several other cities. Local chapters throughout the country are taking the initiative in finding jobs for the hard-core unemployed and in setting up on-the-job training programs. In New York, the American Jewish Committee cosponsors two ghetto housing developments and has attempted to bring the Shanker and McCoy forces together.

The national director of the B'nai B'rith's Anti-Defamation

100 For an account of the Washington Freedom *seder* see the Judith Coburn's article "Passover in the Ghetto: This Year in Washington," in the *Village Voice*, 10 April 1969.

101 One such example has been the setting up of the East-West Grand Concourse community council in the Bronx. The interracial council has outlined a program to (a) establish a children's day care center, (b) open storefront recreational facilities for the elderly, and (c) encourage property owners to use available funds for improvements and rehabilitation projects. *New York Times*, 19 May 1969.

League, Ben Epstein, spoke of an encouraging "new frankness and realism" which had been developing in Negro-Jewish relations, as the result of a series of off-the-record conferences held throughout the country. Spokesmen for the ADL emphasized at these conferences that their concern for anti-Semitism in no way minimized their conviction that the racial crisis could be resolved by unified efforts on the part of the total community. Epstein did not wish to jeopardize the progress being made by identifying the individuals or groups involved in the conferences. He warned that future confrontation between Negroes and Jews could be expected in welfare, health services, and other areas where Jews fill a large number of positions. In accommodating to social change, "Jews and Negroes must seek to avoid racism and anti-Semitism."[102]

The more relaxed mood on the part of the Jewish agencies was sustained by an assessment by authorities on intergroup relations who found no evidence of a significant increase of anti-Semitism despite the Negro-Jewish controversy. The report made by the National Jewish Community Relations Advisory Council affirmed that: "notwithstanding some acute manifestations . . . overt anti-Semitism continues at a low ebb, as it has for a number of years." Despite latent anti-Semitism, "Jewish group status and security are unprecedentedly high in America." The report pointed to the likelihood of continuing clashes of interest arising from Negro demands for greater opportunities in school teaching and other fields where Jews are heavily represented. But as an appended statement by Alex Allen of the National Urban League admonished: "What is essential is that the Jewish community not interpret situational friction and competition and the resultant antagonism as anti-Semitism."[103]

While greater attempts were being made by liberal Jewish groups to communicate with Negro leaders and to learn of the real problems of the ghettos, the fear of black anti-Semitism was not so quickly forgotten by many middle-class and lower middle-class Jews. This concern, strongest among those who live or work in close geographic proximity to Negroes, led to the formation of the Jewish Defense League (JDL). The League represents a new

[102] Ibid. 19 April 1969.
[103] Ibid., 13 April 1969.

militancy among some New York Jews. Its members and supporters include small businessmen, working class people, and some students from proletarian families. Many are from Orthodox backgrounds, and are determined that Jews "never again" shall be an easy mark for their enemies. The JDL followed in the footsteps of the Maccabees, an organization in Brooklyn which provided escort service at night and patrolled the streets after dark in cars to detect and deter crime. The Maccabees were disbanded after city officials objected that the group constituted an unauthorized, para-police force. An immediate purpose of the group was served, however, by better police protection which was subsequently provided in the Crown Heights section of Brooklyn.

The Jewish Defense League was founded in September 1968 during the school strike on the premises that not only was anti-Semitism on the increase but also that the city's political leaders were unconcerned about the phenomenon. As an article in the *National Observer* put it: "like the Black Panthers in Oakland and the Puerto Rican Young Lords in Chicago, the JDL contends a defense force is necessary because of the breakdown of law and order. The group believes the increasing violence of the streets defines the need."[104] The membership of the JDL grew significantly during the spring and summer of 1969 to an estimated six thousand. The founder and spiritual father of the movement, Rabbi Meir Kahane, has sharply chastised Mayor Lindsay for his alleged softness on anti-Semitism and his inability to maintain law and order. Kahane counters his critics among liberal Jewish organizations by asserting that such criticism "almost always comes from a rich Jew who lives in Scarsdale or some other rich suburb. How can a rich Jew or non-Jew criticize an organization of lower and middle class Jews who daily live in terror because of the breakdown of government?"[105]

[104] *National Observer*, 28 July 1969.
[105] Ibid. Kahane continued: "This city is polarized almost beyond hope— There's anger, hate, frustration . . . The Jew is the weakest link in the white chain, and the black militant knows that few non-Jews are concerned with the Jew's plight. The Jew has always been more liberal than other white ethnic groups. So now most Jewish neighborhoods are integrated, and the militant blacks there practice terror, extortion and violence. The establishment Jew is scandalized by us, but our support comes from the grass-root. The People."

The weekly *Jewish Press* served as an organ for Rabbi Kahane to disseminate his views. In enlarged headlines the *Press* underscores every available anti-Semitic incident or remark, thus adding to the tendency toward collective paranoia of its readership. The paper, for example, in its 20–26 December 1968 issue ran a huge front-page headline, "Black Group Hits 'Ruthless' Zionists." The article denounced the "vicious anti-Semitic and anti-Zionist" leaflet which had been circulated by the Tenants' Rights Party in Harlem during the school strike. The leaflet was essentially the work of a few individuals. Nevertheless, an unaware *Jewish Press* reader would be led to believe that the black areas of the city were seething with anti-Semitism and were about to launch a pogrom (with the silent acquiescence of the WASP leadership in City Hall and the Ford Foundation).

Rabbi Kahane has spoken out against those Jewish moderates and liberals who have called JDL street patrols "goon squads" and "a group of self-appointed vigilantes whose protection the Jewish community does not want or need."[106] In a rejoinder he argues that "the B'nai B'rith and the American Jewish Congress along with their non-Jewish counterparts that comprise the liberal establishment have little or no comprehension of the radical mind and less that of the thinking of the masses." It is this ignorance "which is causing them to lead us all astray in this racial crisis that could mean destruction for the country and the Jews."[107]

"To turn the other cheek is not a Jewish trait," Rabbi Kahane contends. In its first nine months the JDL tangled with hecklers on Fifth Avenue during a parade celebrating Israeli independence day, obtained a court order which required the City College of New York to reopen after having been shut down by black and Puerto Rican demonstrators, and "policed" a Model Cities council election in Crown Heights. The JDL also sent about one hundred members to Temple Emanu-El on Fifth Avenue to block an announced visit by James Foreman's group which has been seeking to collect reparations for past exploitation of the black man by American Christians and Jews. (Temple Emanu-El itself objected to the JDL tactic.) "Heads would have been broken" if Forman had

---

[106] *Jewish Press,* 20 December 1968.
[107] Ibid., 27 December 1968.

appeared, said one of the JDL coordinators. "We felt that if they could extort money from one synagogue, black extremists all over the country would do the same thing—If they can enter our synagogues it is just as well that they bring on the machine guns now."[108]

During the summer of 1969 the JDL ran a youth training camp in the Catskill Mountains. The teenagers attending the camp learned karate and shooting. After an eight-week session they returned to their homes in some of the rougher integrated neighborhoods or near the fringes of the black ghettos. A Brooklyn College physics student, Marty Lewinter, who taught karate at the camp, attributed the youngsters' dedication to the fact that "all of us had someone among those six million who walked quietly into German gas chambers. We won't just walk in again. Never again."

How seriously should one take the Jewish Defense League? In reality, America, for all its ills, is not Germany of the 1930s, and the Jews in New York are not surrounded by hostile neighbors like their brethren in Israel. America's Jews, objectively speaking, are not about to be victimized by black pogroms. The most likely target of some hypothetical future pogrom would be the blacks themselves. Therefore, the JDL is understandably condemned by most Jewish human relations groups and service organizations.[109] But, after considering all this, the JDL cannot merely be dismissed as a group of Jews playing a game solely for the sake of bravado. The apprehension of the lower middle-class Jewish community, like other working class groups, is real. The political backlash in America has to be understood as more than just latent white racism coming to the surface. The Wallace phenomenon in 1968 had a strong racial component, but it was also based upon other working class grievances and fears. These are many people who feel

---

[108] *National Observer,* 28 July 1969.

[109] *New York Times,* 30 June, 1969. A coordinating body of Jewish human relations groups representing nine national organizations and eighty-two local communal groups, condemned Jewish extremist groups that threaten "violent and coercive tactics" in defense of Jewish interests. The meeting held in Pittsburgh stressed that groups "not take the law into their own hands." The condemnation did not apply to those who, in cooperation with the police, have patroled areas when violence had been widespread.

threatened by Negro job competition, the rising crime rates, the possible deterioration of their neighborhoods, and integrated schools. Coupled with this is the myth that the established elite in America, in an effort to placate the Negro, is somehow sacrificing the interests of the working class and dispossessed whites.

Overt Negro-Jewish tensions receded considerably by mid-1969. But the events of the previous year had churned up the emotions of Jews for whom the Nazi holocaust is a recent memory. Hopefully, after an end to the Vietnam tragedy, America will strive to reorder its national priorities, taking into consideration the psychological needs of those who have joined or lent their support to organizations such as the JDL, along with those of the historically oppressed black, brown, and red minorities.

}9{

WHERE
DO WE STAND NOW?

BY THE END OF WORLD WAR I THE MASSIVE MIGRATION OF EAST European Jews to urban America was almost complete, while the demographic movement of black Americans northward was reaching its peak. Although Afro-Americans would continue to leave the rural South through the 1960s, it was apparent by the 1920s that the southern Negro had not found his promised land in the North. He had merely exchanged the existence of the sharecropper for that of the ghetto dweller. His image in the eyes of his white countrymen had scarcely been altered.

These two unrelated population movements placed large numbers of blacks and Jews in close proximity for the first time. Contacts between the two minorities prior to the twentieth century had been sporadic. Henceforth, the contacts were to be more frequent. As is the case with almost all white-black relationships, contacts were generally of the abrasion-producing variety: landlord-tenant, housewife-domestic, employer-employee, merchant-customer.

The title of this book, *Bittersweet Encounter,* is in many ways indicative of the relationships, but is also partially misleading. Morally, as well as financially, Negro groups in the twentieth century seeking to ameliorate their condition have received proportionately more support from Jews than from the great majority of other white groups in America. When white-black intermarriages have taken place they have often been between liberated Jews and Negroes in the North.[1] Yet the Afro-American's relationship with Jews as with other white ethnic groups, has been far more bitter than sweet. And for most Jews and Negroes there have been few and sometimes no encounters with individuals of the other group, except on an unequal status basis. Jews and Negroes rarely meet as neighbors or as equals in business. While some Negroes in the North have met Jews or other whites in a friendly situation, the majority of ghetto dwellers today have very few contacts with Jews, and what contacts they have generally reinforce the "bitter" rather than the "sweet" overtones. On the whole, Jews know very little about Negroes, and Negroes about Jews, as people. Most Jews do not fully understand the disabilities which have handicapped the Negroes in America, while Negroes sometimes underestimate the effect of the Nazi experience and previous tragedies in Europe on the Jewish psyche.[2]

In the chapter "Wellsprings of Tension" and elsewhere in this book, we have reviewed those studies which have summarized data on Jewish and Negro attitudes toward each other. Several studies of Negro attitudes are available; however, there is a paucity of statistical data about Jewish attitudes toward blacks. For the most part, we must draw upon statements by Negroes about Jewish conduct and self-appraisals by some Jewish essayists such as Norman Podhoretz to get a sense of residual racism among Jews. Jewish negative feelings about Negroes are often expressed privately but rarely appear in print, so they are not easily "docu-

---

[1] The story of several of these marriages, as appraised by both partners, is related in Albert I. Gordon, "Negro-Jewish Marriages," *Judaism* 13, no. 2 (Spring 1964):164–184.

[2] In an ADL sponsored study measuring the reactions of the inhabitants of Oakland, California, to the trial of Adolph Eichmann in 1961, Negro respondents on the whole were less informed than whites of the proceedings. Of those aware of the trial, Negroes at every level of educational background were slightly less likely than whites to hold Eichmann guilty as charged by the prosecution. (84 percent of the Negroes expressing an opinion judged Eichmann to be guilty, as compared with 95 percent of the whites sampled.) Charles Y. Glock, Gertrude J. Selznick, and Joe L. Spaeth, *The Apathetic Majority* (New York: Harper & Row, 1966), p. 78.

mented." Jews do not express their feelings about Negroes going "too far too fast" as vocally as other white ethnic groups, nor do they attempt the kinds of physical coercion against blacks which other whites have sometimes employed.

Jewish names crop up with regularity in the civil rights movement, and Jewish radicals are conspicuously present in support of the "black revolution." But these Jews constitute a small percentage of the total Jewish-American community. In a seminal article in *Commentary* written more than two decades ago, Kenneth Clark referred to some studies dealing with racial attitudes, especially among college students, which showed "in general that Jewish students are relatively less negative in their attitudes toward Negroes than are average Gentile whites."[3] However, one investigation in a New York community cited by Clark revealed that nearly 60 percent of its Jewish inhabitants harbored some unfavorable stereotyped reaction toward Negroes. Those who held stereotyped views felt Negroes "have no ambition—they are lazy—they drink a lot—they have low intelligence—they are low class, rowdy, dirty and noisy."[4] Many Jews still hold such views.

Speaking about the psychology of young blacks in New York City who make anti-Semitic remarks, Julius Lester commented insightfully that out of frustration blacks sometimes want to say things that will hurt Jews. At the time of the New York school strikes "we were talking about decentralization and education and Shanker starts yelling anti-Semitism."[5] The bitterness of the conflict during the strikes led to some unpleasant incidents over the following months. The anti-Semitic poem by the fifteen-year-old girl read on Lester's WBAI program "was like a zen slap in the face for Jews"; it shocked people.[6]

In a physical sense blacks have no capacity to carry out a pogrom against the Jews, nor do they desire to do so. But Lester

---

[3] Kenneth B. Clark, "Candor about Negro-Jewish Relations," *Commentary*, February 1948, p. 11.

[4] Ibid., p. 10. By the criteria used to measure stereotypes in the above study, 70 percent of the Negroes had some unfavorable stereotyped reaction toward Jews.

[5] Nat Hentoff, "Blacks and Jews: An Interview with Julius Lester," *Evergreen Review*, April 1969, p. 71.

[6] Ibid., p. 72.

believes that Jews can create anti-Semites by the way in which they respond to Negro-Jewish tensions.

If it's very clear that he (a Jew) is brutalizing me for his own ends, then I'm going to retaliate, and I will retaliate in a way that will most hurt him. I don't think I have any other choice. I don't want to be called an anti-Semite for it. And that can be better understood if you understand that black people are a colonized people. You have, you know, two groups—the colonized and the colonizers. And the Jewish community is in the position of being on the side of the colonizers. . . . We are America's Jews, the Jews think we are the Germans.[7]

What Lester and others, black and white, are emphasizing is the fact that in America the Jews are part of the goyim and black people are cast as Jews.

Jewish concern about Negroes in recent years has focused on the issue of anti-Semitism. The term anti-Semitism, as we have used it in this book, involves irrational and stereotyped attitudes about Jewish beliefs and behavior. Resentment of ghetto dwellers to unfair business practices, for example, has nothing to do with anti-Semitism unless, of course, Jewish merchants are singled out as Jews, and unfairly condemned as having less ethical business practices than other white businessmen—an allegation which has no basis in reality. As pointed out in chapter 4, the problem of how to measure anti-Semitism is ultimately a subjective matter. Equally difficult to ascertain is the level beyond which latent anti-Semitism constitutes a real danger to Jews and to the equilibrium of society.

On the basis of research carried out in 1964 for his book, *Protest and Prejudice,* Gary Marx reported that no case could be made for the widely held notion "that anti-Semitism is more widespread among Negroes than among whites, any more than it could be shown that [Negroes] single out Jews for special enmity."[8] Three-quarters of the Negro respondents in the study made no distinction between Jews and other whites. Among the 25 percent who did make such a distinction, "Jews were seen in a more favorable light than other whites by a 4–1 ratio."[9]

Marx noted that blacks were somewhat more accepting of eco-

---

[7] Ibid., p. 73.
[8] Gary T. Marx, *Protest and Prejudice: A Study of Belief in the Black Community* (New York: Harper & Row, 1967), p. 147.
[9] Ibid., p. 139.

nomic stereotypes about Jews,[10] a conclusion which was also reached by Selznick and Steinberg in their study, *Tenacity of Prejudice,* conducted in 1964. On the other hand, blacks "consistently emerge as less anti-Semitic than white gentiles where economic stereotypes are not involved. Furthermore, Blacks were considerably more likely than whites to reject discriminatory practices against Jews."[11] Because they have suffered discrimination themselves, blacks generally decry discrimination against any other minority group. Negroes interviewed by Selznick and Steinberg were considerably less likely than whites to support discriminatory practices against Jews. Almost all Negroes, 91 percent as compared with 69 percent of whites, said that private clubs should not have the right to exclude Jews. Only 51 percent of Negroes as compared with 68 percent of whites held that they would be disturbed if their political party nominated a Jew for president. Negroes, because they have been discriminated against by whites generally, respond to their own situation by decrying discrimination against other minorities—in this case Jewish-American—more than do whites.[12]

Since 1964, America's racial crisis has deepened. Attitudes seemingly have hardened. Yet Marx, in an updated 1969 paperback edition of his book, reiterates his earlier contention that "most Negroes favor integration . . . are opposed to indiscriminate violence and are not consistently anti-white or anti-Semitic" and asserts that this "conclusion would seem still to hold in 1969, if perhaps not as strongly."[13]

A survey carried out by the Bureau of Applied Research at Columbia University for the American Jewish Committee came up with results strikingly similar to those of Marx. The levels of anti-Semitism were "not dramatically higher or lower" than those discovered by the ADL-sponsored study. The anti-Jewishness which existed among Negroes was primarily a function of a generalized

[10] See the earlier chapter on "Wellsprings of Tension" for a discussion of the Marx and the Selznick and Steinberg studies.
[11] See Marx, *Protest and Prejudice,* pp. 147–148; Gertrude Selznick and Stephen Steinberg, *The Tenacity of Prejudice* (New York: Harper & Row, 1969), p. 129.
[12] Ibid., pp. 123–129.
[13] Marx, *Protest and Prejudice,* p. 216.

resentment toward whites. With respect to Negro contacts with landlords, storekeepers, and employees: "Jews are as favorably viewed or more so than are non-Jewish whites." Jews were also seen as the most pro-Negro of the white ethnic groups.[14]

One central conclusion which emerges from these studies is that Afro-Americans are certainly no more negative than white Americans in their views about Jews, and are sometimes less negative. In those areas such as New York City and Chicago where more Negroes are inclined to accept unfavorable stereotypes of Jews, the latter tend to be a conspicuous and readily identifiable part of a system which deals exploitatively with nonwhites.

It would seem that if the same ADL 1964 studies were conducted again in 1969–1970, the percentage of blacks who would "qualify" as anti-Semitic might be slightly higher, especially in New York City. Some blacks hold that New York Jews in a collective sense acted irresponsibly during the period of the school strikes and community control struggle.

A recent survey entitled "Black-Jewish Relations in New York City," which was financed by the Ford Foundation and carried out by Louis Harris, indicated that Jews had serious misapprehensions about blacks. Jews exaggerated the strength of the separatists in the black community. Almost 50 percent of the Jews interviewed believed that Afro-Americans sought to "tear down white society." Black enmity toward Jews was discovered but Jews generally viewed "anti-Jewish feeling as worse than it is in reality."[15]

The fact that American blacks collectively have very little power is no source of comfort for those Jews who live near large concentrations of poor Negroes in urban areas. It should, however, be reassuring for Jews to know that to the extent that anti-Semitism does exist among blacks, it is not ordinarily of the mindless traditional, Christ-killer variety, but is often based on the realities of black-white encounters. Such a realization, hopefully, should lead substantial numbers of American Jews to want to engage in action programs which would help to abate the black anger stem-

[14] Carolyn Olivia Atkinson, *Attitudes of Selected Small Samples of Negroes Toward Jews and Other Ethnic Groups* (New York: Bureau of Applied Social Research, Columbia, 1968), p. 74. The sample used in this study was rather small (48).
[15] *New York Times,* 26 November 1969.

ming from real grievances against white America of which Jews are a part.

It should be noted that the studies sponsored by various Jewish organizations have focused mainly on one side of the picture. While the ADL has an excellent record of seeking to identify and eradicate prejudice, its first concern, indeed its historic raison d'être, has understandably been the problems and needs of American Jewry. Consequently, there has been little effort expended in fighting the discrimination of the dominant white majority against blacks and other nonwhite minorities.

There are class as well as racial components which figure in black-white tensions. A major source of friction in many cities is created by blacks desiring to move up the socioeconomic ladder into occupations presently held by whites. The process of upward mobility in American cities has usually reflected the rank order in which ethnic and racial groups have arrived. Blacks, of course, have always been excluded from this pattern. When Jews moved up the economic ladder in New York their places were often taken by blacks and Puerto Ricans, but Jews continue to dominate the industries in question. Herbert Gans, in a sociological evaluation of Negro-Jewish conflict in New York City, cites the garment industry as the foremost example of this occurrence: while Jews retain many ownership and managerial positions and are the leading officers in the unions, nonwhites hold most of the low paying jobs.[16]

The civil-service protected professions and jobs were an area which large numbers of Jews entered in past decades. Public school teaching became an occupation attractive to many educationally minded Jews of working-class background who sought a respectable position in society along with job security. Even though the number of Jewish entrants into public school teaching has been declining, the percentage of Jews among new teachers in 1960 was still at least 60 percent of the total.[17] By contrast, scarcely 10 percent of New York City's public school teachers are black. Blacks and Puerto Ricans also seek more positions as school administrators, college professors and students, antipoverty workers, and in

[16] Herbert J. Gans, "Negro-Jewish Conflict in New York City: A Sociological Evaluation," *Midstream*, March 1969, p. 4.
[17] Ibid., p. 7.

various municipal services heavily dominated by Jews. In cities other than New York, where other ethnic groups stand in the way of Negroes receiving a representative share of positions in the professions and trades, antagonism between Negro and Jew is less likely to arise.

During the New York school strike in 1968, tensions dramatically rose to the surface. A few blacks who felt the UFT leadership was actively working to discredit the community control experiment resorted to anti-Semitic outbursts. The obscure individuals who made these remarks were given citywide prominence by the UFT and the news media. Some Jews reverted to a racist mood, although their private remarks and thoughts rarely received any public coverage. The Jewish middle class became nervous when Negroes started to ask for community control and for some of the jobs held by Jews.

Jewish public school teachers are concerned over job security. They share similar fears with non-Jewish blue-collar workers who are concerned by black demands for more skilled union jobs. Apprehension that more black workers in their fields will reduce the occupational status of whites is, of course, also present.

To the extent that the fear of job competition is a factor in the "backlash," however, the problem can be largely resolved by industry and government creating more and better job opportunities for whites and blacks alike, taking into careful consideration the nature of what has been termed our "postindustrial" society.

The range of Jewish-Negro conflicts of interest extends into the realm of higher education as well. The situation in the New York City public university came to the fore in 1968, particularly during the confrontations at the City College of New York and Queens College campuses. For decades a high percentage of the students at the tuition-free city colleges have been Jewish. Students have been admitted on the basis of competitive entrance exams and high school averages. The only problem with the prevailing system was that large numbers of blacks and Puerto Ricans, because of their economic and educational handicaps were precluded from entering the city colleges.

Demands by black and Puerto Rican student activists in 1968–1969 centered on the adoption of quotas and open enrollment.

Strong opposition from many elements of the Jewish community flared up on both counts.[18] The whole notion of quotas is anathema to most Jews, because of past experiences where quotas were designed to keep down the percentages of qualified Jews vis-à-vis other white students in colleges and medical schools. On the personal level there is the understandable concern that a qualified son, daughter, or relative might be denied a place in the university because more seats are set aside for nonwhites, and that the educational quality of the institutions will deteriorate.

The crux of the problem is the contradiction existing between the deeply rooted American ideal that individuals advance according to merit and the historical reality that many individuals, because they are part of particular ethnic and racial groups, are at a distinct disadvantage in the competition. From the black point of view, basing admission to universities on the conventional criteria in effect discriminates against them. It is analogous to bringing them to the starting line with their legs manacled and instructing them to race on equal terms.

Admitting more Negroes to the City University need not mean that fewer Jews can attend. The city colleges should be open to all qualified students,[19] and can be if our society and government, from the municipal to the federal level, desires it to be so. If the matter is given the priority it deserves—and this necessitates a general reordering of America's fiscal priorities—funds and personnel can be acquired to provide a quality education for all who seek it.[20]

[18] For a discussion by two Jewish educators, David Haber and Will Maslow, on the pros and cons of a quota system per se, see "College Admission: Are Quotas the Answer?" *Congress Bi-Weekly* 36, no. 9 (9 June 1969):4–8.

[19] "Qualified" is used here in a very broad sense, as criteria other than high school grades and competitive exam scores have to be considered in the problem of providing more intellectual opportunities for those whom society has discriminated against. But it would be a disservice and patronizing to black and Puerto Rican students if large numbers were thrust indiscriminately into the university system. One reasonable direction seems to be in the further developing and improving of programs like SEEK, which since its inception in 1966 through 1969 has helped four thousand educationally disadvantaged students to reach a level of proficiency required for entrance into the seven senior colleges of the New York City University.

[20] If, during a period of transition, poor but qualified Jewish youngsters

Essential to the improvement of Negro-Jewish relations is the maintenance of rationality, especially during times of crisis. Rash accusations of anti-Semitism or racism are invariably counter-productive. Whatever Albert Shanker is, he is not a racist. Prior to the decentralization struggle, he was widely regarded as one of the most pro-Negro labor leaders. Labeling him a racist has not aided the cause of community control in Ocean Hill-Brownsville. If anything, it has further polarized opinion and complicated the already difficult task of finding a modus vivendi.

Calling Rhody McCoy an anti-Semite was clearly irrational and self-defeating. The use of such an epithet only served to convince more blacks that their demands for community control were hopelessly misunderstood. It also led to an oversimplified characterization of the UFT-Governing Board confrontation as an ethnic and class struggle between Jews and Afro-Americans.

In plain terms, namecalling fans the flames of emotionalism and makes meaningful communication almost impossible. At no time was reasoned discourse between Afro-Americans and Jewish-Americans more necessary than during the school strike and its aftermath. Yet, in December 1968, Floyd McKissick, a former national director of CORE, a leading proponent of black economic power, and an advocate of school decentralization, was barred from a Long Island synagogue where he had been invited to speak on the subject of "Black Power and the Jewish Response." Ostensibly the belief, a grossly inaccurate one, that McKissick was "anti-Semitic" prompted the organizers of the program to cancel the speech.[21] This was the same Floyd McKissick who in March 1967, in an interview with the *Morning Freiheit* said: "We are very much opposed to any and all talk, no matter from what source it comes, that Jews are responsible for the bitter fate that has befallen the Negro people in our country and in the ghettos." He added, "Both racism and anti-Semitism are the bitterest foes of everything that is progressive and humanist in the world generally and especially

are denied places in the city university because of the need to broaden opportunities for Blacks the Jewish agencies might well provide funds necessary for them to attend private universities. It would also be desirable if the agencies established substantial scholarship programs for blacks.

21 *New York Times,* 12 December 1968.

in our country. . . . Whether anti-Semitism or racism comes from white or black it is a calamity for the Negro liberation movement and for all oppressed peoples." McKissick urged black people to be vigilant and to vigorously "oppose racism and anti-Semitism because irrational national hatred against any people only serves the interests of the worst oppressors of the Negro people."[22] Twenty-one months later, when bridges between the Jewish and Negro communities were crucially needed, the kind of bridge that McKissick could have helped to construct was thoughtlessly demolished.[23]

One lesson to be learned from the tragedy of the school strike in terms of interethnic group understanding is that overreaction to racial or religious slurs is harmful to all concerned. The authors are not suggesting that defamation of Jews be ignored by Jewish agencies. We are suggesting that they not overreact to smears by obscure, unrepresentative persons and thereby help to create a panic atmosphere by giving these persons the recognition and publicity they crave but do not warrant. Dialogue between representatives of so-called moderate and radical movements and Jewish leaders will surely prove more productive.

Articulate Afro-Americans have sometimes had greater expectations for Jews than for other whites insofar as the black man's struggle is concerned. After all, down through the centuries, Jews had repeatedly known the sting of persecution. In an essay based on his youthful experience working in a Chicago hospital, Richard Wright discovered that "even Jewish doctors had learned to imitate the sadistic method of humbling a Negro that others had cultivated."[24] Wright's use of the word "even" is pregnant with meaning. And Julius Lester in an interview in 1969 asked: "Why is it that they [Jews] can understand Israel and can't let us have Ocean Hill-Brownsville? That's the same thing, they should under-

---

[22] *Morning Freiheit* (New York), 12 March 1967.

[23] Parenthetically, it should be noted that a business associate of McKissick's reportedly characterized the synagogue incident as "racism at its worst." However ill-advised the decision to deny McKissick a platform was, it was inappropriate and distinctly unhelpful to call that decision racist.

[24] Richard Wright, "The Man Who Went to Chicago," *Eight Men* (Cleveland and New York: World Publishing Co., 1940), p. 239.

stand that better than anybody in this country."[25] Somewhat more cynical—or should we say realistic—is James Baldwin who argues that Jews are singled out in the ghetto not because they act differently from other whites, but because they don't, because they have not been "ennobled by oppression." He continued: "One can be disappointed in the Jew—if one is romantic enough—for not having learned from history; but if people did learn from history, history would be very different."[26]

Baldwin's assertion about Jews not acting differently raises a fundamental question. Is it fair to expect more of Jews than of other whites? Nat Hentoff believes the answer depends on whether Jews define themselves in the Prophetic tradition or in the tradition of South Africa's troubled Jewish community.[27] There, a small albeit a noticeably disproportionate minority of Jews actively challenge the nefarious apartheid system, while simultaneously the leaders and the rank and file of the Jewish community acquiesce in the system and profit from it.

For American Jews who enjoy a more secure position than those in South Africa there is much less excuse not to assume the responsibility of the Prophetic tradition.[28] That responsibility is not diminished one whit by the occasional anti-Semitic insult. The Synagogue Council of America put it this way: "As Jews we are committed by our faith to work for racial justice in an integrated society. Any Jew who fails to join in this struggle demeans his

[25] *Evergreen Review*, April 1969, p. 71.

[26] James Baldwin, "Negroes Are Anti-Semitic Because They're Anti-White," *New York Times Magazine*, 9 April 1967, p. 140.

[27] Nat Hentoff, ed., *Black Anti-Semitism and Jewish Racism* (New York: Richard W. Baron, 1969) p. xvi. On this point also see the essay by Rabbi Alan W. Miller in the same work.

[28] Professor E. Feit points out quite rightly that it is easy for others to urge heroic gestures at a distance of many thousands of miles. He further argues that, whereas the much more numerous German Catholics might have successfully opposed Hitler, defiance by the Jewish community would be futile in South Africa. However, it can be counter-argued that with the German nightmare of the 1930s and 1940s still fresh in their minds, South Africa's Jews, both collectively and individually, have an obligation to oppose actively the inhumanity of the Nationalists, not because such opposition is likely to be successful but because it is right. See E. Feit, "Community in a Quandary: The South African Jewish community and *apartheid*," *Race* (London) 8, no. 4 (April 1967):399.

faith." Such declarations of high ideals are necessary, but far from sufficient. The Jewish community is faced with the challenging task of marshalling its considerable resources and energies to assist the black man's quest for freedom and equality. For it has been true of American Jewry as it has been true of America as a whole, that when all is said and done, more has been said than done.

BIBLIOGRAPHY

BOOKS

Abernathy, Arthur T. *The Jew a Negro*. Moravian Falls, N.C.: Dixie Publishing Co., 1910.

Allport, Gordon W. *The Nature of Prejudice*. Garden City: Doubleday, Anchor Books, 1958.

Andrews, C. M. *Colonial Folkways: A Chronicle of American Life in the Reign of the Georges*. New Haven: Yale University Press, 1919.

Baldwin, James. *Notes of a Native Son*. Boston: Beacon Press, 1955.

Berkowitz, Leonard. *Aggression: A Social Psychological Analysis*. New York: McGraw-Hill Book Co., 1962.

Berson, Lenora E. *Case Study of a Riot: The Philadelphia Story*. New York: American Jewish Committee, Institute of Human Relations, 1966.

Berube, Maurice R., and Gittell, Marilyn, eds. *Confrontation at Ocean Hill-Brownsville: The New York School Strikes of 1968*. New York: Praeger, 1969.

Bondi, August. *Autobiography of August Bondi 1833–1907*. Galesburg, Ill.: Wagoner Printing Co., 1910.

Bontemps, Arna, and Conroy, Jack. *Anyplace But Here*. New York: Hill & Wang, 1966.

Breitman, George. *The Last Year of Malcolm X: The Evolution of a Revolutionary*. New York: Merit Publishers, 1967.

————. *Malcolm X Speaks*. New York: Grove Press, 1965.

Brotz, Howard. *The Black Jews of Harlem: Negro Nationalism and the Dilemmas of Negro Leadership*. New York: The Free Press, 1964.

Brown, Claude. *Manchild in the Promised Land*. New York: New American Library, 1966.

Carmichael, Stokely. *Power and Racism: What We Want*. Boston: New England Free Press, n.d.

Carter, Dan T. *Scottsboro: A Tragedy of the American South*. Baton Rouge: Louisiana State University Press, 1969.

Clark, Kenneth B. *Dark Ghetto: Dilemmas of Social Power*. New York: Harper & Row, 1967.

Cleage, Albert B., Jr. *The Black Messiah*. New York: Sheed & Ward, 1968.

Cohen, Henry. *Justice, Justice: A Jewish View of the Black Revolution*, New York: Union of American Hebrew Rabbis, 1969.

Cruse, Harold. *The Crisis of the Negro Intellectual*. New York: William Morrow & Co., 1967.

Dinnerstein, Leonard, *The Leo Frank Case*. New York: Columbia University Press, 1968.

Drake, St. Clair, and Cayton, Horace R. *Black Metropolis: A Study of Negro Life in a Northern City*. 2 vols. New York and Evanston: Harper & Row, 1962.

Du Bois, W. E. B. *Dusk of Dawn: An Essay Toward an Autobiography of Race Concept*. New York: Schocken Books, 1968.

Einhorn, David. *War With Amelek: A Sermon Delivered on March 19, 1864*. Philadelphia: Stein & Jones, 1864.

Elkins, Stanley. *Slavery: A Problem in American Institutional and Intellectual Life*. New York: Grosset & Dunlap, 1963.

Essien-Udom, E. U. *Black Nationalism: A Search for an Identity in America*. New York: Dell Publishing Co., 1964.

Ezell, John Samuel. *The South Since 1865*. New York: Macmillan Co., 1963.

Fisher, Miles Mark. *Negro Slave Songs in the United States*. New York: Citadel Press, 1963.

Franklin, John Hope. *From Slavery to Freedom: A History of Negro Americans*. New York: Alfred A. Knopf, 1967.

Garvey, Amy Jacques, ed. *Philosophy and Opinions of Marcus Garvey or Africa for the Africans*. London: Frank Cass, 1967.

Glazer, Nathan. *American Judaism*. Chicago: University of Chicago Press, 1957.

Glazer, Nathan, and Moynihan, Daniel Patrick. *Beyond the Melting Pot: The Negroes, Puerto Ricans, Jews, Italians, and Irish of New York City*. Cambridge: Massachusetts Institute of Technology Press, 1964.

Glock, Charles Y., Selznick, Gertrude J., and Spaeth, Joe L. *The Apathetic Majority*. New York: Harper & Row, 1966.

Gold, Bertram H. *Jews and the Urban Crisis*. New York: American Jewish Committee, Institute Human Relations, 1968.

Gold, Michael. *Jews Without Money*. New York: Avon, 1965.

Golden, Harry. *A Little Girl Is Dead*. New York: Avon, 1965.

Handlin, Oscar. *Boston's Immigrants: A Study in Acculturation*. Cambridge: Harvard University Press, 1959.

————. *The Uprooted: The Epic Story of The Great Migration That Made The American People*. New York: Grosset & Dunlap, 1951.

Harap, Louis, and L. D. Reddick. *Should Jews and Negroes Unite*. Negro Publication Society of America, 1943.

Hentoff, Nat, ed. *Black Anti-Semitism and Jewish Racism*. New York: Richard W. Baron, 1969.

Higham, John. *Strangers in the Land: Patterns of American Nativism, 1860–1925*. New York: Atheneum, 1963.

Hooker, James. *Black Revolutionary: George Padmore's Path from Communism to Pan Africanism*. New York: Frederick A. Praeger, 1967.

Hühner, Leon. *The Life of Judah Touro 1775–1854*. Philadelphia: Jewish Publication Society, 1946.

Jarrette, Alfred G. *Muslims Black Metropolis*. Los Angeles: Great Western Book Publishing Co., 1962.

Jones, LeRoi, and Neal, Larry, eds. *Black Fire: An Anthology of Afro-American Writing*. New York: Morrow, 1966.

Jordan, Winthrop. *White Over Black: American Attitudes Towards The Negro 1550–1812*. Chapel Hill: University of North Carolina Press, 1968.

Katz, Shlomo, ed. *Negro and Jew: An Encounter in America*. New York: Macmillan Co., 1967.

Kohler, Max J. *The Jews and the Anti-Slavery Movement*. Publication of the American Jewish Historical Society, no. 5. New York, 1896.

Korn, Bertram Wallace. *American Jewry and the Civil War*. Cleveland and New York: World Publishing Co., 1961.

———. *Jews and Negro Slavery in the Old South 1789–1865*. Elkins Park, Pa.: Reform Congregation Keneseth Israel, 1961.

Levine, Naomi, and Cohen, Richard. *Schools in Crisis*. New York: Popular Library, 1969.

Lincoln, C. Eric. *The Black Muslims in America*. Boston: Beacon Press, 1963.

Litwack, Leon F. *North of Slavery: The Negro in The Free States, 1790–1860*. Chicago: University of Chicago Press, 1965.

Lomax, Louis. *When the Word Is Given*. Cleveland and New York: World Publishing Co., 1963.

Lynch, Hollis, *Edward Wilmot Blyden, Pan Negro Patriot, 1822–1912*. London: Oxford University Press, 1967.

McKay, Claude, *Harlem: Black Metropolis*, New York: E. P. Dutton, 1940.

Malcolm X. *The Autobiography of Malcolm X*. New York: Grove Press, 1966.

Mannix, P. Daniel, and Cowley, Malcolm. *Black Cargoes: A History of the Atlantic Slave Trade*. New York: Viking Press, 1962.

Marcus, Jacob Rader. *Early American Jewry*. Vol. I. Philadelphia: Jewish Publication Society, 1961.

———. *Memoirs of American Jews 1775–1865*. 2 vols., Philadelphia: Jewish Publication Society, 1965.

Marsh, Zöe, and Kingsnorth, G. W. *An Introduction to the History of East Africa*. Cambridge: Cambridge University Press, 1965.

Marx, Gary T. *Protest and Prejudice: A Study of Belief in the Black Community*. New York: Harper & Row, 1967.

Mayer, Martin. *The Teachers' Strike: New York, 1968*. New York: Perennial Library Edition, 1969.

Meade, Robert Douthat. *Judah P. Benjamin and the American Civil War*. Chicago: University of Chicago Press, 1944.

Meier, August. *Negro Thought in America, 1880–1915: Racial Ideologies in the Age of Booker T. Washington*. Ann Arbor: University of Michigan Press, 1966.

Meier, August, and Rudwick, Elliot. *From Plantation to Ghetto: An Interpretive History of American Negroes*. New York: Hill & Wang, 1966.

Myrdal, Gunnar. *An American Dilemma*. 2 vols. New York: McGraw-Hill Book Co., 1964.

Negro-Jewish Relations in the United States: Papers and Proceedings of a Conference Convened by the Conference on Jewish Social Studies. New York: Citadel Press, 1966.

Osofsky, Gilbert. *Harlem: The Making of a Ghetto*. New York: Harper & Row, 1968.

Ottley, Roi. *New World A-Coming: Inside Black America*. Boston: Houghton Mifflin Co., 1943.

Pickard, Kate E. R. *The Kidnapped and the Ransomed*. Syracuse: William T. Hamilton, 1856.

Podhoretz, Norman. *Doings and Undoings: The Fifties and After in American Writing*. New York: Farrar, Straus & Giroux, 1963.

Powell, Adam Clayton, Jr., *Marching Blacks: An Interpretive History of the Rise of the Black Common Man*. New York: Dial Press, 1945.

Rice, Madeleine Hooke. *American Catholic Opinion in the Slavery Controversy*. New York: Columbia University Press, 1944.

Riis, Jacob A. *How the Other Half Lives: Studies Among the Tenements of New York*. New York: Charles Scribner's Sons, 1902.

Roche, John P., *The Quest for the Dream: The Development of Civil Rights and Human Relations in Modern America*. New York: Macmillan Co., 1963.

Rogers, David. *110 Livingston Street: Politics and Bureaucracy in New York City Schools*. New York: Random House, 1968.

Rokeach, Milton. *The Open and Closed Mind*. New York: Basic Books, 1960.

Rose, Arnold. *The Negro's Morale: Group Identification and Protest*. Minneapolis: University of Minnesota Press, 1949.

Rudwick, Elliot. *W. E. B. Du Bois: Propagandist of the Negro Protest*. New York: Atheneum, 1968.

Saenger, Gerhard. *The Social Psychology of Prejudice: Achieving Intellectual Understanding and Cooperation in a Democracy*. New York: Harper & Brothers, 1953.

St. John, Robert. *Jews, Justice and Judaism*. New York: Doublday, 1969.

Sartre, Jean-Paul. *Anti-Semite and Jew*. Translated by George J. Becker. New York: Schocken Books, 1965.

Schappes, Morris N., ed. *Documentary History of the Jews of Philadelphia from Colonial Times to the Age of Jackson*. Philadelphia: Jewish Publication Society, 1957.

Scheer, Robert, ed. *Eldridge Cleaver: Post-Prison Writings and Speeches*. New York: Random House, 1967.

Scheiner, Seth. *Negro Mecca: A History of the Negro in New York City 1865–1920*. New York: New York University Press, 1965.

Selzer, Michael. *Israel as a Factor in Jewish-Gentile Relations in America: Observations in the Aftermath of the June 1967 War*. New York: American Council for Judaism, 1968.

Selznick, Gertrude J., and Steinberg, Stephen. *The Tenacity of Preju-*

dice: Anti-Semitism in Contemporary America. New York: Harper & Row, 1969.

Stampp, Kenneth. *The Peculiar Institution*. New York: Vintage Books, 1956.

Tannenbaum, Frank. *Slave and Citizen: The Negro in the Americas*. New York: Vintage Books, 1946.

Thirty Years of Lynching in the United States, 1889–1918. New York: NAACP, 1919.

Wade, Richard C., ed. *The Negro in American Life: Selected Readings*. Boston: Houghton Mifflin Co., 1965.

Wedlock, Lunabelle. *The Reaction of Negro Publications and Organizations to German Anti-Semitism*. Washington, D.C.: Howard University Press, 1942.

Wilson, James Q. *Negro Politics: The Search for Leadership*. New York: Free Press, 1960.

Wirth, Louis. *The Ghetto*. Chicago: University of Chicago Press, 1928.

Wolf, Edwin, II, and Whiteman, Maxwell. *The History of the Jews of Philadelphia from Colonial Times to the Age of Jackson*. Philadelphia: Jewish Publication Society, 1957.

Woodward, C. Vann. *Origins of The New South, 1877–1913*. Vol. IX of *A History of the South*, edited by Wendell Holmes Stevenson and E. Merton Coulter. 10 vols. Baton Rouge: Louisiana State University Press, 1951.

————. *The Stranger Career of Jim Crow*. New York: Oxford University Press, 1966.

Wright, Richard. *Black Boy: A Record of Childhood and Youth*. Cleveland and New York: World Publishing Co., 1950.

————. *Eight Men*. Cleveland and New York: World Publishing Co., 1940.

Yaffe, James, *The American Jews: Portrait of a Split Personality*. New York: Random House, 1968.

ARTICLES

Aptheker, Herbert. "Anti-Semitism and Racism." *Political Affairs* 48, no. 4 (April 1969): 35–44.

———. "Du Bois As Historian." *Negro History Bulletin* 32, no. 4 (April 1969): 6–16.

Baker, Ella, and Cooke, Marvel. "The Bronx Slave Market." *Crisis* 42, no. 11 (November 1935): 330–331, 340.

Bakst, Jerome. "Negro Radicalism Turns Antisemitic—SNCC's Volte Face." *Wiener Library Bulletin* (Winter 1967–1968): 20–22.

Baldwin, James. "The Harlem Ghetto: Winter 1948: The Vicious Circle of Frustration and Prejudice." *Commentary*, February 1948, pp. 165–170.

———. "Negroes Are Anti-Semitic Because They're Anti-White." *New York Times Magazine,* 9 April 1967, pp. 27ff.

Bayton, James A. "The Racial Stereotypes of Negro College Students." *The Journal of Abnormal and Social Psychology* 36, no. 1 (January 1941): 97–102.

Bender, Eugene I. "Reflections on Negro-Jewish Relationships: The Historical Dimension," *Phylon* 30, no. 1 (Spring 1969): 56–65.

Chrisman, Robert. "The Crisis of Harold Cruse." *The Black Scholar* 1, no. 1 (November 1969): 77–84.

Clark, Kenneth B. "Candor about Negro-Jewish Relations." *Commentary,* February 1946, pp. 8–14.

Coburn, Judith. "Passover in the Ghetto: This Year in Washington." *Village Voice,* 10 April 1969, pp. 3, 59–60.

Du Bois, W. E. B. "The Negro and the Warsaw Ghetto." *Jewish Life* 6, no. 7 (May 1952): 14–15.

Ellis, Eddie. "Semitism in the Black Ghetto." *Liberator,* January, February, April 1966. For responses, see letters by James Baldwin and Ossie Davis in *Freedomways* 7, no. 1 (Winter 1967): 77–78.

Emerson, Edwin, Jr. "The New Ghetto." *Harper's Weekly,* 9 January 1897, p. 4.

Epstein, Jason. "The Real McCoy." *New York Review of Books,* 13 March 1969, p. 31ff.

Feit, E. "Community in a Quandary: The South African Jewish Community and *Apartheid.*" *Race* (London) 8, no. 4 (April 1967): 395–408.

Ferretti, Fred. "New York's Black Anti-Semitism Scare." *Columbia Journalism Review,* Fall 1969, pp. 18–29.

Gans, Herbert J. "Negro-Jewish Conflict in New York City: A Sociological Evaluation." *Midstream,* March 1969, pp. 3–15.

Glasser, Ira. "The Burden of the Blame: New York Civil Liberties Union Report on the Ocean Hill-Brownsville School Controversy." In Berube, Maurice, and Gittell, Marilyn, eds. *Confrontation at Ocean Hill-Brownsville:* (New York: Praeger, 1969), pp. 104–119.

Glazer, Nathan. "Blacks, Jews, and The Intellectuals." *Commentary,* April 1969, pp. 33–39.

————. "A New Look at the Melting Pot." *The Public Interest,* August 1969, pp. 180–187.

Goldbloom, Maurice J. "The New York School Crisis." *Commentary,* January 1969, pp. 43–58.

Gordon, Albert I. "Negro-Jewish Marriages." *Judaism* 13, no. 2 (Spring 1964): 164–184.

Gregson v. *Gilbert* in Henry Roscoe. *Reports of Cases Argued and Determined in the Court of Kings Bench, 1782–1785.* London, 1831, III, 233–234.

Haber, David, and Maslow, Will. "College Admission: Are Quotas the Answer? *Congress Bi-Weekly* 36, no. 9 (9 June 1969): 4–8.

Harap, Louis. "Anti-Negroism Among Jews." *The Negro Quarterly* 1, no. 2 (Summer 1942): 105–111.

Hatchett, John. "The Phenomenon of the Anti-Black Jews and the Black Anglo-Saxon: A Study in Educational Perfidy." *Afro-American Teachers Forum* 2, no. 2 (November–December 1967): 1, 3–4.

Hentoff, Nat. "Blacks and Jews: An Interview with Julius Lester." *Evergreen Review,* no. 65 (April 1969): 21ff.

————. "The Siege of WBAI." *Village Voice,* 6 February 1969, pp. 9ff.

Hoffer, Eric. "The Reason for Negro Hostility Toward Jews." *San Francisco Examiner,* 18 November 1968.

Hühner, Leon. *Some Associates of John Brown.* Reprinted from *The Magazine of History,* 1908.

Internal, About NYU: For Faculty and Administration III, no. 35 (13 August 1968): 1–6.

Israel, Edward L. "Jew Hatred Among Negroes." *Crisis* 43, no. 2 (February 1936): 39, 50.

Jabara, Abdeen. "The American Left and the June Conflict." *The Arab World* 14, nos. 10–11 (special issue, n.d.): 73–80.

Jacobs, Paul. "Watts vs. Israel." *Commonweal,* 1 March 1968, pp. 649–654.

Leo, John. "Black Anti-Semitism." *Commonweal,* 14 February 1969, pp. 618–620.

McKissick, Floyd. "Anti-Black and Anti-Jew." *Amsterdam-News,* 8 February 1969.

Miller, Kelly. "Race Prejudice in Germany and America." *Opportunity* 14, no. 4 (April 1936): 102–105.

"Interview with Malcolm X." *Playboy,* May 1963, pp. 53ff.

Moore, Louise R. "When a Black Man Stood Up." *Liberator,* July 1966, p. 7.

Owen, Chandler. "Negro Anti-Semitism Cause and Cure." *The National Jewish Monthly,* September 1942, pp. 14–15.

————. "Should the Negro Hate the Jew." *Chicago Defender,* 8 November 1941.

Pierce, David. "Is The Jew a Friend of the Negro." *Crisis* 30, no. 4 (August 1925): 184–186.

Pilati, Joe. "Orienting the Frosh to the Ivory Tower." *The Village Voice,* 26 September 1968, pp. 24–26.

Poinsett, Alex. "Battle to Control Black Schools." *Ebony,* May 1969, pp. 44–54.

Raab, Earl. "The Black Revolution and the Jewish Question." *Commentary,* January 1969, pp. 23–33.

Reddick, Lawrence D. "Anti-Semitism Among Negroes." *Negro Quarterly* 1, no. 2 (Summer 1942): 112–122.

————. "What Hitler Says About the Negro." *Opportunity* 17, no. 4 (April 1939): 108–110.

Ruchames, Louis. "The Abolitionists and The Jews." *Publications of the American Jewish Historical Society* 42, no. 2 (December 1952): 131–155.

Rustin, Bayard. "The Anatomy of Frustration." Address delivered at the 55th National Commission Meeting of the Anti-Defamation League of B'nai B'rith, 6 May 1968, New York City.

————. "From Protest to Politics." *Negro Protest Thought in the Twentieth Century.* Edited by Francis L. Broderick and August Meier. Indianapolis: Bobbs-Merrill Co., 1965, pp. 408–409.

Sheppard, Harold L. "The Negro Merchant: A Study of Negro Anti-Semitism." *American Journal of Sociology* 53, no. 2 (September 1947): 96–99.

Sobel, B. Z., and May L. "Negroes and Jews: American Minority Groups In Conflict." *Judaism* 15, no. 1 (Winter 1966): 3–22.

Teller, Judd L. "Jews and Blacks: Together." *National Jewish Monthly,* January 1970, pp. 21–29.

————. "Negroes and Jews: A Hard Look." *Conservative Judaism* 21, no. 1 (Fall 1966): 13–20.

Vaxer, M. "Haym M. Solomon Frees His Slave." *Publications of the American Jewish Historical Society,* no. 37 (1947): 447–448.

Weisbord, Robert G. "The Case of the Slave Ship *Zong.*" *History Today,* August 1969, pp. 561–567.

Wellman, David, and Dizard, Ian. "i love ralph bunche, but i can't eat him for lunch." *Leviathan,* July–August 1969, pp. 46–52.

REPORTS AND PUBLIC DOCUMENTS

Atkinson, Caroline O. *Attitudes of Selected Small Samples of Negroes*

Toward Jews and Other Ethnic Groups. New York: Bureau of Applied Social Research, Columbia, 1968.

Ethnic Distribution of Pupils in the Public Schools of New York City. Prepared by the Central Zoning Unit of the Board of Education, 24 March 1965 and 15 June 1966.

Involvement of the City Commission of Human Rights with the Jewish Community of New York during the Chairmanship of William H. Booth. Prepared by the Human Rights Commission of New York City (News Release of 4 February 1969).

Mayor's Task Force Report on the Economic Redevelopment of Harlem. 15 January 1968.

Memorandum from New York Civil Liberties Union to Special Committee on Religious and Racial Prejudice. 26 November 1968.

Report of the National Advisory Commission on Civil Disorders. New York: Bantam Books, 1968.

Statement of the Special Committee on Racial and Religious Prejudices (The Botein Committee Report). 17 January 1969.

Supplementary Studies for the National Advisory Commission on Civil Disorders. Washington, D.C.: U.S. Government Printing Office, 1968.

Subversive Influences In Riots, Looting, and Burning. Part 4. Newark, N.J. Hearings Before the Committee on Un-American Activities, House of Representatives, April 23 and 24, 1968. Washington, D.C.: U.S. Government Printing Office, 1968.

NEWSPAPERS AND MAGAZINES

Specific articles are cited under "Articles."

ADL Bulletin (Anti-Defamation League), September 1967.

African Opinion 8, nos. 1 and 2 (May–June 1967); 8, nos. 3 and 4 (August–September, 1967).

The Afro-American (Baltimore), 22 February 1936, 10 November 1956, 1 December 1956, 3 March 1966.

Amsterdam-News (New York), 19 February 1938, 16 April 1938, 9 November 1968, 1 February 1969.

Ann Arbor News, 27 August 1968.

The Black Man (London), July 1935, July–August 1936, June 1939.

The Black Panther (Los Angeles), 7 September 1968, 12 October 1968, 21 December 1968, 4 January 1969, 2 February 1969, 9 February 1969, 28 February 1970.

Black Power 1, no. 7 (June 1967).

Chicago Defender, 8 November 1941, 10 November 1956.

The Colored American Review (New York), 1 October 1915.

Commentary, 1946, 1948, 1964–1970.

Congress Bi-Weekly, 1966–1970.

Crisis, February 1919, April 1938, May 1933, September 1933, October 1933.

Daily Argus (Mt. Vernon), 4 February 1966, 8 February 1966.

Daily Worker (New York), 2 April 1957.

Hadassah Magazine, 1969–1970.

Islamic Press International News-Gram (New York), October 1967.

The Israel Digest 10, no. 15 (28 July 1967).

Jewish Press (New York), 1968–1970.

The Liberator, 1966–1970.

Long Island Press, 2 January 1969.

Los Angeles Herald Dispatch, 6 August 1960, 29 September 1966, 15 December 1966, 12 January 1967.

Metropolitan Star (New York), January 1969.

Morning Freiheit (New York), 12 March 1967.

Muhammad Speaks (Chicago), 16 June 1967, 23 June 1967.

National Guardian, 16 September 1967.

National Jewish Monthly, 1966–1970.

National Observer (Washington), 28 July 1969.

The New York Age, 14 June 1917, 18 February 1919.

New York Herald Tribune (Paris), 22 September 1967.

The New York Times, 1965–1970

Nite Life (Philadelphia), 10 January 1967, 19 December 1967.

Norfolk Journal and Guide, 10 November 1956.

Pittsburgh Courier, 26 November 1938, 3 December 1938, 24 May 1947, 27 March 1948, 10 November 1956, 29 December 1956.

SNCC Newsletter, June–July 1967.

South End (Detroit), 4 June 1968.

Time, 31 January 1969.

Westmore News (Long Island), 8 February 1968.

UNPUBLISHED SOURCES

Jonas, Franklin. "The Early Life and Career of B. Charney Vladeck: A Study In Political Acculturation." Ph.D. diss. New York University, 1970.

INDEX

Abernathy, Ralph, 191, 198
abolitionism, 23–31
African-American Heritage Association, 98
Africans
  slave ships and, 1
  tragedy in history of, xxiv
Afro-American, use of term, 108–109
Afro-Americanism, as new culture, 67–68
Afro-American studies, 151–160
Alexander, Pat, 91–92
Alexander, Raymond Pace, 198
Alexander, Sanford, 91–92
Al Fatah, 101 n., 107 n., 128, 132
Ali, Noble Drew, 90
Allen, Alex, 201
Allen, James E., Jr., 139, 163, 167
American Jewish Committee, 80, 122, 134, 140, 149, 153 n., 163–164, 210
American Jewish Congress, 73–74, 83, 134, 140, 142, 152–153, 155, 160–161, 164, 170 n., 180, 188, 195, 200, 203
American Jewry
  ghettos of, 7–8
  rights organizations formed by, 133–134
  spokesmen for, 28
  see also Jew(s)
Anti-Defamation League, B'nai B'rith, 77, 92, 104, 134, 140,

153 n., 158 n., 163–164, 176, 180, 186–187, 193 n., 194–201, 207 n., 211
anti-Semitism
  in American cities, 10–13
  anti-Zionism and, 89
  beginings of, 7
  among blacks, 49, 55–67, 69–70, 124–129, 152–160, 209–211
  black-white tensions and, 211–215
  by black extremists, 185–187
  black nationalism and, 148–149
  black view of, 114, 124–125
  denounced by various Negroes, 37–38
  in Detroit, 13
  as expression of hostility, 190
  five-year study of, 78 n.
  in ghetto, 144–146
  in Great Depression, 61
  in "Harlem on MY Mind," 178–182
  Jewish denial of in Ocean Hill dispute, 173 n.
  in Mount Vernon, N.Y., 139–143
  during N.Y. school desegregation disputes, 182–205
  during 1920s, 13
  during 1935 Harlem riot, 81 n.
  in Ocean Hill-Brownsville dispute, 169–175
  in Philadelphia, 144
  psychological explanation of, 65–66

233